A History of Religious Education

A History of Religious Education

Documents and Interpretations from the
Judaeo-Christian Tradition

Robert Ulich

New York: New York University Press
London: University of London Press Limited
1968

Preface

In our secular age we are inclined to underestimate the role of religion in the history of education. All early education was religious, and all early religion was also educational. Both elements were inherent in the rites and ceremonies of birth and death, war, hunting, and harvesting. Even in highly developed civilizations the priests were the educators, often cooperating with the kings, the judges, and the warriors, and sometimes being even superior to them.

In India the Brahman was also the teacher; in the Islamic countries education centered in the Koran; the Jews had the Torah; and in the Christian countries education centered in the Bible and the writings of the Church. The more the teachers were the guardians of the sacred tradition, the more they were respected. The separation of Church and state, which means also the separation of public education from ecclesiastical influence, is relatively recent and even in the nations of Europe still a matter of argument. In some of them the Church supervises the schools, either institutionally or in spirit, and except in totalitarian countries there exists everywhere a denominational or parochial school system.

In regard to their moral teaching and their interpretation of historical events even our secular schools live on a large substratum of religious ideas. Hence, an educator who is unaware of them can neither fully understand our present situation, nor can he participate productively in the current discussion about the relation between religion and the schools. It is the purpose of this book to fill the gap.

During the preparation of this book I received much encouragement from my colleagues Harry Austryn Wolfson and George Huntston Williams of Harvard, and from Lawrence A. Cremin of Columbia University. I have also greatly profited from the expert assistance of Dr. Hedwig Schleiffer. Finally, I wish to express my thanks to those many clergymen who have kindly informed me about the educational activities in their various churches.

Contents

A History of Religious Education

Chapter 1

The Judaic Tradition

Religiously, the West is embedded in the East. The New Testament, on which Christian education is based, cannot be understood without the Old Testament. So powerful and clear is the latter's message that a few quotations will suffice to prove the continuity between the two traditions. [1]

When Moses returns to God who had already spoken to him out of a burning bush, and tells of the evil that the Egyptian Pharaoh has done to the captive people of Israel, he receives the following message:

> I am the Lord. I appeared to Abraham, to Isaac, and to Jacob, as God Almighty, but by my name the LORD I did not make myself known to them. I also established my covenant with them, to give them the land of Canaan, the land in which they dwelt as sojourners. Moreover I have heard the groaning of the people of Israel whom the Egyptians hold in bondage and I have remembered my covenant.

> Say therefore to the people of Israel, "I am the Lord and I will bring you out from under the burdens of the Egyptians, and I will deliver you from their bondage, and I will redeem you with an outstretched arm and with great acts of judgment, and I will take you for my people, and I will be your God; and you shall know that I am the LORD your GOD, who has brought you out from under the burdens of the Egyptians. And I will bring you into the land which I swore to give to Abraham, to Isaac, and to Jacob;

I will give it to you for a possession. I am the LORD."
(*Exodus* 6:2–8.)

Thus the Old Testament interprets the mission of Israel as the history of a covenant between God and His chosen people, or as a process of education toward unity with God.

Then "in the third month, when the children of Israel were gone forth out of the land of Egypt," God reveals to Moses the Ten Commandments. These revelations (before 1200 B.C.) occur with the threat of fire and thunder and in an atmosphere of awe-inspiring distance. In order to placate this supernatural power and to establish an inner communion with it, the Hebrews developed a rich and meticulous ritual that reached deeply into their daily life and became later one of the instruments for the preservation of the children of Yaweh within a hostile world. They preached the virtue of justice and love even for the stranger ("you shall love him as yourself," *Leviticus* 19:34). They spoke of the continual presence of a guarding and judging God and thus had a profound effect on Christianity. A large part of Leviticus is a code of rules concerning sacrifices, offerings, food habits, purification rites, leprosy, ceremonies at the holy place, the scape goat, sexual behavior, the feasts of the Lord, vows, and redemptions.

But there occurred a process of spiritualization. The prophets Isaiah and Jeremiah, who lived during the first part of the seventh century, i.e., two hundred years after the writing of the early books of the Old Testament, protested against the externalism of the tradition.

These prophets are among the first of a period when advanced minds in the civilized ancient nations discovered the divine principle behind the concrete individual idol, as they also intuited unseen laws and forces behind the visible surface of nature. Obviously the two discoveries are intimately connected; mankind began to free himself from the pressure of the immediate and to understand the value of the inner life, of contemplation, and of abstraction.

Confucius (550–478 B.C.) said:

There is nothing more evident than that which cannot be seen by the eyes and nothing more palpable than that which cannot be perceived by the senses.[2]

Lao-Tse (sixth century B.C.) spoke of the mystery of the enduring:

The Tao that can be trodden is not the enduring, the un-
changing name. [Conceived of as] having no name, it is the
originator of heaven and earth; [conceived of as] having a
name, it is the Mother of all things. . . . Under these two
aspects, it is really the same; but as development takes
place, it receives the different names. Together we call them
the Mystery. Where the Mystery is the deepest is the gate
of all that is subtle and wonderful.[3]

In the *Republic* (Book VII) Plato (427–347) had Socrates say:

In like manner, when anyone by dialectics attempts through
discourse of reason and apart from all perceptions of sense
to find his way to the very essence of each thing . . . he
arrives at the limit of the intelligible. . . .

We shall require them (the guardians of the State) to turn
upwards the vision of their souls and fix their gaze on that
which sheds light on all. . . .

Several hundred years before Plato, Isaiah admonished his people
(1:11ff.):

What to me is the multitude of your sacrifice? says the
LORD; I have had enough of burned offerings of rams and
the fat of fat beasts. . . . Wash yourselves; make yourself clean; remove the evil of your doings from before my
eyes; cease to do evil, learn to do good; seek justice, correct
oppression; defend the fatherless, plead for the widow.

Come now, let us reason together, says the LORD.

In other words, it is neither the ritual, nor the gesture, but the
heart and the mind and their dialog with the unseen God which con-
stitute the essence of religion.

Indeed a momentous turning point in the spiritual history of man,
for it is through the great prophets of Judah, such as Isaiah and Jeremiah, that man has heard about the oneness of the divine that trans-

cends the boundaries of nations and makes itself known in the eternal paradoxes of suffering and salvation, of loneliness and inspiration, of the worth of the individual who can forget himself in God, and of the consciousness of spiritual privilege that knows that it can maintain itself only through the consciousness of responsibility and the willingness of sacrifice.

The prophets remind us that cult becomes idolatry unless it involves man's search for the eternal, and that only those who really love their country are willing to suffer persecution for the courage of their criticism.

Out of the prophetic despair in view of the corruption of man arises also the paradoxical hope that with his final judgment over the multitude of nations the Lord will vindicate the hopes of his people.

> He shall judge between the nations, and shall decide for many peoples; and they shall beat their swords into plowshares, and their spears into pruning hooks; nation shall not lift up sword against nation, neither shall they learn war any more. (*Isaiah* 2:4.)

> For as the rain and the snow come down from heaven,
> and return not thither but water the earth,
> making it bring forth and sprout,
> giving seed to the sower and bread to the eater,
> so shall my word be that goes forth from my mouth;
> it shall not return to me empty,
> but it shall accomplish that which I purpose,
> and prosper in the thing for which I sent it.

> For you shall go out in joy, and be led forth in peace;
> the mountains and the hills before you shall break forth
> into singing, and all the trees of the field shall clap their
>   hands.
> Instead of the thorn shall come up the cypress;
> instead of the briar shall come up the myrtle;
> and it shall be to the LORD for a memorial,
> for an everlasting sign which shall not be cut off.
> (*Isaiah* 55:10–13.)

In view of Israel's assurance of the divine covenant and its incumbent moral obligations, it cannot be surprising that the Jewish people developed an elaborate system of guiding the young, or, using a modern term, of pedagogy. Here, too, much has gone over into Christian education.

Apparently, no difference was made between religious and secular wisdom. The older Jewish tradition shows no interest in scholarship and research as a value of its own, or in literature in the sense of belles-lettres—though we do not know what may have been lost. There was no *l'art pour l'art,* except perhaps music. Both Jews and, later, Christians, regarded King David as the master of the harp; he can be seen in many illuminated manuscripts of the Middle Ages. But though the Psalms belong to the very great creations of lyric beauty, with a rhythmical power and a force of expression rarely, if ever, achieved again, their intention was beyond the aesthetic; it was religious. In addition, the prohibition of "any graven image" of the Divine (*Exodus* 20:4) was certainly unconducive to the development of the plastic arts; Islam, another creation of the Semitic world, has also suffered from this restriction imposed on the aesthetic impulse.

Much greater is the Jewish emphasis on the ethical side of education. Two qualities form the foundation for a truly religious development. The first is the fear of the Lord.

> The fear of the LORD is the beginning of knowledge; fools despise wisdom and instruction. (*Proverbs* 1:7.)

The second quality is the preparation of the heart.

> The plans of the mind belong to man, but the answer of the tongue is from the LORD.

> All the ways of man are pure in his own eyes, but the LORD weighs the spirit. (*Proverbs* 16:1-2.)

The third basic virtue is charity.

> Cast your bread upon the waters, for you will find it after many days.

Give a portion to seven, or even to eight, for you know not what evil may happen on earth. (*Eccesiastes* 11:1–2.)

And the fourth postulate is patience, combined with humility.

Then Job answered the LORD: "I know that thou canst do all things, and that no purpose of thine can be thwarted.

Who is this that hides counsel without knowledge? Therefore I have uttered what I did not understand, things too wonderful for me, which I did not know." (*Job* 42:1–3.)

PRACTICAL EDUCATION

In no way were the Jews satisfied with general moral precepts; they had to transfer them into the daily practical life of a nation for whom obedience to the Torah (the Pentateuch or the Law of Moses) was synonymous with the preservation of the Covenant and, consequently, with national survival and salvation. The Jewish historian Flavius Josephus wrote in his book *Against Apion:* [4]

Above all we pride ourselves on the education of our children, and regard as the most essential task in life the observance of our laws and of the pious practices, based thereupon, which we have inherited. (I:12)

All schemes of education and moral training fall into two categories; instruction is imparted in the one case by precept, in the other by practical exercising of the character. All other legislators, differing in their opinions, selected the particular method which each preferred and neglected the other. . . . (II:16)

Our legislator Moses, on the other hand, took great care to combine both systems. He did not leave practical training in mortals inarticulate, nor did he permit the letter of the law to remain inoperative. . . . (II:17)

The center of practical education was the family, and children were considered the greatest blessing. When the Lord rewarded Job for his faithfulness, he gave him not only fourteen thousand sheep and six thousand camels, and a thousand yoke of oxen, and a thousand she asses, but also seven sons and three daughters.

When they blessed Rebekah, who prepared herself for the meeting with her future husband Isaac, they told her:

> Our sister, be the mother of thousands of ten thousands; and may your descendants possess the gate of those who hate them. (*Genesis* 24:60.)

But children are not only a joy and a reward, they are also a religious responsibility.

> Hear, O Israel: The LORD our God is one LORD; and you shall love the LORD your God with all your heart, and with all your soul, and with all your might. And these words which I command you this day shall be upon your heart; and you shall teach them diligently to your children, and shall talk of them when you sit in your house and when you walk by the way, and when you lie down, and when you rise. (*Deuteronomy* 6:4–7.)

But the child is not naturally inclined to obey. It may be necessary to break his opposition by severe discipline.

> Apply your mind to instruction and your ears to words of knowledge.
>
> Do not withold discipline from a child; if you beat him with a rod, he will not die.
>
> If you beat him with the rod you will save his life from Sheol. (*Proverbs* 23:12–14.)

Yet, as everywhere, so also among the Jews of the Old Testament parental love and the sweet melancholy of age caused many an adult to look with indulgence at the cheerfulness of normal youth.

> Rejoice, O young man, in your youth, and let your heart cheer you in the days of your youth; walk in the ways of

your heart and the sight of your eyes. But know that for all these things God will bring you into judgment.

Remove vexation from your mind, and put away pain from your body; for youth and the dawn of life are vanity. (*Ecclesiastes* 11:9 –10.)

The sage or the sages who, living at the post classical period of Hebrew thought, wrote the aphorisms collected under the name of *Ecclesiastes,* were heretics in matters of faith. Only with some pious additions could their work be accepted into the sacred canon. Less impressed by the beatific or threatening visions of the prophets than by the precariousness of human existence, they faced the eternal problems of evil and death, of the success of the wicked and the suffering of the righteous with stoic acceptance. Their God is one who looks with cool indifference at the world he has created, if he cares for it at all.

All go to one place; all are from the dust, and all turn to dust again. Who knows whether the spirit of man goes upward and the spirit of the beast goes down to the earth? So I saw that there is nothing better than that a man should enjoy his work, for that is his lot; who can bring him to see what will be after him? (*Ecclesiastes* 3:20–22.)

As in all older civilizations, education among the Jews was carried through within a strict ritual framework. The prophet Ezekiel compared the nonritualistic upbringing of a child with the earliest infancy of Jerusalem when the Lord had not yet recognized it as his chosen country.

Again the word of the LORD came to me: "Son of man, make known to Jerusalem her abominations, and say, Thus says the Lord GOD to Jerusalem: Your origin and your birth are of the land of the Canaanites; your father was an Amorite, and your mother an Hittite. And as for your birth, on the day you were born your navel string was not cut nor were you washed with water to cleanse you, nor rubbed with salt, nor swathed with bands. No eye pitied you to do any of these things to you out of compassion for you, but you were cast out on the open fields, for you were abhorred, on the day you were born.

And when I passed by you and saw you weltering in your blood, I said to you in your blood, Live and grow up like a plant in the field. And you grew up and became tall and arrived at full maidenhood; your breasts were formed, and your hair had grown; yet you were naked and bare.

When I passed by you again and looked upon you, behold, you were at the age for love; and I spread my skirt over you, and covered your nakedness: yea, I plighted my troth to you and entered into a covenant with you, says the LORD GOD, and you became mine. Then I bathed you with water and washed off your blood from you, and anointed you with oil. . . ." (*Ezekiel* 16:1–9.)

The child was nursed by the mother who, though polygamy was permitted, enjoyed more respect in the days of the Old Testament than in the Arabic nations.

Charm is deceitful, and beauty is vain, but a woman who fears the Lord is to be praised.

Give her of the fruits of her hands, and let her works praise her in the gates. (*Proverbs* 31:30, 31.)

The eighth day the boy is taken into the covenant with the Lord through circumcision.

And God said unto Abraham, "As for you, you shall keep my covenant, you and your descendants after you. This is my covenant which you shall keep, between me and you and your descendants after you: Every male among you shall be circumcised. . . ." (*Genesis* 17:9–10.)

And in Chapter 12 of *Leviticus* we have an elaborate description of the purification rites which the mother has to undergo after the birth of a child. The name which the child receives should remind him of his relation to God or of his descendance from a noble people. "Jona-

than"—the Greek Theodoros—and "Nathanael"—the Greek Doro-
theos—mean "God-given"; "Eliezer" and "Azariah" exhort the bearer
to implore the help of the Lord; also the names "Joel," "Michaiah," or
"Micha" are conjurations of the Divine, while "Amminadab"—the
Greek Aristodemos—means "of a noble people."

Numbers 18:15 describes the portions to be given to the Levites
(the priests) at the occasion of the birth of the first child for the purpose of redeeming.

> Everything that opens the womb of all flesh, whether man
> or beast, which they offer to the LORD, shall be yours;
> nevertheless the first-born of man you shall redeem, and the
> firstlings of unclean beasts you shall redeem.

Families of some wealth invited guests for a feast of the occasion
of weaning. Abraham, at least, "made a great feast on the day that
Isaac was weaned." Apparently, the child was kept much longer at
the mother's breast than in our culture.

In a more advanced state of childhood, the father takes over the
religious education of the child. We have already quoted *Deuteronomy*
6:7 ". . . and you shall teach them diligently. . . ." And in *Deuteronomy* 6:20–25 we read:

> When your son asks you in time to come, "What is the
> meaning of the testimonies and statutes and the ordinances
> which the LORD our GOD has commanded you?" then
> you shall say to your son, "We were Pharaoh's slaves in
> Egypt, and the LORD brought us out of Egypt with a
> mighty hand, and the LORD showed us signs and wonders,
> great and grievous, against Egypt and against Pharaoh and
> against all his household, before our eyes; and he brought
> us out from there, that he might bring us in and give us the
> land which he swore to give to our fathers. And the LORD
> commanded us to do all these statutes, to fear the LORD
> our GOD, for our good always, that he might preserve us
> alive, as at this day. And it will be righteousness for us,
> if we are careful to do all this commandment before the
> LORD our GOD, as he has commanded us.

Since, like the Christians and Moslems, the Jews possessed their revelation in written form, much emphasis was laid on the art of reading, though the Old Testament contains no reference to formal schooling. Nevertheless, Ezra, the priest (*ca.* 536–456) was called "the scribe of the law of the God of heaven." Mehemiah and others of the school of scribes formed an aristocracy of teachers and established special houses of learning. Regular instruction in the Law was given in the halls of the outer temple, as we know especially from the New Testament (*Matthew* 21:23; 26:25; *Mark* 14:49; *Luke* 2:46; 20:1; 21:37; *John* 18:20).

During the Second Commonwealth (515 B.C.–A.D. 70) a great number of schools for adolescent youth or institutions, which we might call secondary, must have existed throughout Israel. They prepared those of their pupils who wished to go further for the college of advanced theological studies at Jerusalem. At the same time, probably in consequence of foreign influences to which Israel became increasingly exposed, the old custom of teaching children within the family seems to have degenerated without formal and elementary education taking its place, until Rabbi Joshua ben Gamala corrected the defect. Nathan Drazin in his *History of Jewish Education from 515 B.C.E. to 200 C.E.*[5] records the following statement from the Talmud tract *Baba Batra* (21a) about the work of this great teacher of the Jewish people (about 64 B.C.):

> Verily let this man be remembered for good, and Joshua b. Gamala is his name, for had he not been, Torah would have been forgotten in Israel. At first everyone that had a father was taught Torah, but he that had no father did not learn the Torah. . . . So they ordained that teachers for children should be set up in Jerusalem. Whence did they deduce this idea? From "For out of Zion shall go forth the Law, and the word of the Lord from Jerusalem." (*Isaiah* 2:3)

> But this measure sufficed not, for he that had a father was brought by him there to be taught, but he that had no father did not go there. In consequence of this, they ordained

that teachers should be set up in every district, to whom children should be sent at the age of sixteen or seventeen years.

Still when a teacher became angry with a pupil, the latter rebelled and walked away. In this condition education remained until the time of Joshua b. Gamala, who ordained that in every province and in every town teachers should be set up to whom children should be brought at the age of six or seven years.

The Jews, politically powerless, knew that they would be absorbed by the surrounding ethnic and religious groups unless they held their youth strictly to the tradition. Thus their schools did not cease to exist even after the destruction of Jerusalem by Tiberius in A.D. 70. In spite of the dispersion, a large number of Jews remained in the smaller towns and continued their teaching, and the Sanhedrin, though no longer functioning as the highest court under the High Priest—its competence having already been restricted by the Romans—remained a source of authority in matters religious under a patriarch. At several places, e.g., at Jamnia or Jabneh, Usha, Zephoris, and Sura, academies that decided about the canonicity of some books of the Old Testament, interpreted the Law authoritatively, and helped in the editing of the Palestinian and Babylonian Talmud were founded for scholars.

Whoever, as a layman peruses the Talmud, cannot help wondering at the medley of wisdom, legal scholasticism, and verbal dialectics of this encyclopedic compilation of Jewish knowledge and thought during the first centuries of the Christian era. But though most of the Talmud consists of legal arguments, it is also a source of understanding later Jewish educational views and practices.

The tractate *Sabbath* (119b) contains the beautiful sentence: "The world is sustained only through the breath of the children in school." There are witty remarks of the Tannaim on individual differences, especially in the tract *Aboth* which says that "there are four types among pupils; swift to hear and swift to lose—his gain is cancelled by his loss; slow to hear and slow to lose—his loss is cancelled by his gain; swift to hear and slow to lose—this is a happy lot; slow to hear and swift to lose—this is an evil lot." (*Aboth* 5:12.) Or, the author of the tract distinguishes (5:15) between "the sponge" (which absorbs everything); "the funnel" (which takes in on one end and lets out on the other); "the strainer" (which lets out the wine and collects the lees); and "the sieve" (which extracts the coarse matter and collects the fine flour). From the same tract we also receive a picture of the sequence of learning considered desirable by the teachers: Tract *Aboth,* "Mishna EE," reports that Jehudah b. Tema used to say:

> One five years old should study Scripture; ten years—Mishna; thirteen years—should practice the commandments; fifteen years old—should study Gemmara; eighteen years old—the bridal; at twenty—pursuits; at thirty—strength; at forty—discernment; at fifty—counsel; at sixty—age; at seventy—hoariness; at eighty—power; at ninety—decrepitude; at one hundred—it is as though he were dead and gone and had ceased from the world.[6]

The historian Moritz Güdeman has shown that, despite all vicissitudes that befell the Jewish people, the tradition of the Tannaim was continued wherever a sufficient number of believers assembled.[7] In Chapter II of his *History of the Education and Culture of the Jews during the later Middle Ages* he gives a German translation of a document, called the "Book of the Ancient Laws of Teaching," probably from the thirteenth century. There the Rabbis and Levites are admonished "to single out and consecrate one of their sons to the study of the Torah," to erect for the thus separated a school next to the synagogue where they will have to remain for seven years with teachers and pupils supported by the community. "Let no teacher instruct more than ten pupils in one subject." He should teach from script and not from memory. "Let the teacher encourage his students that they question one another in the evening, that they sharpen their intellect with their questions and thereby increase the compass of their mind."

Much value is laid on the solemn character of instruction and the protection of the sacred studies from contagion by the profanities of every day life. An atmosphere of complete devotion should surround the place of learning.

The teachers enjoyed the highest veneration of their people. Lewis Joseph Sherrill [8] quotes a passage from Baba Mezia (II, 11) according to which a person must ransom his teacher first if he and his father are in captivity. Sherrill mentions also a ruling (*Kethuboth* 96a; cf. *Mark* 1:7) that "all manner of service that a slave must render to his master a student must render to his teacher, except that of loosening his shoe." And the prophet (*Daniel* 12:3) speaks of the teachers:

> And those who are wise shall shine like the brightness of the firmament; and those who turn many to righteousness, like the stars for ever and ever.

During the whole Middle Ages Christian teaching owed much to Jewish learning. This was the case especially after the works of Aristotle had become an increasingly rich source of speculation for both Jewish and Christian thinkers. Several great Jewish philosophers such as Isaac Israeli, Ibn Gabirol, and Maimonides influenced Christian Scholasticism in several important points. Rashi's commentaries on the Bible enriched and deepened the understanding of the Old Testament by Christian schoolmen. And no one can read the works of the greatest of their representatives, Albertus Magnus and Thomas Aquinas, without realizing that for many centuries two great traditions of religious philosophy, the Jewish and the Christian, had not only gone alongside, but penetrated each other.

In no way, unfortunately, did the Jewish contributions to the religion of the Christians prevent the latter from continuing their hostility against the former. Especially during and after the crusades all Western nations engaged in violent persecutions and attempts at conversion. However, the hardship but increased the belief of the faithful that the Lord had chosen the people of Israel for a special historical destiny.[9] Jewish scholarship was carried on in several academies of which the one of Jamnia (Jabneh) has already been mentioned. But since the Jews were excluded from any kind of public benefits, their education was inevitably limited to their own communities and their synagogues and much of it was restricted to worship. The *Schema,* which together with the reading of the Torah had since old times been the principal Jewish prayer—"the taking upon oneself the yoke of the kingdom of Heaven"—began with the verses from Deuteronomy:

> Hear, O Israel: The Lord our God is one Lord, and thou shalt love the Lord thy God with all thine heart, and with all thy soul, and with all thy might. . . .

Throughout, the *Schema* contains the most emphatic exaltations of the glory of the One God, admonishing His people to obey His commandments, to revere His power and to be mindful of His everlasting reign (*Deut.* 6:4-9; 11:13-21; *Numbers* 15:37-41; *Exodus* 15:11 and 18).

The element that in unity with the synagogue and the cultivation of the sacred language kept the Jews of the diaspora in spiritual communion was the penetration of the spirit of the covenant into their daily life. There was no room for the profane.

The Daily Prayer Book,[10] or the *Siddur,* is one of the world's great documents of devotional literature. And to such a degree was the "Sabbath" or the day of rest respected by the Jews as assuring the permanence of Israel that they forced the Romans to exempt them from military service. As the New Testament tells us, even Jesus and his disciples had to suffer the rebukes of the Pharisees. Indeed, it has been said even by Jews themselves that the Sabbath rules with their thirty-nine prohibitions of work put an excessive strain on the more restless members of the family. On the other hand, even they enjoyed the ceremonial lighting of the candles and the Sabbath table adorned with wine and special food. Thus Sabbath has been called by the rabbis "the joy of the soul" and been personified as the bride whose bridegroom is Israel. A rich wreath of myths surround the Jewish holidays. Apparently, they reflect not merely the history of the people of Yahwe, but the course of mankind as a whole with its continual rhythm between occasions of sadness and reasons for elation.

Only those who have lived in still untouched Catholic communities, with their festivals of saints, ceremonials, processions, and a traditional kind of bakery prepared in honor of the day, can imagine how much the nonverbal side of religious life contributes to religious education. For words do not become alive unless they are embedded in an environment that gives body and color to what they intend to mean. It is here where modern Protestantism, increasingly also modern Catholicism and Judaism, cut off one of the main sources of spiritual strength.

Although the schooling of the young Jew was primarily based on the Torah, secular subjects such as mathematics and astronomy were also taught. The curriculum of the advanced schools, the Yeshivas, spread all over Europe, was certainly not unaffected by the Aristotelian tradition of the seven liberal arts. And as a result of their compulsory communal schooling, the Jews in countries with a high degree of illiteracy, such as Poland, were far better educated than the large majority of their Christian neighbors.

Inevitably, variances developed among the Jews of the diaspora. The Sephardim, the Jews of Spain and Portugal, cultivated a ritual and a language slightly different from that of the Jews of Middle and Eastern Europe, the Ashkenazim. Jewish mysticism, somewhat suspect to the orthodox because of its pantheistic leanings just as Christian mysticism was to the medieval church, flowered among the Hasidim of the East of Europe. Their way of seeing the divine element even in ordinary daily life has now become universally known through the writings of Martin Buber.

But despite differences in expressing the sense of the Holy, as they inevitably occur in every imaginative culture, there never developed within Judaism the splitting sectarianism characteristic of Christendom, and to a degree also of Islam. Apparently, the strength of the faith in the hearts and the continual threats from outside reinforced each other in the maintenance of an unbroken Jewish tradition.

Not before the middle of the eighteenth century and even then only sporadically, were Jews admitted to the professions. All that was open to them in most countries was trading and dealing with money. Living in ghettos, most of them could acquire only a smattering knowledge of the language of their host nation, nor could they fully participate in the intellectual development of Europe after the Renaissance.

Finally, the spirit of the Enlightenment with its emphasis on religious toleration prepared the gradual emancipation of the Jews in the Western countries.

The symbolic figure of the liberation has become the German Jew Moses Mendelsohn (1729–1786), the model of the hero in Lessing's famous drama of tolerance, *Nathan the Wise (Nathan der Weise)*, to which we will refer in the tenth chapter of this book. Moses Mendelsohn translated the Pentateuch and other parts of the Bible and created thereby the instrument from which the Jews learned the German language. Through his many writings on philosophy, religion, and general cultural topics he became also one of the most influential figures in the general emancipation of German literature from foreign patterns. It was also due to his influence that, in 1778, the Jewish Free School in Berlin was organized which then served as a pattern of similar schools in other German cities.

But even at Mendelsohn's time the Jewish situation was precarious. In order to assure his right to reside undisturbed in the Prussian capital, King Frederick the Great had to declare him a "Schutzjude," that is a Jew under the special protectorate of the monarch. And Lessing's several attempts to prove the high moral standards of the Jews were ridiculed by the mob, inside and outside the clergy. Indeed, the Roman Church needed the second Ecumenical Council to solemnly absolve from the guilt of deicide the Jewish people, who according to Holy Script God Himself had chosen as the instrument of salvation.

It was inevitable that the sudden emancipation of the Jews brought to them not only advantages—as it did to the surrounding populations —but endangered the self-identity of the Jewish tradition more than the persecutions and isolations of earlier times. Before Hitler made the world shockingly aware of the sinister undercurrents out of which centuries' old prejudices may suddenly emerge, a considerable number of Jews were ready for amalgamation with their Christian environment. Furthermore, at the present, Judaism experiences the same encounter with secular movements as does Christianity. There are orthodox and reformist groups, and within each of them there are shades of opinion as to the weight that should be given to the tradition. Even

the inhabitants of Israel itself do not agree about the religious upbringing of their children.

Nevertheless, many liberal Jews wish their children to add instruction in Hebrew to their regular schooling in order to give them
the feeling of belonging to the tradition of their ancestors. The family
will still cherish the symbolism of the Jewish festivals and celebrate
the Sabbath. And while some modern Jews may be embarrassed by
the sight of an Eastern Jew as we find him in the big cities of the world
and in the language of the artist in the paintings of Marc Chagall,
others may venerate and perhaps even envy him as a symbol of the
perseverance of his people within a foreign environment.[11]

Chapter **2**

The Early Centuries of Christianity

INTRODUCTION

For the early and medieval Church the whole pre-Christian world was merely a preparation for the central event in the world's history, the coming of the Christ, as was shown by the introduction of a new calendar beginning with the supposed date of Jesus' birth. According to Christian faith, all, Jews and pagans, were headed toward death, unless they realized that the fulfillment of man's destiny lay in his communion with God through Christ, the only begotten of the Father in whom "the Word was made flesh" (*John* 1:14).

Christ's disciples believed in the literal meaning of the "Word made flesh." His crucifixion was interpreted as the act of reconciliation between God, the judge, and man, the sinner; Christ's resurrection and his promise to return were seen as the victory of faith over sin and death.

When the perishable puts on the imperishable, and the mortal puts on immortality, then shall come to pass the saying that is written:

"Death is swallowed up in victory."
"O death, where is thy victory?
"O death, where is thy sting?"
The sting of death is sin, and the power of sin is the law.

But thanks be to God, who gives us the victory through our Lord Jesus Christ. (*I Corinthians* 15:54-57.)

There are many places, especially in the letters of St. Paul, where the essence of the Christian doctrine comes to light, but perhaps none helps more to understand its difference from the pagan and Jewish traditions and the educational implication of this difference than Chapter 2 of the *Epistle to the Ephesians,* going under the name of St. Paul.

The Christian parent or educator who has imbibed the meaning of that chapter will consider it his duty to develop in his disciples, with the help of God's "grace" and "mercy" the new spirit that has delivered man from "the desires of the flesh and of the mind." No one can become a Christian who has not felt the "great love wherewith God loved us" and "quickened us together with Christ" and who has not understood that it is by "grace" and "faith" and not by works, not even by following "the law of commandments" that man can be saved. Through "the blood of Christ" the "middle wall of partition" between God and man has been broken down and the situation of man as a "stranger and foreigner" can be changed into one of fellowship "with the saints" and "the household of God."

The new gospel was bound to have an enormous influence on the life of the "new born."

I therefore, a prisoner for the Lord, beg you to lead a life worthy of the calling to which you have been called, with all lowliness and meekness, with patience, forbearing one another in love, eager to maintain the unity of the Spirit in the bond of peace.

There is one body and one Spirit, just as you were called to the one hope that belongs to your call, one Lord, one faith, one baptism, one God and Father of us all, who is above all and through all and in all. . . .

Assuming that you have heard about him and were taught in him as the truth is in Jesus. Put off your old nature which belongs to your former manner of life and is corrupt through deceitful lusts, and be renewed in the spirit of your

minds, and put on the new nature, created after the likeness of God in true righteousness and holiness.

Therefore, putting away falsehood, let everyone speak the
truth with his neighbor, for we are members one of another.
Be angry but do not sin; do not let the sun go down on
your anger, and give no opportunity to the devil. Let the
thief no longer steal, but rather let him labor, doing hon-
est works with his hands, so that he may be able to give to
those in need. Let no evil talk come out of your mouths,
but only such as is good for edifying, as fits the occasion,
that it may impart grace to those who hear.

And do not grieve the holy Spirit of God, in whom you
were sealed for the day of redemption. Let all bitterness
and wrath and anger and clamor and slander be put away
from you, with all malice, and be kind to one another, as
God in Christ forgave you. (*Ephesians* 4:1–6; 21–32.)

Inevitably, the new concept of personality affected also the concept of community. The main objectives of Greek and Roman education was loyalty to the state, in the first centuries after Christ sym-
bolized by the worship of the emperor. Those who were not citizens,
such as women or slaves, were of inferior status. For the Christian—
here they followed the Jews—one power only could be supreme; one
power only could be worshipped: God. This transcendentalism caused
the persecutions of the Christians by the Romans; also in later centuries it was bound to clash with absolute political power unless
both found a compromise. But as we know from many documents,
for example Tertullian's *Apologeticus,* quoted later, the Christians
prayed for (though never to) the emperor. Also the *Epistle of Clement* to the Corinthians, written about A.D. 100, contains an invocation
that proves that the Christians recognized governmental authority.[1]

. . . Give concord and peace to us and to all that dwell on
the earth, as thou didst give to our fathers who called on
thee in holiness with faith and truth, and grant that we may
be obedient to thy almighty and glorious name, and to our
rulers and governors upon the earth.

Thou Master, hast given the power of sovereignty to them through thy excellent and inexpressible might, that we may know the glory and honour given to them by thee, and be subject to them, in nothing resisting thy will. And to them, Lord, grant health, peace, concord, firmness that they may administer the government which thou hast given them without offence. For thou, heavenly Master, king of eternity, hast given to the sons of men glory and honour and power over the things which are on the earth; do thou, O Lord, direct their counsels according to that which is "good and pleasing" before thee, that they may administer with piety on peace and gentleness the power given to them by thee, and may find mercy in thine eyes. O thou who alone art able to do these things and far better things for us, we praise thee through Jesus Christ, the high priest and guardian of our souls, through whom be glory and majesty to thee, both now and for all generations and for ever and ever. Amen.

Nevertheless, by making all earthly power relative to the divine absolute and to the last judgment which they expected to come soon to end all secular kingdoms, the Christians undermined, in a form of silent and creeping revolution, the ancient society with its polytheistic rituals and ceremonies, its emperor worship, and its philosophical tradition. They did not abolish slavery as an institution; they themselves had slaves. Nevertheless, they accepted them to their worship. Before God there was no distinction. And though the Greek rhetor Isocrates (436–338 B.C.) and the Roman Stoic philosopher Epictetus (ca. A.D. 60–120) had already developed the idea of the essential equality of men, the Christians changed the theory into a creed with corresponding action. This, of course, made them dangerous.

For as in one body we have many members, and all the members do not have the same function, so we, though many, are one body in Christ, and individually members one of the other. (*Romans* 12:4, 5.)

However, as through all human history, the customs, prejudices and pressures of society were stronger than the ideal. Christians brought from the old Greek, African, and Asiatic heritages a concept of womanhood that made the female sex inferior to men. The paradise myth and other parts of the Bible supported that attitude so that, despite the high appreciation of the role of the mother and the increasing veneration of St. Mary, women were at a disadvantage in the life of the Church, the Christian family and with regard to their education.

In honor of Cornelia, "Mother of the Gracchi," the Romans erected a monument. It is doubtful whether they would ever have degraded women (and thus indirectly themselves) as did the church father Tertullian when he wrote the following diatribe against the female sex: [2]

On Female Dress

If there dwelt upon earth a faith as great as is the reward of faith which is expected in the heavens, no one of you at all, best beloved sisters, from the time that she had first "known the Lord," and learned [the truth] concerning her own [that is, woman's] condition, would have desired too gladsome [not to say too ostentatious] a style of dress; so as not rather to go about in humble garb, and rather to affect meanness of appearance, walking about as Eve mourning and repentant, in order that by every garb of penitence she might the more fully expiate that which she derives from Eve,—the ignominy, I mean, of the first sin, and the odium [attacking to her as the cause] of human perdition. "In pains and anxieties dost thou bear [children], woman; and toward thine husband [is] thy inclination, and he lords it over thee." And do you not know that you are [each] an Eve? The sentence of God on this sex of yours lives in this age: the guilt must of necessity live too. *You* are the devil's gateway: you are the unsealer of that [forbidden] tree; *you* are the first deserter of the divine law: you are she who persuaded him whom the devil was not valiant enough to attack. *You* destroyed so easily God's image, man. On account of *your* desert—that is, death—even the Son of God had to die. And do you think about adorning yourself over and above your tunics of skins? Come, now; if from the beginning of the world the Milesians sheared sheep, and the Serians spun trees, and the Tyrians dyed, and the Phrygians embroidered with the needle, and the Babylonians with the loom, and pearls gleamed, and onyx-stones flashed; if gold itself also had already issued, with the cupidity [which accompanies it], from the ground; if the mirror, too, already had licence to lie so largely, Eve, expelled from paradise, [Eve] already dead, would also have coveted *these* things, I imagine! No more, then, ought she *now* to crave, or be acquainted with [if she desires to live again], what, when she *was* living, she had neither had nor known. Accordingly these things are all the baggage of woman in her condemned and dead state, instituted as if to swell the pomp of her funeral. (I, ch. i)

In another treatise, entitled "To His Wife," [3] Tertullian admonishes his spouse—disavowing, of course, all personal motives—that she renounce the temptation of a second wedlock after his death, for the Lord will not acknowledge such unions at the day of judgment, especially since the apostle, though permitting marriage, prefers celibacy. ("Happy the man who shall prove like Paul.") Even gentile widows choose abstinence, for thus they can devote their time "to the memory of beloved husbands."

"Follow companies and conversations"—so he says to his "best beloved fellow-servant in the Lord"—worthy of God. . . . Talkative, idle, winebibbing, curious tent-fellows, do the very greatest hurt to the purpose of widowhood. Through talkativeness there creep in words unfriendly to modesty; through idleness they seduce one from strictness; through winebibbing they insinuate any and every evil; through curiosity they convey a spirit of rivalry in lust. Not one of such women knows how to speak of the good of single-husbandhood; for their 'god,' as the apostle says, 'is their belly'; and so, too, what is neighbor to the belly" (I, ch. viii).

Bishop John Chrysostom (345–407), most famous of the Greek church fathers, though praising Christian women for their warmth and piety and recommending marriage as the means of mutual perfection, was convinced that since the seduction of innocent Adam by Eve a special curse was laid on women. This curse, so he thought, revealed itself in continual protest by the female sex against divine law. In his treatise *On the Priesthood*, he said: [4]

The divine law excluded women from this ministry, but they struggle violently to thrust themselves in; and since in themselves they can do nothing, they perform all their actions through others; and they have acquired such power that they choose and expel priests at their will.

As we can see from the history of divorce law in late antiquity, the Christians, following the Jewish tradition and Christ's words (*Mark* 10:2–12) affirmed the sacredness of marriage and—at least to a degree—protected the wife against the arbitrariness of the husband. Also, women became martyrs and saints, and, up to the fourth century A.D., Christians took no offence at the married life of the mother of Jesus or at the existence of his brothers. Tertullian, for example, uses Mary's marriage after the miraculous birth of her first son as an argument for the incarnation against the Gnostics. Not before the council of Chalcedon in 451 was the quality of perpetual virginity authoritatively attributed to Mary. The Montanist movement, which Tertullian joined, and which, believing in the nearness of the day of judgment, protested against the compromises of the Church with the Roman empire, venerated two women, Prisca and Maximilla, as inspired by God.

Finally, St. Augustine contributed to Christian literature the praise of his mother Monica.[5]

This other great gift thou also didst bestow, O my God, my Mercy, upon that good handmaid of thine, in whose womb thou didst create me. It was that whenever she could she acted as a peacemaker between any different and discordant spirits, and when she heard any bitter things on either side of a controversy . . . she would disclose nothing about the one to the other except what might serve to their reconciliation. . . . It ought not to be enough in a truly humane man merely not to incite or increase the enmities of men by evil-speaking; he ought likewise to endeavor by kind words to extinguish them. Such a one was she—and thou, her most intimate instructor, didst teach her in the school of her heart. Finally, her own husband, now toward the end of his earthly existence, she won over to thee. Henceforth, she had no cause to complain of unfaithfulness in him, which she had endured before he became one of the faithful. She was also the servant of thy servants. All those who knew her greatly praised, honored, and loved thee in her because, through the witness of the fruits of a holy life, they recognized thee present in her heart. For she had "been the wife of one man" (*I. Tim.* 5:9), had honored her parents, had guided her house in piety, was highly reputed for good works, had brought up her children, traveling in labor as often as she saw them swerving from thee. Lastly, to all of us, O Lord—since of thy favor thou allowest thy servants to speak to all of us who lived together in that association before her death in thee she devoted such care as she might have if she had been mother of us all; she served us as if she had been the daughter of us all. (Bk. 9, ch. ix, 21–22)

THE EDUCATIONAL PRINCIPLES OF EARLY CHRISTIANITY

If I speak in the tongues of men and of angels, but have not love, I am a noisy gong or a clanging cymbal.

And if I have prophetic powers and understand all mysteries and all knowledge, and if I have all faith, so as to remove mountains, but have not love, I am nothing. If I give away all I have, and if I deliver my body to be burned, but have not love, I gain nothing.

Love is patient and kind; love is not jealous or boastful; it is not arrogant or rude. Love does not insist on its own way; it is not irritable or resentful; it does not rejoice at wrong, but rejoices in the right. Love bears all things, believes all things, hopes all things, endures all things.

Love never ends; as for prophecies, they will pass away; as for tongues, they will cease; as for knowledge, it will pass away. For our knowledge is imperfect and our prophecy is imperfect; but when the perfect comes, the imperfect will pass away. When I was a child, I spoke like a child, I

thought like a child, I reasoned like a child; when I became a man, I gave up childish ways. For now we see in
a mirror dimly, but then face to face. Now I know in part;
then I shall understand fully, even as I have been fully understood. So faith, hope, love abide, these three; but the
greatest of these is love. (*I Corinthians: 13*)

With these words from the New Testament the groundwork is
laid upon which the principles of Christian education could later be
built. The fifteenth verse of *Mark* 10 contains profound wisdom; we
shall not enter the kingdom of God unless we receive it "as a little
child." Childhood, there, is not merely a biological but an ethical notion, a quality of faithfulness, innocence, and openness to the wonders of the world which the adult must retain, lest he become incapable of opening himself to the influx of the divine power. Even the
sinner in whom this childlike innocence survives may be nearer to God
than the "righteous."

On the other hand, the Christian concept of man counteracts the
sentimental ideas about the children which developed during the
nineteenth and twentieth centuries. St. Paul's idea that the natural
men, or the men who follow "the desires of body and mind," are "by
nature children of wrath, like the rest of mankind" (*Ephesians* 2:3),
has entered deeply into Christianity as well as the concept of "original
sin," framed by later theologians who traced it back to the "fall" of
the first couple. In certain movements such as asceticism and Calvinist Puritanism the belief in man's total depravity became so overpow-
ering that it distorted their whole concept of man and life. Thus the
history of Christian education has been not only one of love, justice,
and discipline, the three of which, according to the Old and New Testaments, should always go together. It has also served as an excuse for
cruelty and sadistic trends. Of the two verses in *Colossians* 3:20:
"Children, obey your parents in all things for this is well pleasing to
the Lord," and 3:21: "Fathers, provoke not your children to anger lest
they be discouraged," the first was remembered, and the second often
forgotten.

This fear-ridden relation between pupils and teachers in some

Christian schools was far from the spirit with which the early Christian communities embraced their members, young and old. We have a description of it in the so-called Didache, or *Teaching of the Twelve Apostles,* which one might call the oldest Christian catechism. It was written *ca.* 120 in a small community of Egypt or Syria and discovered in 1875. Part One contains a collection of moral precepts influenced by *The Two Ways,* which was probably a Jewish manual carried over to the Christian Church. Part Two is a kind of church directory concerning functions, spiritual gifts, services, and the ministry.[6]

The first part is here given in full.

1. There are two Ways, one of Life and one of Death, and there is a great difference between the two Ways.

2. The Way of Life is this: "First, thou shalt love the God who made thee, secondly, thy neighbor as thyself: and whatsoever thou wouldn'st not have done to thyself, do not thou to another."

3. Now, the teaching of these words is this: "Bless those that curse you, and pray for your enemies, and fast for those that persecute you. For what credit is it to you if you love those that love you? Do not even the heathen do the same?" But, for your part, "love those that hate you," and you will have no enemy.

4. "Abstain from carnal" and bodily "lusts." "If any man smite thee on the right cheek, turn to him the other cheek also," and thou wilt be perfect. "If any man impress thee to go with him one mile, go with him two If any man take thy coat, give him thy shirt also. If any man will take from thee what is thine, refuse it not"—not even if thou canst.

5. Give to everyone that asks thee, and do not refuse, for the Father's will is that we give to all from the gifts we have received. Blessed is he that gives according to the mandate; for he is innocent. Woe to him who receives; for if any man receive alms under pressure of need he is innocent; but he who receives it without need shall be tried as to why he took and for what, and being in prison he shall be examined as to his deeds, and "he shall not come out thence until he pay the last farthing."

6. But concerning this it was also said, "Let thine

alms sweat into thine hands until thou knowest to whom thou art giving."

If one wants to understand further why the small, despised, and persecuted Christian communities finally conquered the Roman empire, he has only to read *The Epistle to Diognetus* and Tertullian's description of the community life of the Christians in his *Apologeticus,* both of which we reproduce here in part.

From *The Epistle to Diognetus* [7]

For the distinction between Christians and other men is neither in country nor language nor customs. For they do not dwell in cities in some place of their own, nor do they use any strange variety of dialect, nor practice an extraordinary kind of life. This teaching of theirs has not been discovered by the intellect or thought of busy men, nor are they the advocates of any human doctrine as some men are. Yet while living in Greek and barbarian cities, according as each obtained his lot, and following the local customs, both in clothing and food and in the rest of life, they show forth the wonderful and confessedly strange character of the constitution of their own citizenship. They dwell in their own citizenship. They dwell in their own fatherlands, but as if sojourners in them, they share all things as citizens, and suffer all things as strangers. Every foreign country is their fatherland, and every fatherland is a foreign country. They marry as all men, they bear children, but they do not expose their offspring. They offer free hospitality, but guard their purity. Their lot is cast "in the flesh," but they do not live "after the flesh." They pass their time upon the earth, but they have their citizenship in heaven. They obey the appointed laws, and they surpass the laws in their own lives. They love all men and are persecuted by all men. They are unknown and they are condemned. They are put to death and they gain life. "They are poor and make many rich"; they lack all things and have all things in abundance. They are dishonoured, and are justified. "They are abused and give blessing," they are insulted and render honour. When they do good they are buffeted as evil-doers, when

they are buffeted they rejoice as men who receive life.
They are warred upon by the Jews as foreigners and are
persecuted by the Greeks and those who hate them cannot
state the cause of their enmity.

To put it shortly, what the soul is in the body, that the
Christians are in the world. The soul is spread through all
members of the body, and Christians throughout the cities
of the world. The soul dwells in the body, but is not of
the body, and Christians dwell in the world, but are not of
the world. The soul is invisible, and is guarded in a visible
body, and Christians are recognised when they are in the
world, but their religion remains invisible. The flesh hates
the soul, and wages war upon it, though it has suffered no
evil, because it is prevented from gratifying its pleasures,
and the world hates the Christians though it has suffered no
evil, because they are opposed to its pleasures. The soul
loves the flesh which hates it and the limbs and Christians
love those that hate them. The soul has been shut up in the
body, but itself sustains the body; and Christians are confined in the world as in a prison, but themselves sustain
the world. The soul dwells immortal in a mortal tabernacle,
and Christians sojourn among corruptible things, waiting for
the incorruptible which is in heaven. The soul when evil
treated in food and drink becomes better, and Christians
when buffeted day by day increase more. God has appointed
them to so great a post and it is not right for them to decline it.

From Tertullian's *Apologeticus* [8]

We are a body knit together as such by a common religious
profession, by unity of discipline, and by the bond of common hope. We meet together as an assembly and congregation, that, offering up prayer to God as with united force,
we may wrestle with Him in our supplications. This violence God delights in. We pray, too, for the emperors, for
their ministers and for all in authority, for the welfare of the
ministers and for all in authority, for the welfare of the
world, for the prevalence of peace, for the delay of the
final consummation. We assemble to read our sacred writ-

ings, if any peculiarity of the times makes either fore-warning or reminiscence needful. However, it be in that respect with the sacred words, we nourish our faith, we animate our hope, we make our confidence more stedfast; and no less by inculcations of God's precepts we confirm good habits. In the same place also exhortations are made, rebukes and sacred censuses are administered. For with a great gravity is the work of judging carried on among us, as befits those who feel assured that the most notable example of judgment to come when any one has sinned so grievously as to require his severance from us in prayer, and the meeting, and all sacred intercourse. The tried men of our elders preside over us, obtaining that honour not by purchase, but by established character. There is no buying and selling of any sort in the things of God. Though we have our treasure-chest, it is not made up of purchase-money, as of a religion that has its price. On the monthly collection day, if he likes, each puts in a small donation; but only if it be his pleasure, and only if he be able: for there is no compulsion; all is voluntary. These gifts are, as it were, piety's deposit fund. For they are not taken thence and spent on feasts, and drinking-bouts, and eating houses, but to support and bury poor people, to supply the wants of boys and girls destitute of means and parents, and of old persons confined now to the house; such, too, as have suffered shipwreck; and if there happen to be any in the mines, as banished to the islands, or shut up in the prisons, for nothing but their fidelity to the cause of God's church, they become the nurslings of their confession.

Here we have the description of an ideal community, held together not only by the natural feeling of neighborly sympathy, but even more so by its consciousness of living under the grace of a supernatural power—helpful and forgiving, but judging at the same time.

Chapter 3

The Adaptation of the Christian Community to the Social and Mental Environment

The longer the Christian communities such as described by Diognetus and Tertullian persevered, the more they attracted persons of rank; and the longer the return of the Savior kept them waiting, the greater became the temptation to compromise with the social environment. At the time of Tertullian, about 200, certain elements had already joined the Church who were less eager to suffer as martyrs than to profit from Christian charity. Others joined because they felt lonely. Soldiers and officials had already been baptized, and many of the educated who had become pessimists, were attracted by mystical ideas and inclined to believe that the end of an era had come. But they had been educated in the Greek-Roman philosophical tradition, and though magnetized by the very strangeness of the new gospel, they also needed some persuasion about its credibility.

The Christians themselves felt early the need to relate their ideas to the thought of Greece—following here the Jew Philo who at the time of Christ had attempted a harmonization between the Judaic and the Hellenistic traditions.[1] When St. Paul in Athens was confronted by "certain philosophers of the Epicureans and of the Stoics" who considered him a "babbler" and "a setter forth of strange Gods," he began the explanation of his gospel with reference to the altar of the Unknown God that the Greeks had erected.

So Paul, standing in the middle of the Areopagus, said: "Men of Athens, I perceive that in every way you are very religious. For as I passed along and observed the objects of your worship, I found also an altar with this inscription, 'To an unknown god.' What therefore you worship as unknown, this I proclaim to you. The god who made the world and everything in it, being Lord of heaven and earth, does not live in shrines made by man, nor is he served by human hands, as though he needed anything, since he himself gives to all men life and breath and everything.

"And he made all the face of the earth, having determined allotted periods and the boundaries of their habitation, that they should seek God, in the hope that they might feel after him and find him. Yet he is not far from each one of us, for 'In him we live and move and have our being' and even some of your poets have said, 'For we are indeed his offspring.'

"Being then God's offspring, we ought not to think that the Deity is like gold, or silver, or stone, a representation by the art and imagination of man. The times of ignorance God overlooked, but now he commands all men everywhere to repent, because he has fixed a day on which he will judge the world in righteousness by a man whom he has appointed, and of this he has given assurance to all men by raising him from the dead." (*The Acts* 17:22–31.)

Moreover, the latest of the gospels, the Gospel according to St. John, written in the first decade or decades of the second century, related the Christian God to a central Platonic-Stoic concept, that of the *Logos*, as the symbol of the order and meaning of life.

In the beginning was the Word [Logos], and the Word was with God, and the Word was God. He was in the beginning with God; all things were made through him, and without him was not anything made that was made. In him was life, and the life was the light of men. The light shines in the darkness, and the darkness has not overcome it. (*St. John* 1:1–5.)

More and more did the intellectuality of the Hellenistic world exercise its pressure on the Christian communities. The younger generation needed an adequate liberal education to compete with its pagan contemporaries. Thus every church father felt himself compelled to write about, or touch upon, the problem of the right upbringing of children.[2]

With the broadening of education and the increasing involvement in Hellenistic thought—this to such a degree that modern historians describe our theology as a compound between the Christian message, Judaism and Greek philosophy—the conflict arose whether to keep the gospel of Christ pure and unadulterated, or to melt it into the heritage of the ancient world. The battle raged for several hundred years. In a way, it still persists.

The Syrian Tatian (second century) can be used as a representative of the intransigent.[3] He addresses the Greeks:

> What noble thing have you produced by your pursuit of philosophy? Who of your most eminent men has been free from vain boasting? . . . The reading of your books is like walking through a labyrinth, and their readers resemble the cask of the Danaids. . . . While you arrogate to yourselves the sole right of discussion, you discourse like the blind man with the deaf. . . .

On Tatian's side were many of the Africans; even Tertullian had similar opinions. Certainly his famous words, "*Credo quia absurdum*," and "*Prorsus credibile est quia ineptum est . . . certum est, quia impossibile*,"[4] do not place him on the side of the rational seekers of truth.

Yet, Tertullian is not consistent. For example, in his *On the Testimony of the Soul (De Testimonio Animae)* he recognizes a certain value in ancient knowledge, although it is born of natural reason, and in his *On Idolatry (De Idolatria)*, after severely criticizing the various pagan occupations including those of the teachers, he ventures the following statement:[5]

> If the servants of God are not permitted to teach the letters, they also cannot be permitted to learn them. But since

the knowledge of literature is requisite to any lasting occupation, how without it can one acquire secular wisdom, common sense and efficiency in action? Thus, how can we reject worldly studies, since without them the sacred studies could not exist? Hence we admit the necessity of literary pursuits. Nevertheless, we must be aware that a part of them cannot be allowed but must be shunned, and that the faithful should be versed in literature, but not teach it.

Inconsistency is also evident in the writings of one of the early church fathers, the Syrian Justin Martyr, who was born about 114 and suffered martyrdom in the reign of Marcus Aurelius.

Naturally, he tries to show the fallacies in pagan thought and the superiority of his adopted faith, but, in contrast to the radicals, he does not forget his early philosophical education—instead, he puts it to good use. Thus he sees many monotheistic trends in Greek thought and so many other similarities to the Judao-Christian tradition that, in order to sustain its claim for uniqueness, he takes refuge in a precarious historical contrivance, used also by later Christian authors. The higher truth, he says, did not come from the pagans' own insight, but they borrowed it from Moses, about whose sacred wisdom they had heard in Egypt. He declares in a chapter of his "Hortatory Address to the Greeks": [6]

But Plato, though he accepted, as is likely, the doctrine of Moses and the other prophets regarding one only God, which he learned while in Egypt, yet fearing, on account of what had befallen Socrates, lest he also should raise up some Anytus or Meletus against himself, who should accuse him before the Athenians and say, "Plato is doing harm and making himself mischievously busy, not acknowledging the gods recognized by the state"; in fear of the hemlock-juice, contrives an elaborate and ambiguous discourse concerning the gods, furnishing by his treatise gods to those who wish them, and none for those who are differently disposed, as may readily be seen from his own statements. For when he has laid down that everything that is made is mortal, he afterwards says that the gods were made. If, then, he should have God and matter the origin of all things, manifestly it is inevitably necessary to say that the gods were made of matter; but if of matter, out of which he says that evil also has its origin, he leaves right-thinking persons to consider what kind of beings the gods should be thought who are produced out of matter. For, for this very reason did he say that matter was eternal [or "uncreated"] that he might not seem to say that God is the creator of evil. And regarding the gods who were made by God, there is no doubt he said this: "Gods of gods, of whom I am the creator." And he manifestly held the correct opinion concerning the really existing God. For having heard in Egypt that God has said to Moses, when He was about to send him to the Hebrews, "I am that I am," he understood that God had not mentioned to him His proper name.

In the centuries after Christ the Egyptian city of Alexandria became, besides Athens, the main international center of learning. Its enlightened character influenced also the famous "Catechetical School" for Christians, with the church father Clement (*ca*. 150–220) as one of its instructors, as most of the Christian leaders were teachers. How could it be otherwise at a time when the few Christians, following the command of Jesus and the examples of the apostles, regarded the propagation of the Gospel and the conversion of Jews and Gentiles as their divine mission? As already mentioned, even at the period of Jesus the Jew Philo attempted to prove the compatibility between the Old Testament and Greek philosophy. It was in his tradition that Clement tried to bring about a synthesis between the Christian message and the Platonic heritage. Christianity was for him a religion of universal quality, destined to replace the moribund pagan polytheism. The idea of "one humanity," first envisioned by Alexander the Great and the Stoic school, was now embraced by a religion that added the claim of revelation by "one God" to the humanistic ethics of the Hellenistic culture.

Clement of Alexandria had undergone a thorough philosophical training when he discovered Christ as the divine guide (*paidagogos*) toward unity.[7]

According to Clement, both the Greek sages and the Christian teachers sought to attain a holy life. Plato was God-inspired; the worship of heavenly bodies as we find it among pagans was meant as homage to the Creator. Not to the Jews alone was God's care confined. In the thought of Clement, as in the Gospel of St. John, Christ appears not only as the fulfillment of the Old Testament, but also as the self-realization of reason, or the *logos*. Those who follow this power become transformed persons. And Clement, as those in the Middle Ages and even we today, is concerned with the relation between faith (*pistis*) and intellectual knowledge (*gnosis*).[8] In faith, he believes, the essence of knowledge is contained. A simple man who obeys the Commandments is, in the eyes of God, not inferior to a learned theologian. However, in order to be complete, faith needs the foundation and affirmation of reason. When the two compenetrate, the true light arises in the human soul and "scientific" or "demonstrated" faith is achieved.[9]

> Faith is then, so to speak, a comprehensive knowledge of the essentials; and knowledge is the strong and sure demonstration of what is received by faith, built upon faith by the Lord's teaching, conveying [the soul] on to infallibility, science, and comprehension.

But gnosis is not merely doctrine, it is also commitment.[10]

> For we say that knowledge is not merely verbal, but a kind of divine science. It is that light which is kindled in the soul by obedience to the commandments and which makes manifest all created things and teaches man to know both himself and all that which he may be able to understand through his reason.

Naturally, a man of Clement's erudition was opposed to the "ignorant bawlers" among the Christians who unconsciously revealed the weakness of their faith through their fear that it might be shaken by contact with scholarly knowledge.[11]

> Now, then, many things in life take their rise in some exercise of human reason, having received the kindling spark from God. . . .

> But God's will is especially obeyed by the free-will of good men. Since many advantages are common to good and bad

men yet they are nevertheless advantageous only to men of goodness and probity, for whose sake God created them. For it was for the use of good men that the influence which is in God's gifts was originated. Besides, the thoughts of virtuous men are produced through the inspiration of God; the soul being disposed in the way it is, and the divine will being conveyed to human souls, particular divine ministers contributing to such services. . . . Such are those fit to lead and teach, in whom the action of Providence is conspicuously seen; whenever either by instruction, or government, or administration, God wishes to benefit. But He wishes at all times. Wherefore He moves those who are adapted to useful exertion in the things which pertain to virtue. And it is given either in order that men may become good, or that those who are so may make use of their natural advantages. For it co-operates both in what is general and what is particular. How absurd, then, is it, in those who attribute disorder and wickedness to the devil, to make him the bestower of philosophy, a virtuous thing! For he is thus all but made more benignant to the Greeks in respect of making men good, than the divine providence and mind.

Again, I reckon it is part of law and of right reason to assign to each one what is appropriate to him, and belongs to him, and falls to him. . . .

Philosophy is not, then, the product of vice, since it makes men virtuous; it follows then, that it is the work of God, whose work it is solely to do good. And all things given by God are given and received well.

Further, if the practice of philosophy does not belong to the wicked, but was accorded to the best of the Greeks, it is clear also from what source it was bestowed—manifestly from Providence, which assigns to each what is befitting in accordance with his deserts.

Rightly, then, to the Jews belonged the Law, and to the Greek philosophy, until the Advent; and after that came the universal calling to be a peculiar people of righteousness, through the teaching which flows from faith, brought together by one Lord, the only God of both Greeks and Barbarians, or rather of the whole race of men. We have often called by the name philosophy that portion of truth attained through philosophy, although but partial. . . .

To be sure, if one takes purity of faith as the exclusive criterion, then it is difficult to decide who was nearer the original message of Christ and his disciples, Tatian and his followers, or Justin Martyr and Clement. But it is certain that the Christians would have remained an obscure sect and sooner or later succumbed to the competition of other Asiatic religions, if men such as Clement had not emphasized its indebtedness to the great philosophical legacies of the past.

But was the ideal synthesis between Christian faith and secular knowledge really achieved by Clement? The reader of Clement's *Stromata* and his other works cannot help but feel that in his syncretistic mind neither the proud anthropocentric search of the Greeks nor the God-embedded faithfulness of the early Christians has received its full share. Certainly, the dilemma is not solved by Clement's attempt —already made by Justin Martyr—to prove the common origin of both by the assertion that Plato was influenced by Moses and the prophets. In the course of time the conflict within the Christian tradition between divine and secular knowledge even increased. Sometimes it was precariously bridged over by men such as Erasmus, Hegel, Schelling, and the modern Christian humanists; and sometimes it burst forth, as in the Reformation and Counter Reformation on the one side, and scientific naturalism on the other. Today we read Kierkegaard, but we also read Nietzsche, and it remains to be seen whether the Christian tradition can be sufficiently widened and deepened to embrace the world view constantly expanded by modern science.

Even more than Clement does, his disciple Origen (*ca.* 185–254) insists on the value of secular learning. For him, too, rational believers are superior to the simple-minded, for those who assent to opinions without logical reasoning may easily be deceived. Only those who are deprived of the privilege of higher studies should take Christianity on faith alone.[12]

Moreover, concerning the multitude of believers who have renounced the great flood of evil in which formerly they have used to wallow, who ask this question—is it better that those who believe without thought should somehow have been made reformed characters and be helped by the belief that they are punished for sin and rewarded for good works, or that we should not allow them to be converted with simple faith until they might devote themselves to the study of rational argument? For obviously all but a very few would fail to attain the help which they have derived from simple belief, but would remain living a very evil life. (I:9)

Inevitably, men such as Clement and Origen ran into logical difficulties when they tried to prove the concord between biblical and pagan literature. They often took recourse to nonliteral, allegorical, and parabolic interpretations of the sacred writings. Thus Origen, like Clement, repeated Philo's comparison of the literal meaning of the Scripture to its "body" and "flesh," whereas he described the inner and real meaning to its "soul." [13]

An illustrating example of Origen's idea of scriptural exegesis may be found in his work *De Principiis*.[14]

The way, then, as it appears to us, in which we ought to deal with the Scriptures, and extract from their meaning, is the following, which has been ascertained from the Scriptures themselves. By Solomon in the Proverbs we find some such rule as this enjoined respecting the divine doctrines of Scripture: "And do thou portray them in a threefold manner, in counsel and knowledge, to answer words of truth to them who propose them to thee." The individual ought, then, to portray the idea of holy Scripture in a threefold manner upon his soul; in order that the simple man may be edified by the "flesh," as it were, of the Scripture, for so we name the obvious sense; while he who has ascended a certain way [may be edified] by the "soul," as it were. The perfect man, again, and he who resembles those spoken of by the apostle, when he says, "We speak wisdom among them that are perfect, but not the wisdom of the world, nor of the rulers of this world, who come to nought; but we speak the wisdom of God in a mystery, the hidden wisdom, which God hath ordained before the ages, unto our glory. . . . For as man consists of body, and soul, and spirit, so in the same way does Scripture, which has been arranged to be given by God for the Salvation of men. . . .

Although this manner of explanation gave rise to mythical beauty and profound speculation—we can still find it in modern religious symbolism—it also allowed for ambiguity, confusion, and all kinds of philological jugglery.

Happily, we possess an address to Origen by one of his many grateful pupils, Gregory Thaumaturgus, and a letter of Origen to Gregory. Both reveal how perfectly one of the greatest Christian teachers understood how to implant in his disciples the firm conviction that the Greek concept of education (*paideia*) is not only compatible with Christian revelation, but also finds in it its true fulfillment. In the manner of the flowering panegyrics of the time, Gregory Thaumaturgus gives us a vivid picture of the ways in which the great Christian teachers introduced their students into the sacred lore. After studying law, Gregory had remained for eight years at Origen's school of Caesarea. He represents his master as an inspiring lover of youth who, after laying a groundwork of scientific knowledge, teaches how to

philosophize and collate with all our powers every one of the writings of the ancients, whether philosophers, or poets, excepting and rejecting nothing . . . save only those of the atheists, who have taken leave even of ordinary common sense in a body and deny the existence of God and Providence.

Only after a thorough philological and philosophical preparation did Origen consider his pupils sufficiently mature to understand divine revelation in its full depth and glory.

Gregory Thaumaturgus—*Address to Origen*

IV . . . Let this our Address then be one of thanksgiving, if of men, to this holy man here above all . . . let it be to him who by some great dispensation obtained the lot of governing me from childhood and tending me and caring for me, the holy angel of God who nourished me from my youth up!

VI. And he took us over, and from the first day, veritably the first day, the most precious of all days—if I must say so—when first the true light began to rise upon me, began by using every device to bind us firmly, us who were like some wild beasts, or fishes, or birds, fallen into snares or nets, trying to struggle out and escape away, and wishful to depart from him to Berytus or our fatherland. He used every turn of language, pulled every string, as they say, employed every resource of his abilities, praised philosophy and those enamoured of philosophy in long numerous and apt eulogies, insisting that they only lived the life befitting the reasonable beings who studied to live rightly, who "knew themselves," first their own nature, and secondly, the things essentially good which a human being ought to follow after, and the really evil things which he ought to avoid. . . .

Furthermore, something else was striking the goad of friendship into us, no easily resisted thing; that was the keenness and great urgency of his ability and good disposition, which shone so benevolently upon us in his very tones as he discoursed or talked, trying not to get an easy victory over us in argument, but by his able and kindly and genuine ability to save us and render us partakers of the benefits of philosophy. . . . Like some spark kindled within my soul there was kindled and blazed forth my love both toward Him, most desirable of all for His beauty unspeakable, the World hold and altogether lovely, and toward this man his friend and prophet. Deeply stricken by it, I was led to neglect all that seemed to concern me: affairs, studies, even by favourite law, home and kindred there, no less than those among whom I was sojourning. One thing only was dear and affected by me; philosophy and its teacher, this divine man—and the soul of Jonathan was knit with David.[15]

Gregory then shows how Origen applies his method of teaching to the various disciplines of the Alexandrian program of higher studies.

Origen's *Letter to Gregory*

1. Greeting in God, sir, my most excellent and reverend son Gregory, from Origen.

Mental ability, as thou knowest, reinforced by practice, can undertake work which leads to the expected end (if I may use the expression) of that which one wishes to practise. Thine ability is fit to make thee an accomplished Roman lawyer, or a Greek philosopher in some one of the schools esteemed reputable. But my desire has been that thou shouldest employ all the force of thine ability on Christianity as thine end, and to effect this I would beseech thee to draw from Greek philosophy such things as are capable of being made encyclic or preparatory studies to Christianity, and from geometry and astronomy such things as will be useful for the exposition of Holy Scripture, in order that what the sons of the philosophers say about geometry and music and grammar and rhetoric and astronomy, that they are the handmaidens of philosophy, we may say of philosophy itself in relation to Christianity.

4. But do thou, sir my son, first and foremost attend to the reading of the Holy Scriptures, yea attend. For we need great attend. For we need great attention in reading the Scriptures that we may not speak or think too rashly about them. And, attending to the reading of the divine oracles with a closeness faithful and well-pleasing to God, knock at its closed places, and they shall be opened unto thee by the porter of whom Jesus said, "To him the porter openeth." And attending to the divine reading, seek rightly and with unwavering faith in God for the mind of the divine letters, hidden from most. Be not content with knocking and seeking; for most essential is the prayer to understand divine things. To this the Saviour urged us when he said not merely, "Knock and it shall be opened unto you: seek and ye shall find," but also, "Ask, and it shall be given unto you."

These words have I ventured of my fatherly love toward thee. Whether they are well ventured or not, God perchance knows and His Christ, and he that partaketh of the spirit of God and the spirit of Christ. Would that thou mightest partake, and ever increase thy participancy, that thou mightest say not merely, "We are become partakers of Christ," but even "We are partakers of God." [16]

When the ancient Church became more and more immersed in the complicated society of late Antiquity, it could no longer educate its youth for the *"parousia,"* the new coming Christ, but had to prepare it also for participation and even leadership in the secular community. As a consequence, the separatists had to yield ground to the conciliatory minds. A few decades after the Council of Nicea (325), the three Cappadocians, Basil the Great, his brother Gregory of Nyssa, and Gregory of Nazianzus and their contemporary, John Chrysostom, amalgamated pagan philosophy and Christian theology to the degree that the latter represents the richest, and most bewildering conflux of thought known in the history of ideas: Old Testament, especially its Prophetic literature, New Testament, Greek-Roman philosophy, especially Platonism, Aristotelianism, and Stoicism, elements of Gnosticism and even of ancient mystery cults—a complex of contradictions, but also an inexhaustible source of inspiration, beauty, and vitality. In all likelihood, pagan youth studied at the famous catechetical schools of Alexandria, Antiochia, Edessa, and others, though these schools were originally established for the catechumens eager to receive instruction in the new doctrine. On the other hand, Christians studied at the famous pagan universities of Alexandria, Pergamon, and especially Athens.

Certainly, in this mingling of ideas the Hellenistic civilization and the Greek language offered greater riches than the Latin-speaking world of Africa and western Europe. Yet, the genius, second to none in the formation of the Christian world-view in the West, wrote in Latin and knew very little, if any, Greek. St. Augustine (354–430), Bishop of Hippo in Africa, was born at Tagasta in the province of Numidia, and trained at a school of grammar at Madaura. Searching for inner security in the battle of opinions, he traveled as a young man with his son and the son's mother to Rome, and then, in 384, to Milan where his pious mother Monica joined him. There he came under the influ-

ence of the great Bishop Ambrose and was converted to Christianity
(387). After returning to Africa, he was consecrated as bishop of the
small seaport of Hippo, where he remained for the rest of his life.

Of his enormous literary work two writings are significant for
Christian education: one, *On the Instruction of Beginner (De Catechi-
sandis Rudibus)*; the other, *On Christian Doctrine (De Doctrina
Christiana)*.

The first, *On the Instruction of Beginners*, gives us a complete
map of the way in which, probably since the time of Origen, adult
men and women of all social strata were introduced into the Christian
community. It is addressed to his "dear brother Deogratias" who
had asked him for guidance and encouragement in the difficult task of
catechization. According to St. Augustine, the main purpose of instruction is to give the catechumen the inner experience of the revelation
of God's love as it is already anticipated in the Old Testament, but
manifests itself fully in Jesus Christ. Through listening, the pupil
must arrive at faith; through faith he must arrive at hope; through hope,
love.

After the historical-theoretical part, St. Augustine, emphasiz-
ing how difficult it is to give an adequate impression of good teaching
by writing about it, gives first a longer, and then a shorter example of
catechesis, or, as we would say, two master lessons. These are the
main points: First, prepare yourself for receiving salvation by avoiding
sin, not for fear of punishment, but for fear of alienation from divine
love and peace. Then understand how God, in analogy to the six days
of work of the creation, has led mankind through five historical periods toward the era when He reveals Himself through Christ and the
Holy Ghost and adds the gospel of love between men and God, and
men and men to the covenant of the Old Testament and the Decalogue. Then follows the description of the first Christian community
with its apostles and martyrs, the promise of the victory of the Church,
and of the final unification of the faithful with the Holy Trinity through
the mystery of the Resurrection. Apparently, the whole instruction
was given in a series of lectures with the assumption that the love of
the teacher for his pupils and his identity with the subject would radi-
ate upon the audience, two factors which are still the ultimate requisite of

success, however much the methods of teaching may have been improved.

St. Augustine's other educational work, *On Christian Doctrine,* has two main purposes: one, to help the reader find and assimilate the truth of the gospel; the other, to aid him in the task of explaining his insight to others (*modus inveniendi quae intelligenda sunt, et modus proferendi quae intellecta sunt*). In other words, St. Augustine intends to provide a handbook for the teacher in which, in encyclopedic form, he would find the necessary general and theological material for his instruction, and in addition, some device by which to present it in organized form.

In the second book of *The Christian Doctrine,* the author discusses the relation of Christianity to Greek-Roman wisdom which he defends with the argument that not everything that has sometimes been misused is therefore objectionable. Though all human work is spoiled by superstition, luxury, and foolishness, it nevertheless may be helpful. Clothing, script, coins, and measures have been used falsely, but they also have made civilization possible. In addition, humanity has produced the various sciences related to nature, society, and the human mind which are not essential but nevertheless useful for a Christian life. But ultimate wisdom is to be found only in the Gospel.

St. Augustine, whose relation to antiquity was ambiguous because while he admired it, he also distrusted it, arrived finally at the reconciling insight—also found in other Christian authors before and after St. Augustine—that the true and good Christian is one who recognizes that truth, wherever discovered, has its source in God.

Origen (185–254) and St. Augustine (354–430) were the masters in the art of catechizing. After St. Augustine it declined. Constantine the Great (272–337) had made the once-despised message of Christ and his apostles the official state religion, and it required more courage to remain a pagan than to become a Christian. Only the Emperor Julian (*ca.* 331–363)—called later "The Apostate" by the Church, but was in reality the last, though desperate, conservative of the Hellenistic tradition—endangered for some years the peace of the Christian communities, some of which now became the prosecutors.

Naturally, many of the newcomers were reluctant to go through the long process of spiritual scrutiny, and the Church did not close its door to them. The severest blow to the old form of catechesis came with the development of infant baptism in the centuries after St. Augustine, though sporadically it had already been practiced before him. Baptism, then, was no longer the end of the catechetical instruction and the decision of an adult, but became the symbolic act of a person's incorporation into the fellowship of the body of Christ, or the *communio sanctorum*.[17]

Also the term catechesis changed its meaning. The Greek *catechein* and the Latin *catechisare* no longer involved oral instruction. They indicated now primarily the liturgical and educational functions which the Church performed in communion with the God-parents who promised to support the parents and the priests in the Christian education of the child.

The large number of admonitions by councils and bishops indicate that those entrusted with this duty were often lax in the performance of their duties. Mostly it was the priesthood which, despite all its defects, carried the main burden of catechization or, as we now say, of religious instruction. This included the teaching of the creed, of prayer, of the Ten Commandments, and of the seven sacraments (baptism, confirmation, the Eucharist, penance, extreme unction, holy orders, and matrimony).

CONCLUDING REMARKS TO CHAPTERS 2 AND 3

The development of Christianity during the first five centuries of its existence offers us one of the most amazing spectacles in the history of mankind. From the "carpenter of Nazareth," derided, tortured, and finally crucified by the Roman soldiers at the demand of the leaders of his own people, there comes a message more persuasive than the great schools of philosophy and more revolutionary in its impact on individual and social life than any revolution in the Western world. Its periods of persecution are at the same time its periods of flowering, while its periods of peace often coincide with its decay. Like the religion of the Jews it grows through suffering. The contradictions and confusions emerging in the discussions with its sometimes intellectually superior environment merely contribute to the strengthening of its convictions. Alien elements are absorbed that would have absorbed or destroyed any other community of believers. Martyrs are willing to die, even though the Messiah, whose coming the early Christians expected from year to year, does not appear. Finally, compromises have to be made with the secular powers, and the quarrels and corruptions within their own ranks compel the Christians to establish an organization which, though certainly not what Christ and his disciples ever dreamt of, gives hope, solace, charity, and a sense of dignity to seeking men.

According to the purpose of this book, we have concentrated only on one aspect of this amazing development—the function of teaching, or, in the wider sense, on Christian *paideia*. Again and again Jesus called himself "the teacher." The word "Master" used in the King James version—like the Jewish "Rabbi"—meant "the teacher" (*magister*) and was the correct translation of the Greek "*didaskalos*." Clement and Origen called Christ the "divine *paidagogos*." St. Paul gave it the character of universality through his missionary activities outside the Jewish world, and the Church fathers, as we have seen, soon engaged in discussions with the Greek and Roman philosophers. They became not only catechists, teachers of the catechumens, but also the founders of a new civilization.

Out of the function of teaching developed the second cause of Christianity's strength—the formulation of dogma. It was understood and communicated, not as concepts born in the brains of men, but as the selfrevelation of God through Christ and the Spirit; and its understanding was considered necessary for salvation and life eternal. Herein lies the superiority of the Christian teachers to the ancient philosophers' philosophizing: they did not invent the truth, but they believed to have received it through supernatural grace.

As could not be otherwise in a religion with its roots in the Jewish tradition, the covenant between man and God required obedience to the divine commandments, or a life which—as far as the original sinfulness of man permitted—tried to reflect the ethical purity of Christ. Yet, the early Christian communities were not places of grim moralistic austerity. To be sure, fanatics for whom we now would use psychiatric terms entered the new congregations, as happens wherever the mystical and unusual breaks through the routines of convention. But on the whole, the Christians helped each other and even their enemies; they cherished hospitality and charity, celebrated their festivals in a mood of gratitude, and, living in the Hellenistic world with its sublime sense of symbolic beauty, developed rituals not only for the purpose of regulating their daily lives, but also for giving rare and elevated form to the rare and elevating experiences connected with their religion.

All this—teaching as a divinely ordained mission and not merely as an educational enterprise; the knowing of God's nearness; the moral commandments; the *imitatio Christi* in a spirit of love, forgiveness, and sacrifice; and the urge for ritual expression—all this would have created the desire for strong and hierarchical organization, even if there had not been the threat of persecution during the first four centuries. So strong became this capacity for organization, constantly reinforced by the central consciousness of a divine mission, that under Constantine the Great (323–337) the Christian Church became recognized by the state because it offered the best guarantee of order in a general confusion of ideas and political forces. It continued in this role even when, after the end of the fourth century, more and more provinces of the Roman empire succumbed to foreign invaders.

But with these remarks we have already left the age of the early Church and the Church fathers and entered the medieval period.

Chapter 4

The Middle Ages

Historians have often described the so-called "barbaric invasion" which caused the final breakdown of the West-Roman Empire, as the "end of ancient civilization." This is correct to a degree. Yet, in view of all the destruction, the change of population and the rapid rise and decline of Germanic principalities ranging from the eastern parts of Europe to Spain and Africa, one may sometimes wonder that so much of ancient learning has been preserved, especially since the creativeness of Greek-Roman thought had been fading for centuries. When, in 476, the last West-Roman Emperor Romulus Augustulus was deposed by a Germanic warrior, Theodoric the Great, who himself was soon overthrown by the founder of the kingdom of the Ostrogoths in Italy, almost the only form of higher training in such ancient seats of learning as Rome, Pavia, and Milan was a bombastic form of rhetoric connected with the study of law. But the Ostrogoths in Italy, the Vandals in Africa, and the Visigoths in Spain, rather than destroying what was left, willingly acknowledged the superiority of the older civilization. Carthage, under the Vandals, was called the "African Rome." Elementary schools still existed in the urban districts, and the teachers of oratory and law still found willing listeners among the Germanic youth. One part of the old culture that impressed the newcomers through its dignity and doctrine was the Church to which they became converted from the fourth century on.

This was the time when Boethius, the author of the famous *Consolation of Philosophy* (*De Consolatione Philosophiae*), Isidor of Sevilla, Marcianus a Capella, and Cassiodorus wrote the Encyclopedias that, though in diluted form, transmitted the old *artes liberales* to later generations. The old catechetical schools were mostly closed. In the sixth century we hear only of Nisibis in Mesopotamia. Aside from the loss of purpose afflicted upon them by the introduction of infant baptism, they apparently participated in the general decay of learning.

A modest revival occurred under Pope Gregory the Great (590–604). In order to preserve the old religious hymns, he founded at Rome the first music school which sent its pupils, the *pueri symphoniaci,* as teachers of religious hymns and liturgy over the whole of occidental Christianity. Otherwise Gregory the Great was, if not an enemy as some documents say, at least not an active friend of theoretical studies. Concerning the value of the classical authors he would have agreed more with Tatian than with Clement and Origen. Though he had lived for years in Constantinople as papal legate, he had not learned Greek; in his Latin he did not try to avoid barbarisms, rather he was proud of them. He forbade the Bishop Desiderius in Gaul the study of grammar (classical literature) "because the same mouth cannot praise Jove and Christ. And think what a crime it is for a bishop to recite what would not be decent for a simple cleric." [1]

Between the period of the Church fathers and the era of Charles the Great, or Charlemagne, the schools of the monasteries saved at least a degree of learning. Monasticism was, and still is, by no means exclusively Christian. It had its beginnings in pre-Christian times in India and other parts of Asia; among the Jews the Essenes were a kind of holy order. Before the third century pious Christians lived the life of hermits. Despite predecessors, the Egyptian St. Anthony (*ca.* 250–350) is generally regarded as the father of Christian and especially of Eastern monasticism. While he and his followers represented the eremitical type of withdrawal into solitude, St. Pachomius, also an Egyptian, assembled, about 340, a number of anchorites (hermits or recluses) near the Nile river in a convent community, establishing hereby the form of monachism, generally called "cenobitical" (Greek *koinos* =

common, *bios*=life). Definite rules ordered the conduct of the monks and thus prevented the further spread of undesirable elements who for doubtful motives preferred to live in seclusion. Around four hundred Pachomian monks numbered about seven thousand. Men such as Origen and St. Jerome favored asceticism also among women as a special sign of Christian devotion [2] and as a protest against the growth of worldliness they observed among their Christian brethren. Monasteries were for them the best places for the holy surrender of the sinful self to God. Almost at the time of Pachomios, St. Basil adapted monasticism to Greek Christianity so ingenuously that the rule he drew up for his monastery at the banks of the Iris in Cappadocia (*ca.* 360) became the pattern for the Greek monasteries to which Eastern Europe owes much of its intellectual and artistic treasures. However, the merit of the successful organization of Western monastic life and its purification from vulgar associates belongs to St. Benedict of Nursia (480–543). He founded in 528 at *Castrum Cassinum,* an old Roman fortress with a temple of Apollo, the still famous monastery of Monte Cassino, almost the same year that two edicts of the emperor Justinian made an end to the once-glorious University of Athens.

For two main reasons could St. Benedict's work spread within the orbit of Western Christendom. He adapted monasticism to Western mentality and climate, and instead of laying too much value on pious ecstasies with their often pathological ingredients, he emphasized the value of labor. Thus the Benedictines could become not only spiritual guides, but also teachers of the crafts and agriculture wherever they settled.

We quote here those passages of the Rules (*Regulae*) which have general educational significance and omit those which pertain to the inner order of the monastery.

The Rule of Saint Benedict [3]

THE PROLOGUE

Listen, my son, and turn the ear of thine heart to the precepts of thy Master. Receive readily, and faithfully carry out the advice of a loving Father, so that by the work of obedience you may return to Him, whom you have left by the sloth of disobedience. . . .

First, beg of Him with most earnest prayer to finish the good work begun; that He who now hath deigned to count us among His children may never be grieved by our evil deeds. . . .

We are therefore now about to institute a school for the service of God, in which we hope nothing harsh nor burdensome will be ordained. But if we proceed in certain things with some little severity, sound reason so advising for the amendment of vices or the preserving of charity, do not for fear of this forthwith flee from the way of salvation, which is always narrow in the beginning. . . .

Chapter I of the Rule of Saint Benedict contains a historically interesting evaluation of "the several kinds of monks and their lives." The Cenobites live in a monastery under a rule or an abbot and are therefore the most disciplined and reliable members of the religious. The Anchorites or Hermits, well prepared by long trial in a monastery "go forth from the ranks of the brotherhood to the single combat of the desert." The Sarabites shun the life of discipline, are monks only in appearance and "lie to God by their tonsures." Finally there are the Gyrovagi, or Wanderers, who stay as guests at different places and monasteries and live a "wretched way of life of which it is better to be silent than to speak."

CHAPTER II

WHAT THE ABBOT SHOULD BE

The abbot should ever be mindful that at the dread judgment of God there will be inquiry both as to his teaching and as to the obedience of his disciples. Let the abbot know that any lack of goodness, which the master of the family shall find in his flock, will be accounted the shepherd's fault. . . .

Let him make no distinction of persons in the monastery. Let not one be loved more than another, save such as be found to excel in obedience or good works. Let not the freeborn be put before the serf-born in religion, unless there be other reasonable cause for it. If upon due consideration the abbot shall see such cause he may place him where he pleases; otherwise let all keep their own places, because *whether bond or free we are all one in Christ* (*I Cor*. xii, 13) and bear an equal burden of service under one Lord: *for with God there is no accepting of persons.* (*Ephesians* vi, 9) For one thing only are we preferred by Him, if we are found better than others in good works and more humble. Let the abbot therefore have equal love for all, and let all, according to their deserts, be under the same discipline.

The abbot in his teaching should always observe that apostolic rule which saith, *Reprove, entreat, rebuke*. . . .

The abbot ought ever to bear in mind what he is and what he is called; he ought to know that to whom more is entrusted, from him more is exacted. Let him recognize how difficult and how hard a task he has undertaken, to rule souls and to make himself a servant to the humours of many. One, forsooth, must be led by gentle words, another by sharp reprehension, another by persuasion; and thus shall he so shape and adapt himself to the character and intelligence of each, that he not only suffer no loss in the flock entrusted to his care, but may even rejoice in its good growth. Above all things let him not slight nor make little of the souls committed to his care, heeding more fleeting, worldly and frivolous things; but let him remember always that he has undertaken the government of souls; of which he shall also have to give an account. And that he may not complain of the want of temporal means, let him remember that it is written, *Seek first the kingdom of God, and His justice, and all things shall be given to you.* (*Matthew* vi, 33) And again, *Nothing is wanting to such as fear Him.* (Psalms xxxiii, 19)

He should know that whoever undertakes the government of souls must prepare himself to account for them. And however great the number of the brethren under him may be, let him understand for certain that at the Day of Judgment he will have to give to our Lord an account of all their souls as well as of his own. In this way, by fearing the inquiry concerning his flock which the Shepherd will hold, he is solicitous on account of others' souls as well as his own, and thus while reclaiming other men by his corrections, he frees himself also from all vice.

CHAPTER XLVIII

OF DAILY MANUAL LABOR

Idleness is an enemy of the soul. Because this is so the brethren should be occupied at specific times in manual labor, and at other fixed hours in holy reading. . . .

CHAPTER LIX

OF THE SONS OF NOBLES OR OF THE POOR WHO

ARE OFFERED TO GOD

If any nobleman shall offer his son to God in the monastery, let the parents, if the child himself be under age, make the petition for him, and together with the oblation wrap the formal promise and the hand of the boy in the altar cloth and thus dedicate him to God. With regard to any property let the parents promise in the document under oath that they will never either give or furnish with the means of obtaining anything whatever, either themselves or by any other person or by any means. Or, if they will not do this, and desire to give some alms to the monastery, as a free gift, let them hand over to the place where they wish, reserving, if they wish, the income for themselves. Let all these matters be so managed that the child have no expectations by which he may be deceived and perish (which God forbid), as by experience we have learned is sometimes the case. In the same way let those who are poorer act. But such as have nothing whatever let simply promise and offer their son before witness with the oblation.

Like Pope Gregory the Great, St. Benedict was more interested in Christian practice than in theory and literature. Gregory calls him *"scienter nescius et sapienter indoctus."* [4] The scholarly contributions of the Benedictines began under Cassiodorus who, in the sixth century, founded two abbeys in the province of Calabria and advocated in his *Institutions* [5] the study of Christian theology and history as well as the study of the liberal arts. Since then the schools of the Benedictine monasteries promoted not only the industrial arts, but side by side with the gradually rising cathedral schools the learned disciplines also. Without such action the scholastic studies of the later Middle Ages and, to a degree, the literary renaissance of the fifteenth century would hardly have been possible. In the course of time the monks divided their instruction into a *schola interior,* for their pupils destined for divine orders, and a *schola exterior,* for those who intended to use their learning as laymen. A long list could be drawn of those monasteries which, before the rise of city schools and universities during the twelfth and thirteenth centuries, preserved the cause of learning: Poitiers, Ferrières, Soissons, and Fonteney in the French-speaking parts; St. Gallen, Reichenau, Fulda, Hersfeld, and Corvey in Switzerland and Germany; Bobbio, Classe, Pomposa in Italy; and Armagh and Clonard in Ireland.

But however great the merits of these monks in transmitting ancient and patristic literature to later generations, they did not advance the frontiers of Christian knowledge. They and the secular clergy, trained by them or in the growing cathedral schools, reveal sometimes a profound and touching simplicity; but their main ambition was to save and teach a unique body of wisdom they considered so great, profound, and superior to their own knowledge, that any attempt to add or to change would have been considered frivolity. This applies even to the men whom Charles the Great, one of the foremost educators of Christianity, assembled at his residence. We do not know where his court school (*schola palatina*) had its domicile. Perhaps it went with the emperor who mostly resided at Aachen and Paris. The legend that Charles was the founder of the University of Paris may have had its origin in the memory of later writers that there existed at his time a famous school either at the French capital or at neighboring St. Denis. New centers of learning were certainly necessary, for, except in Italy, even the members of the ruling families of Europe were mostly illiterate. In spite of all his endeavors Charles the Great himself did not succeed in the art of writing. Yet, not only for political but also for educational reasons, he justified the title he gave himself in one of his first messages, the *Capitulare Primum* of 769: "*Devotus sanctae ecclesiae defensor atque adjutor in omnibus.*" His insistence on the foundation of schools was motivated by the desire to procure a somewhat literate clergy that would be able to teach everyone—young or old, man or woman—the Lord's Prayer and the fundamentals of the creed.[6]

Of course, the emperor could not even have begun his educational work had he not availed himself of the advice and cooperation, first of some learned Italians, then of men from transalpine regions among whom the Irish Alcuin of York was the most prominent. Alcuin met Charles in 782 in Northern Italy and, on the monarch's invitation, assumed the leadership of his palace school and the general supervision of the educational and cultural activities of the realm. It is largely due to him that we speak of a "Carolingian Renaissance."

Alcuin's central position as Charles's personal teacher and his influence at the court enabled him to transplant the more advanced learning of Ireland and Britain to the continent. The source of his inspiration was the conception of a state in which the secular government and the Church would cooperate in the creation of a Christian civilization.

Alcuin's work was continued by Theodulf, a Goth by descent whom Charles invited from Italy and who died as Bishop of Orleans in 821. Theodulf, like Alcuin not only a theologian and administrator, but also a poet of merit, issued several capitularies to the priests of his bishopric.[7]

> The presbyters on the farms and in the villages should have schools, and if one of the faithful wants to entrust his sons to them for studying, they should accept and not reject them. And they should teach them with greatest care, being mindful of what Scripture says: "And they that be wise shall shine as the brightness of the firmament; and they that turn many to righteousness as the stars for ever and ever." And while they teach their pupils they should not ask for money or accept anything, except when parents offer it voluntarily for the sake of learning.

It may be doubted that, as some German historians say, we have at the time of Charles the beginning of universal schooling. But certainly there appears the idea that the whole lay population should be acquainted with the basic tenets of Christianity. To be sure, the Germanic warrior resisted successfully the encroachment of the Carolingian Renaissance on his style of life. However, a number of women from noble houses answered ardently the call to pious learning and living. To them belonged Dhuoda (Latinized, Dodora). In 824 she married Duke Bernard, the son of William the Saint of Aquitania. Louis the Pious made Bernard ruler over the borderland that reached along the Pyrenees and severed the Frankish realm from that of the Saracens. In 843 Dhuoda wrote a Christian manual for her son William, who was educated far from her at the court of King Charles the Bald. Some parts of this manual are here reproduced.

Dhuoda believes in the occult significance of numbers, a superstition that has lasted from the dawn of civilization up to our days. Some of the church fathers also indulged in it. In addition, Dhuoda's work is filled with allegories and quotations from the Bible and ancient pagan and Christian writers that detract from, rather than add, to its impressiveness. All this, though giving the manual its special historical flavor, has been omitted here, but that which remains is enough to convince us that Dhuoda's manual is in no way merely imitative. Rather it reveals a deep sense of piety, the mysteriousness of life, and the loving concern of a lonely mother with her own and her family's station before God.

In The Name of The Holy Trinity [8]

Here begins the manual of Dhuoda addressed to her son, William.

Since I see many parents who in this world enjoy living together with their children, but since I, my son William, see myself far from you, I have written this little work under my name, filled with anxiety and with the desire that I may be of some use to you. . . . [Here follows the following invocation, written in free Latin verse.]

God, the highest, creator of the light of heaven, ruler over the stars, eternal and holy king, look kindly on the works I am beginning. Ignorant as I am, I am searching for Thy help, for the present and the future. Thou who are three and one, Thou ever blessest Thy people and awardest Thy servants according to their merits. . . . Thou who art in the centre and the orbits of the skies, Thou who holdest in Thy hands the oceans and the continents, I confide to Thee my son William. I pray that Thou allowest him to prosper all his life, that he love Thee above all, and that he, together with Thy children, ascend to the summit of happiness. That his mind always be aware of Thy presence. . . . Thou who never failest to give, teach him to believe in Thee, to love Thee, and to praise Thee with zeal overflowing. That Thy grace enter into him. That he have peace and health in body and mind and that he and his children flower forever. Take away from them all hatred. May he read at the right time and in the right spirit. That he follow the examples of the saints and receive from Thee the right understanding. That he be helpful to others, that he practice the four virtues and even more, that he be generous and prudent, pious and brave, and that he never leave the path of temperance. . . . Though I am but an unworthy mother, I implore Thee by day and by night, hear him when he asks, have pity with him. I am surrounded by the hosts of anxiety. . . .

CHAPTER I

ON THE LOVE OF GOD

God must be loved and praised, not only by the heavenly powers, but by each human creature that walks over this earth and wishes to lift himself up. Among them you, my son William, should always strive to climb to the height together with virtuous men and lovers of God. In their community you should attempt to enter the Kingdom that will remain forever and ever. . . .

CHAPTER II

ON SEEKING GOD

You and I, my son, must always seek God, for on His will we thrive, live, and are moved, and exist. Certainly I, in all my unworthiness, frailty, and darkness, I search for Him with all my might and pray for His assistance. He is most necessary to me, for it happens sometimes that even a little dog, waiting with others, catches some of the crumbs from the master's table.

[There follow several chapters on the attributes of God and the Holy Trinity, on Faith, Hope, and Charity, and on Prayer.]

CHAPTER X

ON DEVOTION IN PRAYER

. . . Hence one should pray not with a loud voice and long protracted words, but in silence and with deep emotion that He deign to give us from His plenitude. . . . And pray not only in church, but pray whenever you see an occasion: "God, full of pity and compassion, just and good, kind and true, have pity with the miserable creature that Thou hast created and redeemed with Thy blood, and grant me that I walk in Thy paths and Thy laws. Give me the mind and insight that I understand how to believe in Thee, how to love, fear, praise and thank Thee, and that in all my work I act according to right faith and intention. My Lord and God. Amen."

(The following chapters deal with the conduct due to father, parents, relations, superiors and the king, with behavior in council and in contact with one's councillors, with the reverence one owes to priests, and with the Christian virtues and the patience one should show in times of affliction and sickness. Dhuoda also admonishes her son to pray for the deceased, especially for dead relatives; she devotes several chapters to the mystical meaning of letters and numbers, and finally writes the epitaph she wants to have on her tomb.)

Read O Reader, The Verses of this Epitaph
To the Manes.

In this tomb reposes the body of Duodana created from dust,
King of infinity, receive her!
The earth has taken back the clay from which she was made,
King of kindness, forgive her!
Steeped in sin, there remains nothing for her but the soil of the grave,
God, pardon her trespasses!
You, of all age, men and women, who will come and return to this place, say these words:
God, in Thy greatness and glory, deliver her from her chains!
Pierced by the abyss of wounds, in a life of bitterness,
She has finished her life of misery;
God, do not count her sins!

That the serpent of evil may not seize her soul, you who
    pray, say these words:
God of clemency, help her!
May no one pass who has not read these words.
I conjure you all to pray and to say:
God of kindness, grant her to rest,
And order that in the community of the saints she may fi-
    nally live in the light of eternity—
That she may receive the Amen after her death!

At many places Dhuoda's manual reveals that her life was one
of suffering. We know that her tyrannical husband, who took her children away and soon deserted her, was accused of plotting against his
godfather, King Louis the Pious, was convicted of treasonable alliances
with the Spanish Moors, and finally was caught and sentenced to death.
Her son William followed in his father's steps and was killed after
a lost battle at Barcelona, and her younger son Bernard became a way-
layer in grand style, also ending his life dishonestly—all characteristic of a period when piety and learning in a few was unable to pene-
trate the armor of barbarism in their warrior environment.

A hundred years after Dhuoda, another woman gave proof of ex-
ceptional gifts, Hrotsvith or Hroswitha, who, perhaps related to the
house of the Saxon kings and emperors, entered the Benedictine nun-
nery of Gandersheim in the middle of the tenth century. She wrote an
epic with Otto I, the Great (936–973), as the hero, in which she
praises him as the restorer of the Roman Empire; she composed a series of legends on the theme of Christian chastity. Among historians
of literature she is mainly known for her attempts to translate the come-
dies of Terence into the moral environment of a Christian convent.
Terence was much read at Hrotsvith's time for his style and probably
also for his frivolity—for, despite asceticism and martyrdom in some
places, even the clergy was not always prudish. Hrotsvith herself describes as her purpose: "In the same poetic style which so far was used
to picture the shameful fornication of voluptuous women, I now wish
to celebrate the laudable chastity of holy virgins." But however much
she tried in terms of content, she certainly failed in terms of dramatic art. Says the historian of German literature, Friedrich Vogt: [9]

Certainly, they are not dramatic characters, these heroines whose whole life consists of the negation of life, whose greatest merit lies in their withdrawal from the natural function of their sex, whether they refuse marriage to their suitor or marital relation to their husband, whether they seek martyrdom or whether they let themselves be walled in a solitary cell—and all this with nothing else in view but the end of life with which the true life is going to begin, and always expecting the embrace of Christ, the heavenly bridegroom, who will lead them into the world beyond.

Nevertheless, we must assume this kind of literature to be one of the most appealing means of religious education, though not at all of the same significance and public attractiveness as the processions, the passion plays and other forms of religious drama which, with their mixture of seriousness and robust jest, gave to a largely illiterate public a visual picture of Christ's suffering, of hell, heaven, and salvation. These processions and plays allowed the laymen the degree of personal participation which we still can observe in the towns and villages of the old Catholic regions of Europe and which is so much more effective than any of our modern mechanical instruments of oral and visual mass communication.

Other writers of the time, among them Hrabanus Maurus, deal with religious education on a more scholarly level than Dhuoda and Hrotsvith. Hrabanus Maurus, sometimes called "the first teacher of Germany," was the most beloved disciple of the great Alcuin. Born at Mainz about 776, he entered the monastery of Fulda as a child, returned after a brief time of study at Tours, reigned from 822 to 842 as abbot, and laid during these years the foundation of Fulda's reputation as one of the foremost Christian schools of Europe; in 847 he became Archbishop of Mainz. His main work was his *De Universo* in which he copied whole chapters from the *Etymologiae* of Isidor of Sevilla. Like Isidor, and Beda of England, he collected almost the whole body of knowledge taught at his time. He began his twenty-two books with speculations about the nature of God and the angels—a pattern followed for a long time in writings of this kind—and dealt then with biblical history, with nature, chronology, the gods and writers of antiquity, with language, and then passed over to more practical subjects such as medicine, agriculture, war, and the domestic arts. As much as the book shows Hrabanus as a learned man and avid reader, it also reveals the uncritical acceptance of ancient knowledge characteristic of the period. Nevertheless, a beautifully illuminated manuscript of *The Universe* was still made in the eleventh century for the monastery of Monte Cassino.

But here we are especially interested in Hrabanus Maurus' *The Education of the Clergy*.[10] In it he deals first with the various obligations of the clergy and the desirable scholarly preparation of a priest in terms of the *artes liberales,* which are most primitively explained. Despite the professional emphasis, the author touches also on topics of more general interest, especially on the old issue of the relationship between pagan knowledge and Christian wisdom. The philosophical systems of the pagans, so he finally concludes his section on the Seven Liberal Arts,

> contain not only mendacious and superstitious works of poetry and an overwhelming weight of useless work which everyone of us who is led by Christ will detest and avoid, but they also have transmitted to us the liberal arts which are better fitted for the service of truth, as well as some quite useful rules for life, and one can find even ideas about the veneration of the One and True God. Of course, they have not themselves created this gold and silver, as it were, but they have received it out of the depths of divine providence that permeates everything, though they use it pervertedly and unjustly for the service of the devil. However, the Christian, who will flee their miserable company, must take it from them in order to use it for the proclamation of the Gospel.

It was the good fortune of the northern parts of Europe that at a time of extreme turmoil there were nevertheless three "renaissances," each of them connected with the appearance of a personality rightly named "the Great": Charles the Great, whose work we have already mentioned; Otto I, the Great (912–973) of the House of the Saxons, who after the breakdown of the Carolingian empire brought about a revival of learning in the Germanic countries of the continent; and in

the interval between these two monarchs, Alfred the Great (849–900),
who served as a protector of Christian learning in Britain. Even more
than is the case with Charles and Otto, Alfred, who fought about
fifty battles, combined in himself the warrior, the statesman, and the
patron of literature, being himself an author and translator. Like Charles
he found at the beginning of his reign an almost illiterate clergy. According to the preface to his translation of Gregory's *Pastoral Care,*
only a very few clergymen "on this side of the Humber" understood
their breviary or could translate a letter from Latin into Anglo-Saxon,
and south of the Thames river there were none. Also, Alfred had to
call men from other countries to support him and his native helpers
in the work of the restoration, among them his most intimate friend,
teacher, and counselor, Asser of Wales, to whom we owe the only
existing record of his life.[11]

King Alfred's introduction to his translation of Gregory's
Pastoral Care: [12]

King Alfred bids greet bishop Waerferth with his words
lovingly and with friendship, and I let it be known to thee
that it has very often come into my mind, what wise men
there formerly were throughout England, both of sacred and
secular orders; and how happy times there were then throughout England; and how the kings who had power of the nation
in these days obeyed God and his ministers; and they preserved peace, morality, and order at home, and at the same
time enlarged their territory abroad; and how they pros-
pered both with war and with wisdom; and also the sacred
orders how zealous they were both in teaching and learning,
and in all the services they owed to God; and how foreigners
came to this land in search of wisdom and instruction, and
how we should now have to get them from abroad if we were
to have them. So general was its decay in England that there
were few on this side of the Humber who could understand
their rituals in English, or translate a letter from Latin into
English; and I believe that there were not many beyond the
Humber. There were so few of them that I cannot remember a single one south of the Thames when I came to the
Throne. Thanks be to God Almighty that we have any

teachers among us now. And therefore I command thee to do
as I believe thou art willing, to disengage thyself from worldly
matters as often as thou canst, that thou mayest apply the
wisdom which God has given thee wherever thou canst. Consider what punishments would come upon us on account of
this world if we neither loved it [wisdom] ourselves nor suffered
other men to obtain it: we should love the name only of
Christian, and very few of the virtues. When I consider all
this I remembered also how I saw before it had been all rav-
aged and burnt, how the churches throughout the whole of
England stood filled with treasures and books, and there was
also a great multitude of God's servants, but they had very
little knowledge of the books, for they could not understand
anything of them, because they were not written in their own
language. As if they had said: "Our forefathers, who formerly held these places, loved wisdom, and through it they
obtained wealth and bequeathed it to us. In this we can still
see their tracks, but we cannot follow them, and therefore
we have lost both the wealth and the wisdom, because we
would not incline our hearts after their example!" When I
remembered all this, I wondered extremely that the good and
wise men who were formerly all over England, and had perfectly learnt all the books, did not wish to translate them into
their own language. But again I soon answered myself and
said: "They did not think that men would ever be so careless, and that learning would so decay; through that desire
they abstained from it, and they wished that the wisdom in
this land might increase with our knowledge of languages."
Then I remembered how the law was first known in Hebrew, and again, when the Greeks had learnt it, they translated the whole of it into their own language, and all other
books besides. And again the Romans, when they had learnt
it, they translated the whole of it through learned interpreters into their own language. Therefore it seems better to me,
if ye think so, for us also to translate some books which are
most needful for all men to know into the language which
we can all understand, and for you to do as we very easily
can if we have tranquility enough, that is that all the youth
now in England of free men, who are rich enough to be able
to devote themselves to it, be set to learn as long as they
are not fit for any other occupation, until that they are well

able to read English writing: and let those afterwards taught more in the Latin language who are to continue learning and be promoted to a higher rank. When I remembered how the knowledge of Latin had formerly decayed throughout England, and yet many could read English writing, I began, among other various and manifold troubles of this kingdom, to translate into English the book which is called in Latin Pastoralis, and in English Shepherd's Book sometimes according to the sense, as I had learnt it from Plegmund my archbishop, and Asser my bishop, and Grimbolt my mass-priest, and John my mass-priest. And when I had learnt it as I could best understand it, and as I could most clearly interpret it, I translated it into English; and I will send a copy to every bishopric in my kingdom; and on each there is a clasp worth fifty marcs. And I command in God's name that no man take the clasp from the book or the book from the minister; it is uncertain how long there may be such learned bishops as now, thanks be to God, there are nearly everywhere; therefore I wish them always to remain in their place, unless the bishop wish to take them with him, or they be lent out anywhere, or any one make a copy from them." . . .

Like Charles the Great, Alfred opened a school at his court as a center from which some learning spread even to the older administrators of the realm, who, according to Asser, compared with envy their own neglected upbringing with that of the younger generation which could enjoy the study of the liberal arts (*qui liberalibus artibus feliciter erudiri poterant*). In Alfred's mind, as in that of Charles, there appears the vision of general public education, especially the free-born youth of the country should be able to read Anglo-Saxon, into which the Lord's message should be translated. Latin should come later for those who intend to devote themselves to sacred or other studies. Patiently he urged the clergy to give an example of learning; only when persuasion failed did he make use of his regal prerogatives to take sterner measures.

Chapter 5

The Scholastic Period

With the eleventh century there began a new era in religious education. Gregory VII (Hildebrand, 1073–1085) opened the series of great popes who, through their moral strength, but also through intrigue and war, shook off the tutelage of the German emperors and claimed to be not only the spiritual, but also the political rulers of Europe. For about two centuries the Church could hope to succeed in this power struggle, but it paid for its political entanglements in the fourteenth century. Then the kings of France, on whom the popes had relied in their struggle against the emperors, transferred the papal see from Rome to Avignon (so-called "Babylonian Captivity" 1309–1376). Certainly, the popes were not treated more respectfully by the French than by the Germans; if anything, less.

While the German Emperors needed the support of their increasingly powerful princes for the wasteful wars in Italy, the French monarchy succeeded in suppressing the big vassals and in centralizing its power. In the eleventh century, French monasticism revived itself after a period of decay and then molded the regular clergy all over Europe into the strongest army of the fighting Church. Through its university, the capital Paris became the center of scholastic learning. From France the crusades started and united the European nations for some time under a purpose supposed to be pleasing to the Almighty, but also superstitious and contaminated by cruel instincts and ambitions. The crusades ended in a period of disillusionment and diminution of ecclesiastical authority, not only because of the futile bloodshed, but also because the contact with the East had opened new horizons of thought to the European mind. Since from the seventh century onwards Islam had conquered large parts of Asia and Africa and destroyed the Christian kingdom of the Visigoths in Spain, and since there had been little contact with the East Roman Empire, the central European countries had been almost secluded from the great arteries of economic and intellectual traffic. The crusades broke the isolation, and comparison was not always in favor of Western culture and the Western Church. A dangerous sectarianism arose which even the cruelty of the Inquisition, established at the beginning of the thirteenth century and administered by the Dominican monks, was unable to destroy. Arabic philosophy attracted some of the most advanced minds of the period. All these conflicts contributed, at least in part, to one of the most powerful movements in Christian theology, Scholasticism. It culminated in the works of Albertus Magnus of Cologne and Thomas Aquinas, but there were other thinkers of equal mental acumen.

In its essence, Scholasticism was the attempt to support the Christian creed by a philosophical structure of sufficient strength to withstand the ever rising doubts among Christian theologians who, partly because of Arabic influences, no longer felt as safe in their faith as did their predecessors of earlier centuries. Strangely enough, the tool that Christian Scholasticism used to reestablish unity was of pagan origin, the philosophy of Aristotle. Understandably, in the beginning the Church protested against the rapidly increasing interest in the works of the heathen, newly translated from Greek and Arabic; and conservative churchmen condemned the doctrines of Thomas Aquinas with their Aristotelian logic so that Albertus Magnus had to go to Paris in his defense (1277).

But the appeal of the scholastic movement to the intellectual vitality of the time was too strong to be successfully opposed. The *Summa Theologica* of Thomas Aquinas is one of the greatest masterpieces of the art of dialectics and, in spite of many ideas foreign to us, full of deep insights into the relation of man to himself and the cosmos. The theology of the Catholic Church is still based on the *Summa*. The scholastics enriched the Christian teaching of the time through the acceptance of Greek psychology and science. And through founding great centers of learning in Paris, Bologna, Oxford, and other places, they took learning and theological education out of the narrow walls of monasteries where there was little chance for further development.

Nevertheless, the merits of Scholasticism were at the same time its demerits. Within the realm of Christian devotion, it was primarily a movement of sophistication and argument. It destroyed the teaching of "grammar" as the study of literary masterpieces; it relied one-sidedly on the power of rational deductions and consequently was unhistorical as is every intellectualism; and it was poor from an aesthetic and emotional point of view. The Latin written by the scholars of the time, though more capable of philosophical abstraction than that of Cicero and Seneca because of centuries of Christian speculation and controversy, was nevertheless often abominable. In spite of modern admiration for medieval philosophy, Scholasticism can be interpreted not only as the acme of Christian philosophy, but also as a symbol of the waning of the faithful simplicity of the early Christians, such as Alcuin, Hrabanus Maurus, and Alfred the Great. It was an enterprise of the learned that caused as much doubt as it created faith. As Luther asserted, (and the papacy itself thought so at the beginning of the movement) it was a kind of rationalization of the Gospel; it placed Aristotle, called "The Teacher" or "The Philosopher," beside Jesus as the supreme authority. Without the one-sidedness and increasing barrenness of scholastic speculation and language, the rebellion of the humanists against the medieval universities would not have been so passionate, nor would the Protestant reform have had its appeal to the educated. For they despised not only the corruption of the Church, they despised also the universities which gave no answers to their search for the meaning of existence in the turbulent centuries before and during the Renaissance.

Certainly, every scholastic philosopher considered himself a Christian educator, for what did he attempt but to prove faith by reason (as understood in his time)? But as a surprising number of documents proves, even the students at the universities were not always moved, either religiously or morally. Life at the big centers of learning was often riotous, undisciplined, and even cynical. The great architects of the time, the sculptors and glass painters, and Dante's *Divine Comedy* certainly inspired the soul of the layman more profoundly than all the disputations in the halls of the universities. And so did the great hymns such as *"Dies Irae"* and *"Stabat Mater,"* the one attributed to Thomas a Celano, the other to Jacobone da Todi. Both belonged to the Franciscan order that produced the great preachers who spoke not Latin, but the people's language when they told of St. Francis' praise of poverty [1] and the impending end of a world ripe for God's punishment. But even St. Francis' order degenerated after the end of the fourteenth century.

Occupied with their primarily intellectual interests, most of the scholastic philosophers showed little immediate concern for the religious education of the people. At the University of Paris, Thomas Aquinas held about 1257 a disputation "Concerning the Teacher" (*De Magistro*) as the eleventh of the discussions on the *Problems of Truth* (*Quaestiones Disputatae de Veritate*).[2] But this disputation also is more concerned with metaphysical and epistemological, than with educational issues. The "light of reason," so Thomas says, is given to us by God, and since without this light human teaching can have no good and lasting effect, God is ultimately the true and real teacher. As in other writings of St. Thomas, the goal of man's learning and striving can only consist in the identification of the human soul with the divine principle, or in the unity of intellect and will. For the achievement of this state of "felicity" we need, of course, divine assistance.

As much as Christian philosophers of the time attempted a synthesis of various strands of thought and thus contributed to the sharpening of minds, they also helped to undermine the firmness of the tradition. For rationality, once awakened, does not stop before the premises on which a system of thought is built, and in spite of all the Aristotelianism, the premises of Christian Scholasticism were not rational, but mystical. The inevitably emerging dilemma between divine reason and the Revelation on the one hand, and human reason and its searching logic on the other hand proved finally to be the stumbling block of medieval Christian philosophy. The time had come for new ventures of the religious spirit.

Even those of the scholastics who gave some thought to education proper, were primarily concerned with the preparation of the prospective theologian and with the systematic teaching of the liberal arts —as they understood them. However, their writings contain also general religious wisdom, as relevant for the layman as for the priest. For example, Hugh of St. Victor (1097–1141), author of many commentaries on the Bible and of the *Didascalicon, or Eruditio Didascalica,*[3] the first systematic medieval work on education, reveals his religious concept of human existence in the following statement "On Exile."[4]

> It is a good foundation of virtue if the mind becomes gradually accustomed to free himself of all things visible and finite, so that later on, it can leave them. The one to whom the fatherland is sweet is still too vulnerable. On the other hand, strong is the man who can feel at home in every land, truly perfect is he to whom the whole world is a place of exile. The first has attached his love to the world, the second has dispersed it, the third has extinguished it. From early youth I have been in foreign lands and so I know of the sorrow one feels when leaving even the poorest home, but I also know of the freedom with which one looks down at marble places and luxuriously paneled halls.

We are here interested especially in the fourth, fifth, and sixth books of the *Didascalicon,* which deal largely with the preparation of the theologian. Interspersed with pious observations, they discuss the list of canonic books according to St. Jerome, the historical, allegorical, tropological, and ethical meaning of the Bible, and the fruits of sacred reading. The fifth book (Ch. 9) describes besides sundry related topics the five steps on which man can climb to perfection: (1) reading (*Lectio sive doctrina*), which provides understanding; (2) meditation (*meditatio*) which provides right ideas (*consilium*); (3) prayer (*oratio*), for without God's help all our decisions are ineffectual; (4) work (*operatio*) which also requires God's grace; (5) contemplation (*contemplatio*), or anticipation of the fruits of piety in the life beyond. In this chapter the author has words of real depth and beauty, as for example:

"God desires to work with you. He will not force you, but [if you will so] He will help you" (*Tecum operari vult Deus. Non cogeris, sed juvaris*).[5]

One of the chapters in Hugh's *Didascalicon* is of historical interest because it gives us a picture of the medieval hierarchy of human activities and the low esteem for the practical.[6]

Two activities restore the similarity to God in man, the exploration of truth and the practice of virtue. For man is similar to God in so far as he is wise and just. But while God is constantly wise and just, man is never constant. Those activities which serve the needs of our earthly life, are threefold; first the means necessary for nature's survival; second that which protects us against molestation from outside; third that which serves as remedy against such molestations after they have occurred.

Hence, if we try to restore our original nature before the fall that is a divine activity, but when we care for the necessities of our weak physical life, that is a human activity. Therefore each activity is either divine or human. The first, coming from above, we may rightly call intelligence [*intelligentia*]; the second, coming from below and in need of guidance [*et quasi quodam consilio indiget*] may be called science [*scientia*]. If, therefore, as said before, wisdom [*sapientia*] regulates all our activities that come from reason [*ratio*], it is evident that wisdom contains these two qualities, namely intelligence and science.

Further we divide intelligence, because devoted to the exploration of truth and the consideration of morality, into two species: theory, which is speculative, and practice which is active and may also be called ethics or theory of conduct. On the other hand, we call science, because dealing with the works of man, mechanics, i.e. adulterate [7] [*mechanica, id est, adulterina vocatur*].

Hugh's *Didascalicon* was widely read even up to the sixteenth century and is still mentioned in historical treatises, though it is of second rank. Neither in content nor in volume can it be compared with that great compendium of medieval knowledge, the *Speculum Maius* [8] by Vincent of Beauvais (*ca.* 1190–1264).

Though the *Speculum* is not a work on religious education in the strict sense of the word, it deserves mention here as one of the great documents of medieval Christian learnings. It is a gigantic encyclopedia, consisting of three main parts: the *Speculum Naturale,* the *Speculum Doctrinale,* and the *Speculum Historiale.* It is divided into eighty books of almost one thousand chapters. According to Ludwig Lieser [9] it contains references to about two thousand different works of four hundred and fifty authors. Because of the lack of distinction, typical of the Middle Ages, between what is natural and what is supernatural, between the factual and the doctrinal, the empirical and the mythical, it is difficult to analyze the book by using modern scholarly categories.

Although its first part is called the *Naturale,* it begins, like other medieval works, with a description of the qualities of the Godhead and the angels. The story of the creation gives the author a welcome opportunity to enlighten his readers about all the natural phenomena that appeared in the first days of the world's existence: light, the firmaments, water, plants, all kinds of animals including fighting dragons, finally man and the properties of his soul. Of course, Lucifer, too, is given his part. Since God entrusted to man the care of flora and fauna, horticulture, agriculture, and husbandry are extensively dealt with; all the knowledge from ancient to medieval times is used.

The felicity of Paradise is broken by the sin of the first couple which can be repaired only through the work of redemption in which Christian education plays a major part.

While these chapters contain nothing which could not be read elsewhere, though rarely in the work of one author, the following parts, contained in the *Speculum Doctrinale,* are of unique interest to the historian of culture and education because, interspersed with an enormous number of quotations, they contain an account of the learning of the time, divided into the *"scientiae seminales"* (*trivia*) and the *"scientiae doctrinales"* (*quadrivia*). Particular emphasis is placed on ethics and its various ramifications for husbandry, social life,

and law. Also the "mechanical" arts, from cloth-making and archi-
tecture to chemistry, are dealt with; and three whole books are devoted to medicine, followed by a book on natural philosophy, mathematics, and a probably incomplete book on theology.

The *Speculum Historiale* begins with the history of the world
from Adam to Christ. Naturally, the Bible and the Church fathers
serve as the main source, but the author draws freely from an apparently rich library. Throughout all his works one feels that in the
early Christian struggle between the puritans and the liberals, he would
have taken the side of the latter. As a matter of fact, he quotes several
authors whom the Church had disapproved.

About one half of the first book of the *Speculum Doctrinale*
is given to the discussion of education proper. But whatever is said
there is extensively repeated in Vincent's *De Eruditione Filiorum
Nobilium*.[10]

This work, small in comparison with the *Speculum Maius,* yet
still of considerable size, was written at the request of Queen Margue-
rite. Like the *Speculum,* it overflows with quotations, mainly from Christian writers. Hugh of St. Victor's *Didascalicon* serves as the model.
In the first chapters the author discusses the nature and aim of education, the ideal teacher, and the nature and desirable qualities of
the learner. Then follows a series of chapters on the curriculum and
the order and meaning of studies, connected with practical suggestions on writing and publishing. Inevitably, Vincent devotes a large
part of the book to moral values and the social implications of education, and he ends with a then not unusual medley concerning family
life and the education and proper conduct of the various ages and sexes.

Despite the variety of topics and the multitude of quotations,
Vincent's book on education reveals a profound inner unity. This
unity stems from the conviction that education is one of the means
by which sinful man can attain salvation, for it helps him—though
he needs God's grace—to understand his place in the order of nature
and to harmonize it with the order of the Spirit.[11]

For to educate is to lift man above the state of rawness
[*ruditas*]. The infant's soul, freshly infused into the flesh,

draws from its corruption the darkness of ignorance as regards the intellect, and the foulness of concupiscence as regards the affective life, and so it is incapable of good thinking and acting.

The contrast to the state of *ruditas* is wisdom, which is not only a theoretical quality, i.e., knowledge of the divine as well as of the natural orders, but also the capacity for wise action to be acquired through self-discipline and participation in the practical responsibilities of life. There are, of course, many obstacles that may deflect man from the path of righteousness: five of them are of mental nature, namely pride, envy, anger, sloth, and greed; and two of carnal nature, gluttony and wantonness. In accordance with Hugh of St. Victor, to whom Vincent of Beauvais often refers as his authority, three qualities are considered essential for progress in studies: nurture, practice, and discipline.

Just as Vincent emphasizes the aims and conditions of learning, he also stresses the methods of teaching to be followed by the teacher. His chapter *De modo docendi* contains many statements which are still valid today, as, generally speaking, one cannot read Vincent's treatise without a sense of the continuity that prevails in the educational tradition. The qualities most necessary for the teacher are: clarity, brevity, attractiveness, moderation, and a sense for the useful.[12] Most of all, the scholar should show the student how to study, contemplate, write, and debate,[13] to choose the right books, instead of many which merely confuse the mind; and above all, he should combine learning with humility, for humility teaches the scholar to respect the whole realm of knowledge, to learn from those who have something to say, and to respect also the less learned. Many like the mere show of erudition; they pretend to be more than they really are, and think they are great when, though still lacking in the elements, they deal with big problems.[14]

Vincent is an eclectic; he is not one of the great architects of medieval thought like Albert of Cologne, Thomas Aquinas, and Duns Scotus. Yet, he is not a mere compiler. He assimilates what he has read; he observes; he prefers balanced wisdom to one-sidedness; and he knows how to select because his mind works within a framework of thought that provides for him order and direction.

Vincent's *Speculum* has overshadowed a work which is at least as characteristic of medieval religious education, Peraldus' *On the Education of the Nobility (De Eruditione Principum)*.[15]

Guillelmus Peraldus, in French, Perrault, was born in Southern France, became a Dominican and, in 1245, administrator of the diocese of Lyon. His *Education of the Nobility* was ascribed to Thomas Aquinas and taken into his collected works—a great honor indeed!—though it requires no great philological skill to discover the differences between the two authors. The content of the book can easily be deduced from Peraldus own introduction.

> I have considered it opportune to divide this work into seven books so that the content of each of them can be more easily found and memorized.
>
> In the first book some general topics about earthly power and true nobility are dealt with.
>
> In the second I will show how princes and men of power should act in relation to Him who is *above* them, to God and His Church.
>
> In the third: how they should act in regard to *themselves*.
>
> In the fourth: how they should act in their relations to those *around* and *beside* them, their friends, their advisers and their administrators.
>
> In the fifth: how they should act in relation to those coming *from* them, i.e. their children, especially in regard to education and erudition.
>
> In the sixth: how they should act in relation to their *inferiors,* that is their subjects.
>
> In the seventh: how they should act in relation to those who are *against* them, i.e. their enemies and adversaries.

To us the fifth book is of special importance, and so it seems to have been to Peraldus, because it is almost as large as the rest.

Peraldus strongly believes in original sin and is therefore a severe disciplinarian.

> Mere instruction by word of mouth is not enough; on the contrary, discipline must use strictness, and even blows are necessary. . . . Blows have a great effect; by them also animals, which have no reason, are instructed and tamed. (Ch. 1)

He warns against negligence and undue postponement of education. Bend the twig while it is elastic.

> Whoever fails to acquire good habits while he is young behaves badly against God, against the guardian angel whom God has placed on his side, and against himself. (Ch. 8)

Much value has to be placed in the choice of the tutor. He must be a man of talent and immaculate conduct; he must be humble in his knowledge; he must possess the gift of eloquence; finally, "he must have practical experience and skill in the art of teaching, in order to instruct according to right form and method" (Ch. 10). Indeed, Peraldus devotes a whole chapter to this topic (Ch. 11). According to it, instruction must be (1) clear, (2) brief and precise, (3) useful, (4) agreeable and pleasing, (5) "it must proceed with the right measure of time, i.e. it must keep the right middle between speed and slowness." (6) "The teacher will live up to all these demands if, similar to the good orator, he tries to achieve three things, namely to enlighten, to delight, and to motivate his pupil toward goodness."

And just as with good methods of teaching, Peraldus is also concerned with the conditions of good learning. Good learning for him means good living, humility, absence of envy and of false curiosity, industriousness, devotion, moderation, prayer, methodical procedure, and continuous exercise.

A large number of chapters (15-71) are given to physical and mental discipline, to the cultivation of a noble style of living, and to marriage, which God Himself has deigned to sanctify, though an unmarried life is better in His eyes. He anticipates the content of his later deliberations in an early chapter (15), where he speaks about the main purpose of education.

> In order to produce good habits in children, the educator has to pay attention to both, physical culture and discipline, as well as to virtues of the soul. Six points are especially important in regard to the body: first, posture; second, clothing; third, speaking; fourth, food and drink; fifth, chastity and the entering into marriage; sixth, the choice of virginity. In regard to the virtues of the soul the children of noble families have to be taught humility and voluntary endurance, respect before parents and childlike obedience, the right choice of friends and social company; and when growing up they must feel compelled to abandon childishness for manly perseverance and firmness.

There is hardly one major admonition which the author does not support by quotations from the Bible, from St. Augustine, and other Christian writers; from the ancients he selects especially Seneca.

The warmest feeling for youth among the scholastic academicians we find exactly in the man who, as chancellor of the University of Paris, as French leader of the ecclesiastical reform movement, and as delegate to the stormy reform councils of Pisa (1409) and Constance (1414–1418) was involved in the most decisive conflicts of the time, Jean Charlier Gerson (1363–1429). Gerson lived at the period of the great schism, with two or sometimes three popes and their parties fighting against each other, and heresies appeared in many countries. His sympathetic temperament and his burning concern with the corruption of the time turned his interest to the youth around him.[16] Gerson is not a scholastic philosopher in the pure sense of the word. He is profoundly suspicious of the subtle abstractions discussed at the University of Paris; between him and Thomas Aquinas lie not only one and a half centuries, but also the nominalist philosophies of Duns Scotus and William of Occam; and he was influenced by mystical theology. Not through reason, but through love do we arrive at the knowledge of God. In Gerson, the accent has shifted from the brain to the heart.

Although for Gerson the rod was an indispensable tool of education, he loved youth and tried to understand it. He was not only a
teacher of minds, but also a true curate of souls. To be sure, for him
too every human being stands under the curse of original sin; nevertheless, he believed that children are open to all that is good, and
susceptible to kind persuasion. It is the task of the teacher to help
them to overcome the evil in man by motivating them toward the
virtues of self-negation, humility, work, and prayer, and by explaining to them the saving effect of the sacraments, especially of confession.

When Gerson, probably in years of political disorders which interrupted his work at the University, devoted much of his time to the
care of youth, he was criticized for offending the elevated dignity of
his position. Thus he wrote his tractatus, *On Leading Children to
Christ (De Parvulis Trahendis ad Christum)*, in which he refuted at
length the arguments of his adversaries, asserting that he knew of
no greater duty besides his obligations as a chancellor and preacher
than, "with the help of God, to tear the souls of children from the jaws
of the hell-hound and the doors of the inferno." [17] Each of the four
meditations in this treatise begins with an educationally pertinent quotation from the Bible, and each ends with reference to *St. Mark*
10:14, "Suffer the little children come unto me, and forbid them not."

Love is for Gerson the secret of education. When speaking of
his role as confessor he says, "There has never, with my will, remained
in my heart a trace of revenge or hatred during someone's confession
of sin, were it even the murder of his parents." And no one will lead
the young toward a better life

> unless he smiles kindly at the laughing ones, encourages
> those who play, praises their progress in learning, and even
> in correction avoids bitterness and insult. Then the children
> will feel that he does not hate them, but loves them like a
> brother.

This concern for the souls of youth at a time when, as so many
of his pedagogical writings reveal, children of the large cities were
exposed to the most lewd and vulgar influences, caused him also to

appeal to the authorities that they should prevent the exhibition of "lascivious pictures and other ignominies through which youth becomes corrupted." [18] Gerson also composed several treatises on the instruction of pupils of which the *Ordinance for the Pupils of the Cathedral School of Paris* is the most important.[19] It deals with the guidance and instruction of youth destined for priesthood and contains, besides the usual pious entreaties, the following which give us a vivid picture of medieval school life.

7. The cantor [*magister cantus*] should instruct the pupils especially in plain, or Gregorian, chant and in *"cantus contrapunctus,"* but not in impudent cantilenae. [Here follow interesting remarks about medieval church music.]

8. At meals one of the boys should read from a useful book while the others keep silent, thus following the advice: Speak little at table.

9. The boys should have a well ordered schedule.

10. Each pupil is urged to denounce his fellow student in regard to the following points: When he hears him talk in French; when he curses or lies; when he cheats, abuses or beats an other; when he uses lascivious language or permits himself to touch another student improperly; when he has risen late, missed classes, and chatted in church, etc. Those who fail to denounce a sinner, shall suffer the same punishment for him and with him. These transgressions may also be put down as points in a little notebook that can be given to the director at the end of the week so that he can wisely correct the delinquent. But if one cleric has beaten an other severely, he shall immediately be sent to the penitentiary.[20]

11. The pupils should be forbidden all plays that may lead toward covetousness, dishonesty, vulgar shouting, ire and rancor (games at dice and of hazard).

12. Without permission the boys should not go to any place, not even into the church for singing.

13. According to old custom, there should burn in the boys room and during the whole night, and at a safe place, a lamp before the image of the holy virgin, partly for prayer, partly for the easier satisfaction of natural needs which often come with boys, partly also because they often rise for the mattins. They should do only that which is permitted and

can be seen by light. No boy should go from one bed to another, each should remain with the companion allotted to him. Nor should it be permitted that some hold special conventicles or gatherings, separated from the others, neither by day or night; rather they all should always be together and under the eyes of all. Also, they should not keep and feed animals or dangerous birds.

14. Nobody from outside should be allowed to enter the house and take out a boy except with special permission of the superiors.

15. There should be no undue familiarity with the attendants of the house, nor should the pupils be seen ever with clergymen, servants, or chaplains from outside, except in a teacher's presence. If, nevertheless, the pupils disobey, they should be punished severely. The punishment has to be administered moderately and with a rod, but not with a slender and flexible switch and other dangerous tools; abusive words must be avoided. The boys should feel that they are loved, not derided. Not through harshness, but through mildness should they be lead toward virtue so that they not, as says the apostle, be discouraged.[21]

16. All excess in eating, at morning and the day over, should be avoided, otherwise their voice may be ruined and the rules of moderation be violated. But we wish that they have a sufficient amount of healthy and nourishing food and that their rooms, beds and cloths, etc. be kept proper and clean. Also the sick should be taken care of diligently. The magister should report twice a year about the discharged and the accepted.

17. In the choir they all should sit separated and be absolutely silent and of dignified conduct.

18. Finally the pupils should be well instructed to observe diligently all the activities and ceremonies since long customary in our Church. They should know exactly when to appear, when to bow, when to leave, and in which order to sing, etc. This, in great measure, has already been written down and posted at a visible place of their house.

Whether these rules were always followed, we do not know. But from what we know from other sources about medieval discipline, they are very humane. However, Gerson was at the same time a severe persecutor of what he considered heretical ideas. He made a journey to Pope Clement VIII to procure the condemnation of the Dominican John of Montesono who had dared doubt the dogma of the Immaculate Conception (which had not been a dogma of the early Church). And it is painful to know that at the Council of Constance he presided over the process against the Czech reformer John Huss who, in spite of the Emperor Sigismund's promise of "free conduct," was burned at the stake. From this act resulted the cruel wars of the enraged Hussites in Eastern Germany and—directly and indirectly—the final rebellion of an increasing number of pious Christians against the Catholic Church, to the reform of which Gerson himself had dedicated his life.

Among the many who, like Gerson, were profoundly concerned with the reform of Christendom and, incidentally, also, with the education of youth, was the Belgian Dionysius the Carthusian (1402–1470), the friend and cooperator of the greatest and freest mind of the fifteenth century's theologians, Nicholas of Cusa (from the German city of Kues). From Dionysius we possess almost two hundred writings on Christian exegesis and liturgy, on problems of dogma and canonic law, on various parts of the Bible, on Thomas Aquinas, and on Dionysius Areopagita. Like Gerson, the Carthusian owed much to mysticism, and, with some of his learned contemporaries, he believed he could avert the growing danger from the Turks in Europe by convincing them of the errors of Mohammed and the Koran. They would then convert to the truth of Christianity.[22] Dionysius also devoted much of his literary activity to the improvement of the moral life of both the clergy and the laymen.[23] Among these writings there exists a treatise *On Scholars*,[24] which goes beyond the conventional moral tracts only through the inclusion of an admonition directed to "the authorities in villages and towns to see to it that the pupils have erudite and pleasing teachers." Some sentences in this chapter remind one of Luther's later message to the magistrates of the German cities. We find also an illustration of the life in a medieval community and the desirable role of its teachers in the following paragraph:

Hence the magistrates of the towns should generously care for an adequate salary to be paid annually to fitted and capable teachers. And in order to prevent the older pupils from too great excesses, quarrels and offences against temperance, a public decree should be issued that no foreigner be allowed to live in the town unless he declares himself willing to obey the teachers and to be punished as he deserves. If he refuses, he should be expelled. But the teachers should be enjoined by the authorities that their salary will depend on their willingness to insist on severe discipline without regard of person; they should treat delinquents in such a way that they and others can be kept within the bounds of fear and order. (Art. 24)

More original than any other of Dionysius' educational writings is his *Dialogue between Jesus and the Boy* [25] (*Inter Jesum et Puerum Dialogues*), in which he addresses older adolescents who might consider going from the *scholae particulares* (with Latin and the trivium of grammar, rhetoric, and logic in their curriculum) to the university. Unless one takes into account the spirit and style of the time one may have a feeling of blasphemy when one listens to Brother Dionysius' Christ who speaks, not as the "divine *paidogogos*" of Clement of Alexandria, but as a moralizing schoolmaster. However, the Carthusian shows at least a measure of taste in that he allows Jesus to abstain from supporting his words by quotations from Aristotle, Xenocrates, and other ancient writers to whom we find so many references at other places. Only the Bible is Christ's authority; he quotes it again and again.

Whereas Gerson's dealing with youth is more than of loving encouragement, Dionysius prefers, in the *Dialogue* as elsewhere, the brimstone and hellfire approach. As we saw, Gerson speaks also of the hound of hell, but Dionysius, though speaking through Christ, really gloats over the torments of the inferno (Article VI).

> Consider how insufferable it would be to lie but for an hour with your naked body in a glowing furnace. How then can you endure the heat and tortures of purgatory for many days and years, or, still more, how could you stand the pains of hell without end and hope of salvation? Not only the agonies of the inferno, but also the torments of purgatory surpass all sufferings of life, though the martyrs, as we can read, have borne the most inhuman forms of punishment.

The boy answers.

This frightens me immensely. For to be confined to bed for only a year or even a month seems to me an intolerable and cruel torture.

Jesus

How much more insufferable would it be for you to lie naked for a month, or a year, in the midst of the most poisonous and horrid beasts, basilisks, dragons and toads, to be ensnared by them, embraced and clasped?

Boy.

The mere image fills me with unspeakable horrors.

A profound pessimism, as is characteristic of the late Middle Ages, permeates all the works of Dionysius. The Church itself is corrupt.

At the present and deplorable state of the Church—so Jesus tells the boy—it is most perilous indeed to stay in the world. For one finds today even with the superiors and prelates of the Church only little, if any, regard for the divine commandments and the decrees and laws given by the holy fathers. They are blind leaders of the blind. And if the blind lead the blind, both shall fall into the ditch [*Matthew* 15:14]. But the highest shepherd, God Almighty, will not desert His chosen sheep.

After this the boy is ready "to leave this sullied world and to enter a holy order." And this, indeed, is the intention of the *Dialogue*, to persuade the child to leave the natural bonds of life.

You are obliged—so Jesus says—[Article V] to love spiritually your parents, relations and friends and must wish for them most of all eternal salvation, and for their life here on earth all those graces and virtues through which they can achieve this high state of felicity. . . . This will happen if in your devotion and love of God you withdraw your physical presence from your parents and relatives, when you abandon all mortal comfort, deny yourself all worldly intercourse and offer yourself completely as a servant to the Almighty in a holy order or a pious society. . . .

Needless to say, besides withdrawal, asceticism is the way toward salvation. The horrors of the sins of the flesh, decried everywhere in Dionysius' exhortatory writings, are most passionately depicted in the following paragraph of his already-mentioned treatise *On Scholars* (Article 13).

This cursed pestilence, this worst of all beasts, this most irrational monster is unspeakably dangerous to all young people. It lies in ambush in order to lead them away from the sincerity of their studies, from the beauty of virtue, and from the splendor of the sciences in order to see them wallowing in vice, tainted with dirt, and, torn from Christ, slaves of the devils. This profligate enemy of chastity fights against virtue, generates insolence and leads toward arrogance, disobedience and wrath. It particularly displeases the glorious and immaculate virgin Mary, the sweet and sublime mother of Christ, as on the other hand, she is pleased by nothing as much as by chastity. The abominable sins of the flesh suppress reason, make beasts out of men, vitiate his true qualities, deprive him of the gifts of grace, strip the miserable of divine glory and drag the mad into the eternal torments of hell.

Therefore Jesus feels compelled to warn, (Article 4) his young friend also of the universities.

The universities (*universalia studia*) were rightly founded for useful and necessary reasons. On the mystical body of Jesus Christ, namely the Church, the universities are, as it were, the eyes, having the purpose to resist the errors of faith. And if one lived at these universities for the salvation of the soul and according to the prescribed laws, then for pious and chaste young men the danger would not be so great. But just as in other estates, grades and ranks of the Church there often reign lawlessness and ruin, so they reign also in the universities; hence they are hazardous for pious and chaste young people. Alas, how miserably and rapidly their virtues are there undermined and their souls stained and seduced. Hence, if a boy has been sufficiently educated in the minor schools, it may be better and safer for him to enter a religious order or a pious congregation than to postpone this decision because of a desire for greater knowledge. If such a pupil is diligent, capable, and works devotedly for the purity of his soul and the growth of his virtues, then in a monastery or congregation he will sooner than in a university arrive at a profound understanding of the sacred scriptures and at a deep insight into the things spiritual, wholesome and divine. For a sound knowledge is more easily achieved by appointment in retreat than by public disputation, more by divine illumination than by human instruction, more by the purity of the heart than by verbal argument, more by passionate prayer than by noisy quarrel, more by the depth of silence than by ostentatious bombast. Hence some of the saints fled into a holy order when they saw that at the universities many lived in the abysses of vice, the fires of lust and the traps of bodily and spiritual perversion. . . . About this you can learn from the lives of St. Aegidius, Benedict, and Bernard.

About the corruption of the universities, we have so many testimonies [26] that Dionysius does not seem to be exaggerating. Apparently, the time was ripe for change. It came with the rise of humanism and the Protestant Reformation, both representing that turn of Western civilization we call the Renaissance.

It would be wrong to leave the reader of this chapter on the Middle Ages with the impression that the writings of the learned give us a full picture of Christian education at this period. It may be that, in the larger cities of upper Italy, Germany, Flanders, Brabant, and England, one half of the male population was literate to a degree; in the rural districts only the priests could read. Most of them—if they really possessed any books—owned only those which contained the essentials of liturgy, and the calendar of the festivals and of the days of the saints. Throughout the Middle Ages the *Ecloga Theoduli*,[27] still printed at Leipzig in 1492 and in Lyons in 1504, was used by the clergy not only for their own edification and entertainment, but also for giving the unlearned the story of the great biblical events. The *Ecloga,* written by a not-yet-identified author who was influenced by Vergil, contains in verse a series of coordinated pagan myths and biblical stories. Thus the pagan myth of Saturn and the golden age is placed beside the story of the Paradise and the Fall; the myth of Jupiter and the defeat of Saturn is likened to the expulsion of the first couple; the tale of Cecrops, the first king of Attica who was credited with the introduction of bloodless sacrifices, to the story of Cain and Abel.

All around there were pictorial representations of things holy and a rich symbolism, which was destroyed partly by the Reformation and, even in Catholic countries, by growing rationalism and the spread of the printed word. And while the rich enjoyed their precious altars and prayer books, beautifully illuminated and bound in covers with rare stones, the poor profited, at least indirectly, from the many editions of the *Biblia Pauperum* which represented the transition to illustrated Bibles, made possible by the invention of blockbooks and individual woodcuts.[28] The lower clergy used its illustrations (about 35–50), accompanied by explaining texts in Latin and in German, as a kind of concordance and visual reminder of the earthly life of Christ. The artists used it for their paintings and many other works of art that decorated the churches and the public buildings. Thus even the many who could not buy or read a book profited from the "Poor Man's Bible."

Among the educated, the dominance of Scholasticism declined as early as in the fourteenth century. Bearers of great names were responsible for this decline. In Italy Petrarch (1304–1374) protested against the Aristotelianism of the schoolmen; even in the work of Dante, who lived a generation before him, there appear signs of a new attitude of mind and of a new piety. At the time of Petrarch, German mysticism became a powerful force, represented by Master Eckart, Heinrich Suso, Johann Tauler, and Thomas a Kempis. The Dutch participated in the new Movement, mainly in the person of Jan van Ruysbroeck. Influenced by Eckart, they all considered the *unio mystica,* or the unity of the soul with the divine element, more important than doctrinal tradition. And the already-mentioned Nicholas of Cusa developed a system of thought with such completely new perspectives concerning the relation of man to himself, to nature, and to God that some historians regard his work as the first document of modern philosophy. Piety is for him the knowledge of oneself as part of a universal order that can be understood both by intuition and by scientific investigation, though the Ultimate will always remain in the realm of mystery.

In connection with mystical trends there arose outside the monastic orders loosely knit fraternities that averred the religion of the heart and a truly pious life over and above the theology of the learned, e.g., the Friends of God (*Gottesfreunde*) in the South and West of Germany, and the Brethren of the Common Life in the Netherlands. They represented movements that the always-suspicious Church could not persecute as heretical as it had done with the Waldenses, the Albigenses, and the Hussites, but that, nevertheless, like vernal plants growing under the leaves, prepared the gradual transition from medieval ecclesiasticism to the religious individualism of the reformers. Often these new minds received their inspiration not only from inward forms of religiosity, but also from the revival of classical studies.

Among them was Alexander Hegius (*ca.* 1433–1498, of Heek in Westphalia), a pupil of Thomas a Kempis. He insisted on the reading of classical texts and new methods of instruction instead of the ones followed in the old textbooks. This attitude explains, at least in part, that from his famous school at Deventer there came Erasmus of Rotterdam, a number of outstanding humanists, and Pope Hadrian VI, who, though too late, insisted on the reform of the Church including the Curia which he considered largely responsible for the abuses of ecclesiastical power. A contemporary of Hegius was the Dutchman, Rudolph Agricola, a scholar of remarkable philological learning who after wide traveling lectured on the classics in Holland and at the University of Heidelberg. He had that deep influence on his pupils which distinguishes the great teacher from the mere instructor.

But though Agricola wrote a work *On the Dialectical Method* (*De Inventione Dialectica*) [29] in which he criticized the mechanical spirit of scholastic philosophy, he and all his friends adhered faithfully to the tradition of the medieval Church. They wished to improve it, but, whatever criticism there was in them, it was not rebellious or satirical. Yet, in the minds of many of their pupils they planted the seeds out of which there grew the new intellectual and religious vigor of the Renaissance and the Reformation about which we will speak in the next chapter.

SUMMARY

The society of the Middle Ages, as all advanced societies, can be described only in contrasts, and that which applies to a society as a whole applies also to its education.[30]

At the end of the Migration of the Nations, only a part of the clergy were literate, and most of the nobles could neither read nor write. A woman such as Dhuoda, who could compose a Christian manual for her son, was probably unique. Only in cloisters might she have been able to find her like. All the education the ordinary layman could receive consisted of the barest essentials of the creed, and even they were understood more in magical than in a truly religious sense. How could it be otherwise? But at the end of the Middle Ages, say the fifteenth century, the cities and towns had their schools, and the privileged of the older areas of civilization were highly sophisticated, steeped in luxury, and blasè to the degree of Weltschmerz.

Yet, even in the early centuries the bells tolled from the churches; their altars could not be stained, and it was sacrilege to kill the enemy who had taken refuge in a sacred place. The symbols of worship reminded the people of love, death, and eternity; the holy was present even though the words were not understood. The great festivals and the days of the local saints provided the opportunity for processions and religious plays with their mixture of the sacred and the vulgar.

After some centuries of slow development, the "dark ages," the intellectual surge of Scholasticism began. Truly, some of the logical exercises of the later masters remind one of a vortex of concepts with little or no empirical substance. Nevertheless, the motive as well as the result was of enormous significance. The motive came from the will to organize the Christian faith by means of logic and at the same time to harmonize it with the divine and natural laws of the universe as far as they were understood in a prescientific age. The result was an impressive intellectual edifice, still acknowledged as a canon by Catholic theologians. Without the ordering work of the schoolmen there could have been written neither the Protestant nor the Catholic catechisms which for centuries formed the foundation of religious education, and in many places still do today.

In no way were the scholastic scholars remote from the urgent problems of the time. They knew that the intellect is for thinking, but that thinking is also a kind of politics, hidden perhaps, but nevertheless a force that moulds the environment. From their quiet cells they influenced the course of Christendom. They lived not only within monastic walls and universities; they advised the courts, they went to councils, and they traveled to foreign lands. Thomas Aquinas' thesis on government influenced the political thought of later centuries, and Marsilius of Padua and William of Occam defended the rights of the princes against the usurping tendencies of the popes. And while certainly some of the schoolmen lectured over the heads of many of their students, the mendicant friars preached to the peasants, shared their bread, and slept in their barns—perhaps not always alone.

We are sometimes shocked by the reveling in cruel visions with which men such as Dionysius the Carthusian describe the horrors of hell and damnation (the Puritan preachers were also famous for that). but within the same men we find also kindness and human sympathy. Those within the Church were human and could be forgiven in the name of Christ. Those who doubted had either to be converted or to be eliminated. Constantly we are reminded of that most characteristic medieval monument, Mt. Saint Michel, where the dark and humid dungeons lie right below the lofty halls of worship.

At the time when the disputativeness of the professors turned sometimes into verbally exquisite triviality and the popes were as far away from the spirit of St. Peter as any other fighting and intriguing princes, the mystics broke through the walls of formalism and spoke of the inner wealth of the soul that has discovered the poverty of all things human and, above all, its own poverty before God. Thus Master Eckhart could say: [31]

Love is the foundation of all virtues without which there is no virtue even in the most efficient work. Whenever a man does good deeds they must come from love, not from him. Only love gives our actions the power that leads men into the God-head.

In another sermon he says: [32]

The humblest work done within the soul is higher and nobler than the greatest work done without the soul. Yet even the noblest inner work must stand in silent awe if God is to appear to the soul in His whole light and purity. . . . In order to achieve this unity with the divine, the soul must have divorced itself not only from all external, but even from all intellectual and inner doings: so that God alone be the doer, whole and straight, and the soul be passive before the work of God, obey and submit, so that God be free to create his inborn son in the human soul as within Himself. This is the union through which the soul in one instant is more united with God that through all works it can do, corporeal or spiritual.

These sentences, of course, reveal that mixture of individualism and pantheism which we often find in modern religious poetry. No wonder the Church discovered that these ideas "seem to some people to contain error, and, what is worse, to smack of heresy." [33] Thus, in 1326, Master Eckhart had to defend himself before an ecclesiastical court. His death in the following year closed the books.

Master Eckhart and other mystics built the bridge between medieval ecclesiastic and modern mentality. Amazing though it may seem to the superficial observer, there is a spiritual connection between Master Eckhart's concept of the "divine spark" in the human soul as the source of all religious experience and the educational philosophy of men such as Rousseau, Pestalozzi, and Froebel, whose individualism was also based on the assumption of an inner communion between the human soul and the divine universe.

Chapter 6

The Renaissance

One might call the Renaissance and its humanism an individualist self-assertion against tradition, a new and more empirical testing of the values and depths of human existence, and a search for new forms of verification. All this is true only in part, for in some respects the humanists believed more in authority than the scholastics; though no longer Aristotle, it was now Plato, Cicero, and Quintilian. There were humanists who were more or less pagans within a Church that itself had lost its spiritual moorings, but several among the greatest humanists had no more urgent purpose than to restore it to its ancient purity. Erasmus worked during his whole life for reform without revolution, and Thomas More became a martyr for upholding Christian ethics against his monarch.

Nevertheless, a new era began when the humanists entered the historical scene. The world had widened. Some of the new men envisioned a natural and immanent, not merely a transcendental order of the cosmos. Some thought that the old feudal system was in need of reform. They had a sense for the beauty of life and the preciousness of the human person even here on earth; doubt and curiosity about things so far unknown were for them no longer a vice, but a virtue.[1]

Compared with the greatness of the leading artists and thinkers of the Renaissance, the typical educational writings of the humanists, especially of the Italians such as Pietro Paolo Vergerio, Lionardo Bruni,

Aenea Sylvio (later Pope Pius II), Battista Guarino, and Matteo Vegio are disappointing. In their suggestions about physical and mental hygiene and the methods of teaching and learning they do not go far beyond the late medieval writers. However, the Renaissance reveals itself in the different conception of the purpose of education. The world is no longer an "exile" as for Hugh of St. Victor and Dionysius the Carthusian, but a challenge for the independent, disciplined, and all-around educated man. The new *uomo universale* is everything but an ascetic. He is a "gentleman" who cultivates himself and his taste in contact with men and women of excellence. Poetry and the fine arts, style and form are for him values of the highest order, and he wants his children to study literature and history, not merely the legends of martyrs. The old trivium and quadrivium gives way to a more timely program of study.

Leon Battista Alberti, one of the universal geniuses of the time, writes in Italian—no longer in Latin—a treatise *On the Family* (*Della Famiglia*) in which the glory of the family appears to be one of the main responsibilities of a gentleman.[2]

At the end of the *Proemio* the author asserts his eagerness

to contribute to the praise and exaltation of our family Alberta which always deserved to be esteemed and honored. To its name all my studies and industry, my thoughts, mind and energy will be dedicated.

And the elder Lorenzo, Leone's father, admonishes his children:

And so, my children, aim at virtue, flee vice, honor your elders, be well minded, and live as free, happy, honored and loved men. . . . Do not be difficult, harsh, obstinate, frivolous and vain, but strive to be easy, tractable, interested in many things, and when the age demands, stately and dignified. And try by all means to be grateful, reverent, and obedient to older people.

Everywhere, what a difference between the new spirit and the monastic ideals of earlier times! "Glory" replaces "humility." The service for the prince, the laurels of the soldier, and the art of states-

manship become the goals of ambition. Certainly, they did so also in
earlier times; the knight at the tournament and the warrior in battle
had always fascinated the minds of man. But, at least in theory, the
divine word stood high above the worldly world, whereas now the
two come closer to each other, even in the literature on religious education. Of course, the Christian virtues are recommended, but the new
relation between God and man is conceived in a different key.

As a man who stands in between the older religious and the new
humanistic tradition, with an obvious trend toward the latter, the Italian Cardinal Jacopo Sadoleto (1477–1547) deserves our particular interest because of his work *On Education*.[3]

In this dialogue, which, as so many dialogues of the time, is
merely formal without any real give and take of ideas, Sadoleto speaks
first of the problem of rearing children and of moral training, and
then of scholarly education. The author emphasizes the aesthetic quality of the personality and a rather autonomous concept of man is
shown in the following statement.[4]

> It (the new way of education) must lead our youth to a
> position from which, not content with following the footsteps
> of others, they will learn to look, as if from a watch tower,
> with their own eyes, choosing their goal and electing the
> path towards it under the command of their own judgment
> and will.

> It is the arts which produce man's similarity with God.[5]

> Moral training sets out with the object of ensuring that all
> our words and actions may be marked by moderation and
> may keep a fit and proper rule of conduct, the correct beauty
> of which may delight not only the mind of the learned but
> even the eyes of the ignorant. . . .

Sadoleto's appreciation of the dignity of the person motivates
him to reject severe punishment of a son by his father, for flogging
"may reduce a generous nature to the condition of a slave. . . ."[6]

The idea of original sin gives way to a more lenient interpretation of the nature of man and consequently also to a more lenient pedagogy.[7]

> For there is no reason to anticipate that when a youth has been brought up by such a father and on such a system and has been trained to walk in the right path of virtue, his nature and taste can turn to depravity.

The horrors of hell are no longer pictured in this enlightened form of education. One would enjoy this change even more if the idea of the person's dignity were extended to all humanity and not merely restricted to the privileged.

> For—so Sadoleto says—flogging may be allowed against a servant or workman who, let us admit, is of such a breed that, as an old proverb says of the Phrygian, that he is usually made better by flogging [Cicero, *Pro L. Flaccus,* 27]. On the other hand, it is the essence and significance of scholarly education that it elevates and perfects the mind—which is our real self but which we have received in the state of crudeness and imperfection—in such a way that it becomes similar to the divine.

Besides casual remarks on the value of piety, there are several paragraphs that deal with religion. It is—so the Cardinal says—the duty of both mother and father to plant the fear of God early into the soul of the child. But, in contrast to prehumanist writers, throughout the treatise faith is no longer considered the all-permeating and enduring aim of education, but only one of several components in the growth of the harmonious personality. In the following paragraphs which deal with elementary reading and writing and with the initiation into Latin and Greek, we find the following statement: [8]

> And here at once we note a most admirable practice, customary among us, together with his letters to instill into a boy the elements or simplest characters of Christian Religion, for, . . . there can be neither goodness, nor learn-

ing, nor any hope of an honorable life, unless virtue attends and accompanies. And at the same time there should be put before him pregnant maxims of authors of high authority bearing upon holiness of life and the example of virtue to be copied and evils to be shunned, maxims that the impressionable mind may well receive and carry with it through the rest of life.

While religion recedes, other subjects occupy the open field. In the seven liberal arts, poetry, or the study of poets, neglected by the scholastics, receives its old importance. But in typical humanist fashion, not the poets of the vernacular, but the Greek and Latin authors are recommended, though Dante had already written his *Divine Comedy* about two hundred years before Sadoleto.[9]

But what am I to say about the poets? You know what a multitude of them there are in Latin and in Greek, you know how potent is their art, not only to soothe but to rouse our spirits. The race of poets has ever been held sacred, and dear to the gods: for it is not so much by the effort of human thought as by the breath of some inspiration from heaven that they pour forth those strains which, fashioned with sound and measure, take our senses, and, streaming in upon minds, deeply stir them in such sort that no resistance seems possible to their compelling influence.

The influence of Quintilian, though not expressly mentioned, appears in the praise of eloquence and rhetoric, and for Sadoleto, as for all the other humanists, Cicero was the unsurpassable example. But the crown of all studies is philosophy.[10]

. . . all knowledge or learning is liberal, but those arts of which we have so long been speaking are, as it were, members of that one great body, the object of our quest, philosophy itself; for every process of handling and learning facts of nature—of whatever kind they may be—and all that is involved and implied in the contemplation of nature—all this falls within the province of philosophy, and is illuminated by its light, as by a ray of truth.

This is good humanism, but it is certainly not Christian education in the genuine sense of the word. As a matter of fact, there are several heresies in Sadoleto's writings for which a minor figure might have been punished.

His work on education was highly praised by his friends. Most humanists were generous in mutual epithets of admiration. However, the upright Englishman, Cardinal Reginald Pole, Archbishop of Canterbury, put this finger on the crucial point of Sadoleto's book.[11]

> What—so he asked his friend in whose house at Carpentras he had lived—is your real opinion about the hierarchy of knowledge? Apparently, it is philosophy. This would be justified if you lived at the times of Plato, Aristotle, or Cicero. But since God and His Son have given us now a much better haven for our souls in which Sadoleto himself occupies the position of a helmsman, has your Paulus [the disciple in the dialogue] not a right to complain in that he is left in a strange and insecure post while the cardinal himself has chosen the best and most secure? . . . Do not believe, my friend Sadoleto, that you have really fulfilled your promise concerning the education of your young man after having lead him to the threshold of philosophy or even made him an expert in it. You must go farther and never rest until he has landed in the harbor where you yourself live in complete peace of mind.

An interesting exchange of ideas followed Pole's letter, with an attempt on Sadoleto's part to show the inclusiveness of his humanism in regard to the Christian education, but he didn't convince the English statesman and cardinal—nor does he us.

More religious than Sadoleto was the Spaniard Juan Luis Vives (1492–1540), friend of Erasmus and a teacher at Oxford until punished by Henry VIII for his objection to the king's divorce from Catherine of Aragon. In his treatise *On the Teaching of the Arts* [12] he followed more the convictions of Gerson than those of the humanists. He writes in the fourth chapter of the first book:

> As everything so also man must be judged according to his purpose. . . . But which other goal can man have than

God Himself, or where can man find his peace but in God in Whom, as it were, he becomes absorbed? We came from Him, so we must also return to Him. The cause of our creation was love, for God created man for the sole purpose to make him happy. This is the dearest sign of His love. Out of love, namely self-love, we have separated ourselves from Him. But out of love He has called us back and restored us through the love of Jesus Christ. Thus through love we must return to Him who is both our origin and our goal: through love to God. For only through love can those of the spirit be united.

Through Vives' essay *On the Teaching of the Arts* is probably the finest of the Renaissance writings on education, two other of his books are more widely known. One is his treatise on psychology, *De Anima et Vita,* in which he anticipates Descartes and Bacon and, to a degree, even modern behaviorism by his emphasis on the inductive method of inquiry. What the essence of the soul may be, so he says, "is of no concern for us to know. The main objective is for us to describe its manifestations." Vives' most famous work, however, is *On the Causes of the Corruption of the Arts (De Causis Corruptarum Artium)*. It contains the most serious accusation of the rotten conditions prevailing at the universities in the late Middle Ages, though, in the struggle between the reformers and the Catholic Church, Vives preferred to remain loyal to the latter.

Despite all his indignation about the impiety and looseness of the academic life of his time, Vives himself is far from being bigoted. His piety is that of a thoroughly Christian humanist. Though he knows that there is no knowledge, however good, that cannot be poisoned by false—i.e., for him anti-Christian—doctrines like those of Epicurus, he nevertheless hopes for a synthesis between ever-widening scholarship and a living Christian tradition. We know that the question to which degree this synthesis is possible was discussed among the early Christians and it still is a matter of controversy.

The same objections that Pole raised against Sadoleto he could also have raised against the most universal of the humanist scholars, Desiderius Erasmus of Rotterdam (1466–1536).

Occupied though he was with a Greek and Latin edition of the New Testament and with a whole series of editions of Church fathers, he proved himself the humanist with the most spirited vision of the future. He hoped for a society ready to understand the true meaning and simplicity of religion in contrast to historically grown dogma and ecclesiastical institutionalism (though himself a priest and adhering officially to Catholicism, he deviated from the custom of bequeathing money to the Church, nor did he invite a confessor to his death bed.) He wanted a political organization with peace and justice for all, resembling the ideals of a modern democratic state, and an education that would combine the training of an intellectual elite with the enlightenment of the people as a whole. *"Summa nostrae religionis pax est et unanimitas"* (The essence of our religion is peace and concord).[13] He hoped to achieve the mentality necessary for such a society by restoring the simplicity of Christ's teaching on the one hand and, on the other hand, by opening the minds to the wisdom and beauty of the classics—in this respect being in the line of Origen, Clement, and his friend Louis Vives.

Erasmus' point of view reveals itself also in his educational thought.[14] He was concerned with awakening the pupil's interest and his love for the teacher and strongly averse to harsh treatment which he described most realistically in all the terrible excesses of the time. The school should be the place that children enjoy because they are understood, and it should prepare young minds for the cultivation of good style in speaking, writing and living. "Hence, let us establish this threefold unity, that reason should lead nature and practice perfect reason." [15] In a mature person, knowledge should lead to commitment. Urbanity, erudition, and a Christian faith firmly anchored in the evangel but otherwise undogmatic should constantly interact. There is an atmosphere of liberality in whatever Erasmus wrote.

But the spirit of the time had become unfriendly to liberal minds. For with the advent of Protestantism, against which even the Inquisition was helpless, the Catholic Church finally realized that it had only the choice between losing most of Europe or strengthening its authority by inner reform, severe discipline, and a thorough reexamination of its dogma. The chance for lenity in matters religious was gone.

Humanism became caught between the fighting armies. Its attempt at a reconciliation of the tradition and the new mode of life was frustrated. Pushed off from the religious arena, it became philosophical, aesthetic, but also the seed ground of modern science. Luther was bitter against Erasmus for his desertion of the cause of the Reformation, while the Catholic Church distrusted him in spite of all the honors he received for his loyalty and scholarship.

"Erasmianism" was persecuted in Catholic countries, and the Council of Trent (1545–1563) put some of his books on the *Index Librorum Prohibitorum*. His famous *Proverbs or Adages out of the Chiliades* (*Adagiorum Chiliades*) were condemned; an expurgated edition did not even have his name mentioned on the title.[16]

The three men who more than any others decided the future of Christian education were Luther and Calvin on the Protestant, and Ignatius of Loyola on the Catholic side. Nevertheless, humanism had by no means been in vain. There are people who do not forget the blue skies of freedom even on cloudy days. A few years before Erasmus' death, another man who had escaped the frock, namely Rabelais, wrote his *Gargantua,* and almost the same year, Montaigne, the great sceptical essayist, was born. And without the humanists preparing the atmosphere, the Reformation would not have captured the minds of people. The German theologian and biographer, Melchior Adam, wrote about 1600 that Erasmus' satire against ecclesiastical corruption (expressed particularly in his *Praise of Folly*) had done more harm to papacy than Luther's direct attacks. Men such as Luther's friend, Melanchthon, planted Erasmian scholarship deeply into the educational literature of the Protestants; and both parties—the Catholics and, still more, their opponents—insisted upon the cultivation of the ancient languages and upon the combination of humanist *eloquentia* with Christian *pietas* much more than the men of the Middle Ages to whom Greek had been almost unknown and Latin just a means of communication and not an object of aesthetic culture.

Nevertheless, there was a profound tragical element in the life and work of the great Dutchman. Being at the same time a critic and a believer, a liberal and a traditionalist, a destroyer and a conserver, he was caught between the fighting camps. He was considered a trimmer by those who did not understand that insistence on balance might be more difficult than a quick resolution or who did not want to acknowledge that he had shown courage on several occasions, e.g. in the defense of the humanist Johann Reuchlin who was on trial before the Roman Inquisition because of his interest in Jewish literature.

Of the several letters that reveal to us the dilemma of Erasmus few are so revealing as the one to Duke George of Saxony of which we quote here a part.

> No wonder you are displeased at the aspect of things. None can deny that Luther had an excellent cause. Christ had almost disappeared, and when Luther began he had the world at his back. He was imprudent afterwards, but his disciples were more in fault than he. The fury is now so great that I fear the victors will exact terms which none who love Christ will endure, and which will destroy the Christian faith. You are a wise prince, and I will speak my mind freely. Christendom was being asphyxiated with formulas and human inventions. Nothing was heard of but dispensations, indulgences, and the powers of the Pope. The administration was carried on by men who, like Demas, loved the life that now is. Men needed waking. The Gospel light had to be rekindled. Would that more wisdom had been shown when the moment came. Stupid monks and sottish divines filled the air with outcries, and made bad worse. Nothing was in danger but the indulgences; but they replied in language disgraceful to Christian men. They would not admit that Luther was right, and only cursed. Seeing how the stream was running, I kept out of it, merely showing that I did not wholly go with Luther. They wanted me to answer. I had thought from the first that the best answer would be silence. The wisest men, cardinals and others, agreed with me. The Pope's furious Bull only made the flame burn hotter. The Emperor followed with an equally savage edict, edicts cannot alter minds. We may approve the Emperor's piety, but those who advised that measure were not his best councillors. ("To Duke George") [17]

Of the famous *Colloquia,* widely read all over Europe, none gives such a clear picture of Erasmus's desire to restore pure and genuine piety as the one "Concerning Faith," which is remarkable also for the catechetical style as the author has found it in St. Augustine. Like Gerson, Erasmus also had to defend himself against the reproach of "Childishness" because of his interest in teaching youth.[18]

> . . . if any one shall cry out that it is an unseemly thing for an old man to sport himself thus childishly, I care not how childishly it be, so it be but profitably. And if the ancient teachers of children are commended who allured them with wafers, that they might be willing to learn their first rudiments, I think it ought not to be charged as a fault upon me that by the like regard I allure youths either to the elegancy of the Latin tongue or to piety.

Among the teachers of Latin Erasmus became famous for his *Colloquia*. But only a superficial reader would fail to detect in them more than mere exercises in an ancient tongue. They contain, for example, a dialogue concerning faith between a certain Aulus who examines his friend Barbatus about matters of faith. Unfortunately, the dialogue consists of too long a sequence of short questions and answers to be read today without a feeling of fatigue. Also, in order to discover its finesses—often contained in between the lines—one should read it in the original. We give, therefore, only a brief abstract of the content.

Barbatus is suspected of heresy and has, therefore, been struck by the "thunderbolt" of excommunication. However, the examination by Aulus proves that he has the right faith in all the essentials of Christian dogma: the nature of God, Christ, the Holy Spirit, the miracle of salvation, and the spiritual role of the Church that can claim holiness not as an institution administered by "deceived and deceiving" men, but only as a congregation of believers. It appears that Erasmus uses the dialogue for expressing his opinion about the uselessness of force in matters of conscience and about the futility of excommunication by a pope whom he no longer considers the "Vicar of Christ." The dialogue ends with a satirical remark about customs "that are besides our creed" such as eating fish on Friday.

CONCLUDING REMARKS

If we except Erasmus of Rotterdam, the greatness of the Renaissance is only dimly reflected in its thought on education, both secular and religious. The minor authors use a pious, but conventional vocabulary, assuring the reader of the necessity of a Christian life, while the greater men move in the twilight between the religious tradition and the admiration of the ancients without admitting its incongruence with the Christian gospel. To a degree, this kind of religious education mirrors the writings of some humanist poets in whose literary products the Olympus of Jupiter encroaches upon the heaven of Christ and St. Mary. Erasmus ridiculed these writers in his dialogue *Ciceronianus.*

Yet, it would be wrong to underestimate the impact of the Renaissance on education, even on religious education. For it developed the philological and historical interest in the Christian tradition which was represented, among others, by Erasmus, Thomas More, and by Johann Reuchlin, one of the first students of Jewish literature. This interest made possible not only the Lutheran and later translations of the Bible, but also the reorganization of the Protestant theological faculties which, in turn, influenced Protestant religious education on the more advanced levels of schooling. Against the intention of the reformers, it eventuated in the modern historical and critical analysis of Scripture.

But the humanism of the Renaissance influenced Christian educators in other respects also. As a natural response to the widening knowlege of foreign cultures, the man of the Renaissance developed a certain spirit of internationality. It was not that of the medieval universities which, though crossing national boundaries, remained within the Christian world. Nor was it the idea of the unity of mankind toward which we strive today. The time was then still less ripe for it than it is today. Nevertheless, the foreign was no longer identical with the inferior, but an object of curiosity. The first signs of a desire to use reason with more perspective and in a more universal sense than the scholastics, and the first glimmer of tolerance, about which we will speak later, appeared. The Italian humanist Count Giovanni Pico della

Mirandola, to whom we owe the magnificent *Oration on the Dignity of Man,* studied Arabic, Hebrew, and Chaldee.[19] His Hebrew teachers introduced him to the Kaballah. Like Master Eckhart, he also was not free from the suspicion of heresy.

But more clearly than the idea of internationality the humanists recognized the value of humaneness and wished to see it applied in the relation between adults and youth, teachers, and pupils. It appears in Cardinal Sadoleto's disinclination to hard forms of punishment and in Erasmus' hatred of the brutality in the schools of the time from the lower to the highest grades. The humanist, Vittorino da Feltre (1378–1446), was probably the first Christian educator after many centuries whose school at Mantua could be called "the house of joyfulness."

Renaissance humanism developed also the notion of the *uomo universale,* or the man equally versed in the various arts of knowing and noble living.

The ideal of the *uomo universale* reflected the change from the other worldly transcendentalism of the Middle Ages to a more autonomous aspect of the person as well as a higher appreciation of earthly values such as honor, the glory of the family, the striving for personal excellence, the emphasis on manners, and the elevation of service to country above all other duties. Many of these values are more Greek than Christian. They have helped produce a spirit of nationalism from which we still suffer. They have also created the image of the "gentleman" which has penetrated the schools of the privileged and which, if viewed from the point of view of an Erasmus, would be more a compromise between selfishness and polite behavior than an ethical solution, even when combined with the adjective "Christian."

Yet, the gentleman ideal, because it aimed at the formation of character within the affairs of life rather than at erudition, could adopt itself to social and ethical changes until it received its finest formulation by Cardinal John Henry Newman in his *Idea of the University.*[20]

Chapter **7**

Reformation and Counterreformation

MARTIN LUTHER

As all great men of his period, Luther was medieval and modern at the same time. At the beginning of his historical career he did not intend to become a revolutionary. Rather his intention was conservative, namely the preservation of the pure Church through the pure faith. One could well call him a counterrevolutionary against the Aristotelian revolution of the scholastics. He became a rebel when he saw that the Church, his spiritual mother, refused to extricate herself from idolatry and corruption. There had always been saintliness and charity among the clergy and the people. But since Gregory VII, the papacy had arrogated to itself absolute power not only over the souls, but also over the governments of men, had thrown a network of international conflict, taxation, exploitation, venality and fraud over Western Christianity, and stubbornly defied the accusations and implorations of the pious. As a delegate of his Order to Rome, Luther had personally seen the frivolity of the Holy City; and as a curate in his German community of Wittenberg, he had observed the disastrous effect of the sale of indulgences on the souls of his parishioners.

> Sobald der Pfennig im Kasten klingt,
> Die Seele aus dem Fegfeuer springt.

(Soon as the coin in the coffer rings,
    The soul from purgatory springs.)

The young Luther suffered from a tremendous sense of guilt. In this he was by no means alone. Paroxysms of asceticism and repentance broke out from time to time all over Europe. The monk Savonarola (1452–1498), condemned by the Church and burned at the stake for his arousal of the people of Florence against heathen luxury and humanist frivolity, was only one of many symbols of the time's perturbation. Luther's sensitive mind could not imagine how "Jehovah," the stern "God of Justice," could ever pardon the sinfulness of the human race until, while preparing his course on St. Paul's Letter to the Romans, he understood the meaning of the apostle's words:

> For therein is the righteousness of God [*iustitia dei*] revealed from faith to faith: as it is written, the just shall live by faith.

This decisive insight into the central significance of faith in the process of salvation turned Luther away not only from the Catholic stress on "good works" as a means of salvation, but also provided him with a specific conception of religious truth. This conception was not entirely new; almost everything said by Luther, including the description of the Pope as the "Antichrist," can be found in the Christian tradition, but it was certainly distinct from scholastic Aristotelianism. Not by logical inquiry and rationality, but by the truth that reveals itself to him in faith can man be reconciled with God and God be reconciled with him.

In addition to the despair concerning the spiritual recovery of the Catholic Church, the reinterpretation of St. Paul, and the ensuing concept of religious truth, there was a further factor which made a revolutionary out of the monk of Wittenberg; this was his disappointment in the teaching of the late scholastic universities. More and more he understood that Christ's teaching, rather than being clarified, had all but been obscured by the learned theologians, the councils, and the disputations in the universities. So he sought to understand and restore the "pure Word of God" as laid down in the Bible. The Catholic emphasis on sacramental institutionalism changed into a more indi-vidualistic relationship between man and the voice of God. Luther is revolutionary, not only because he burned publicly the papal bull of excommunication, but also because he restored the idea that every man who has his faith through his inspiration from the Bible could be his own priest, however much he might need the Church and his min-isters.

As a consequence of all these experiences and insights Protestant education assumed a new aspect, both in the lower and in the higher schools. Luther's ideal was not the man who talked about truth but who lived in truth. Hence the Protestants rejected the dialectics of the scholastics, the learned commentaries which had pollulated like rank weed, and Peter Lombard's *Sententiae* which in the medieval university every candidate for the master's degree had to expound before his senior colleagues. In his emphasis on languages, Luther came close to the humanists, though not for the glorification of the Muses, but for the glory of God.[1]

> And let this be kept in mind that we will not preserve the Gospel without the languages. The languages are the scab-bard in which the word of God is sheathed.

The Protestant pastor, and, if possible, the educated layman, should be able to listen to the word of God as revealed in Hebrew and Greek; he had also to be familiar with Latin in order to understand the Western Christian tradition, especially St. Augustine to whom Luther's religious personalism was deeply indebted. The humanists were not entirely wrong in their fear that the religious excitement caused by the Reformation put into shadow their own literary interests. Nevertheless, Luther was influential in founding chairs for the ancient tongues, including Hebrew, and the cultivation of these languages in the secondary schools.

Furthermore, nothing seemed to Luther of greater importance than good public schools which should enable every Christian to read the Bible. Certainly, the religious emotionalism that, right after the Reformation, hit the Protestant universities and swept away the old scholastic Aristotelianism, was unconducive to methodical academic studies, though they had already exhausted themselves during the preceding century.[2] Luther himself expressed his concern several times that the simple people were not sufficiently mature for his work. They enjoyed—so he feared—the freedom from the old ecclesiastical authorities but did little to justify it in terms of a deepened concept of Christian life.[3]

Within the framework of his total work as a Christian reformer Luther has influenced religious education mainly in the following aspects: First, through his rejection of ecclesiastical abuses, beginning with the ninety-five theses against the sale of indulgences (1517); second, through his translation and interpretation of the Bible; third, through his various appeals to establish Christian schools and to give a better education and a higher prestige to the teachers; fourth, through the publication of his Large and Small Catechisms; and fifth, through the creation of the Protestant hymn.

It is impossible to do justice to Luther's educational ideas by means of some extracts. There should be reprinted here almost completely his *Letter to the Christian Nobility of the German Nation Respecting the Reformation of the Christian Estate* (1520) and his *Letter to the Mayors and Aldermen of All the Cities of Germany in Behalf of Christian Schools* (1524), and also the *Sermon on the Duty of Sending Children to School* (1530).[4]

In order to characterize Luther's attitude toward humanism we quote here part of a letter he wrote on March 29, 1523, to Eobanus Hessus, the leading humanist poet at the University of Erfurt, which had become the center of the new movement. Luther himself had studied at Erfurt without, however, belonging to the humanist group.

> Do not be disturbed by the fears, which you express, that our theology will make us Germans more barbarous in letters than ever we have been; some people often have their fears when there is nothing to fear. I am persuaded that without knowledge of literature pure theology cannot at all endure, just as heretofore, when letters have declined and lain prostrate, theology, too, has wretchedly fallen and lain prostrate; nay, I see that there has never been a great revela-

tion of the Word of God unless he has first prepared the way by the rise and prosperity of languages and letters, as though they were John the Baptists. There is, indeed, nothing that I have less wish to see done against our young people than that they should omit to study poetry and rhetoric. Certainly it is my desire that there shall be as many poets and rhetoricians as possible, because I see that by these studies, as by no other means, people are wonderfully fitted for the grasping of sacred truth and for handling it skillfully and happily. To be sure, "Wisdom maketh the tongues of those who cannot speak eloquent," but the gift of the tongues is not to be despised. Therefore I beg of you that at my request (if that has any weight) you will urge your young people to be diligent in the study of poetry and rhetoric. As Christ lives, I am often angry with myself that my age and manner of life do not leave me any time to busy myself with poets and orators. I had bought me a Homer that I might become a Greek. But I have worried you enough with these little things. Think as well of Luther as you can think of your *Captiva,* and farewell, strong in Christ. Amen.[5]

Of particular significance for Luther's attitude toward education is his *Sermon on the Duty of Sending Children to School (Eine Predigt, dass man Kinder zur Schulen halten solle,* 1530).

Part Second. THE TEMPORAL BENEFIT OR INJURY ARISING FROM THE SUPPORT OF THE NEGLECT OF SCHOOLS. In the first place, it is true the secular authority of station is in no way comparable to the spiritual office of the ministry, as St. Paul calls it; for it is not so dearly purchased through the blood and death of the Son of God. . . . For secular authority is an image, shadow, or figure of the authority of Christ; for the ministerial office (where it exists as God ordained it,) brings and imparts eternal righteousness, eternal peace, and eternal life, as St. Paul declares in the fourth chapter of 2 Corinthians. But secular government maintains temporal and transitory peace, law, and life.

But it is still a beautiful and divine ordinance, an excellent gift of God, who ordained it, and who wishes to have it maintained as indispensable to human welfare; without it men could not live together in society, but would devour one another like the irrational animals. . . .

. . . You must indeed be an insensible and ungrateful creature, fit to be ranked among the brutes, if you see that your son may become a man to help the emperor maintain his dominions, sword, and crown—to help the prince govern his land, to counsel cities and states, to help protect for every man his body, wife, child, property, and honor—and yet will not do so much as to send him to school and prepare him for this work! Tell me, what are all the chapters and cloisters doing in comparison with this? I would not give the work of a faithful, upright jurist and secretary for the righteousness of all the monks, priests, and nuns at their best. And if such great good works do not move you, the honor and desire of God alone should move you, since you know that you thereby express your gratitude to God, and render Him a service of surpassing excellence, as has been said. . . .

. . . If you now have a son capable of learning; if you can send him to school, but do not do it and go your own way asking nothing about temporal government, law, peace, and so on; you are, to the extent of your ability, opposing civil authority like the Turk, yea, like the Devil himself. For you withhold from the empire, principality, state, city, a savior, comforter, corner-stone, helper; and so far as you are concerned, the emperor loses both his sword and crown, the state loses protection and peace, and it is through your fault (as much as lies in you) that no man can hold in security his body, wife, child, house, property.

I will not here speak of the pleasure a scholar has, apart from any office, in that he can read at home all kinds of books, talk and associate with learned men, and travel and transact business in foreign lands. For this pleasure perhaps will move but few; but since you are seeking Mammon and worldly possessions, consider what great opportunities God has provided for schools and scholars; so that you need not despise learning from fear of poverty. Behold, emperors and kings must have chancellors, secretaries, counsellors, jurists and scholars; there is not a prince but must have chancellors, jurists, counsellors, scholars, and secretaries; likewise counts, lords, cities, states, castles, must have councils, secretaries, and other learned men; there is not a nobleman but must have a secretary. And to speak of ordinary scholars, where are the miners, merchants, and artisans? At the end of three years where are we to find educated men, when the want has already begun to be felt? It looks as if kings would have to become jurists, princes chancellors, counts and lords secretaries, and mayors sextons. . . .

When they are not engaged in war but govern by law, what are emperors, kings, princes, (if we speak according to their work,) but mere scribes and jurists? For they concern themselves about the law, which is a legal and clerical work. And who governs the land and people in times of peace? Is it the knights and captains? I think it is the pen of the scribe. Meanwhile, what is avarice doing with its worship of Mammon? It can not come to such honor, and defiles its devotees with its rust-covered treasures. . . .

We should duly praise all the offices and works ordained of God, and not despise one for the sake of another; for it is written, "His work is honorable and glorious" (Ps. cxi, 3). And again, Psalm civ, 24: "O Lord, how manifold are thy works! in wisdom hast thou made them all." And especially should preachers constantly inculcate such thoughts upon the people, school-teachers likewise upon their pupils, and parents upon their children, that these may learn what stations and offices are ordained of God. When they come to understand this, they should not despise, mock, or speak evil of them, but honor and esteem them. That is pleasing to God, and contributes to peace and unity; for God is a great Lord, and has many servants. . . .

If I had to give up preaching and my other duties, there is no office I would rather have than that of school-teacher. For I know that next to the ministry it is the most useful, greatest, and best; and I am not sure which of the two is to be preferred. For it is hard to make old dogs docile and old rogues pious, yet that is what the ministry works at, and must work at, in great part, in vain; but young trees, though some may break in the process, are more easily bent and trained. Therefore let it be considered one of the highest virtues on earth faithfully to train the children of others, which duty but very few parents attend to themselves. . . .

Therefore, let him who can, watch; and wherever the government sees a promising boy, let him be sent to school. If the father is poor, let the child be aided with the property of the Church. The rich should make bequests to such objects, as some have done, who have founded scholarships; that is giving money to the Church in a proper way. You do not thus release the souls of the dead from purgatorial fire, but you help, through the maintenance of divinely appointed offices, to prevent the living from going to purgatory—yea, you secure their deliverance from hell and entrance into heaven, and bestow upon them temporal peace and happiness. That would be a praiseworthy, Christian bequest, in which God would take pleasure, and for which He would honor and bless you, that you might have joy and peace in Him. Now, my dear Germans, I have warned you enough; you have heard your prophet. God grant that we may follow His Word, to the praise and honor of our dear Lord, for His precious blood so graciously shed for us, and preserve us from the horrible sin of ingratitude and forgetfulness of His benefits. Amen.[6]

Besides his hymns, Luther's greatest contribution to Christian education are his *Catechisms* of 1529.[7] As with regard to so many other points, Catholic and Protestant educators have claimed priority for the origin of the new type of catechism that emerged in the period of the Reformation. We have shown in the chapters on Origen, St. Augustine, and the Middle Ages that the art of catechizing was originally used for the Christian indoctrination of adults who wished to be baptized. After the establishment of infant baptism the institution of catechizing became connected with the obligations of the godparents. There also existed in the Middle Ages a considerable number of customs and books that had the same purpose as the later catechisms of the Protestants and their Catholic opponents, namely to familiarize the faithful, young and old, with the main tenets of the Christian tradition, especially the Creed, the Ten Commandments, the Lord's Prayer, and the Sacraments. Some catechisms in the form of questions and answers were compiled in the eighth and ninth centuries, and the sectarian movements before the Reformation used a catechism, first printed in 1498 and based on St. Augustine's *Enchiridion* (Waldenses, Brothers of the Common Life). For the Moravian Brethren (*Unitas Fratrum*) the Bishop Luke of Prague had published a catechism that was widely used in Switzerland and Germany and attracted Luther's attention. But there can be no doubt that with the coming of Luther there began a new and vital phase in the history of the catechism. There now were large denominations, no longer mere sects persecuted by the secular authorities and the one and only officially acknowledged Catholic Church. Inevitably, in this age of theological controversy, propaganda and counterpropaganda, persecution and revenge, every denomination felt compelled to issue its catechism. Thus we have the catechism of Calvin or the *Instruction and Confession of Faith for the Use of the Church of Geneva* (1537), followed in 1542 by a more handy edition, used in Geneva and Scotland. Two of Calvin's disciples composed the *Heidelberg Catechism* (1562–1563) which, revised by the Synod of Dort in 1619, served as the pattern for the Reformed Churches of Central Europe and America. The Church of England included a catechism in the Book of Common Prayer.

We quote here in part from Luther's Small Catechism the Preface, Part I which contains the explanation of the Ten Commandments, and Part II, "The Creed," according to the translation by Joseph Stump with the title: *An Explanation of Luther's Small Catechism, A Handbook for the Catechetical Class.*[8]

The *Small Catechism* includes also the Lord's Prayer (Part III), the Sacrament of Holy Baptism (Part IV), Of Confession, The Sacrament of the Altar, or the Lord's Supper (Part V). It ends with a brief section on Prayer and a Table of Duties.

Luther's Preface [9]

Martin Luther to all faithful and godly Pastors and Preachers: Grace, Mercy and Peace, in Jesus Christ, our Lord!

The deplorable condition in which I found religious affairs during a recent visitation of the congregations, has impelled me to publish this Catechism, or statement of the Christian doctrine, after having prepared it in very brief and simple terms. Alas! what misery I beheld! The people, especially those who live in the villages, seem to have no knowledge whatever of Christian doctrine, and many of the pastors are ignorant and incompetent teachers. And, nevertheless, they all maintain that they are Christians, that they have been baptized, and that they have received the Lord's Supper. Yet they cannot recite the Lord's Prayer, the Creed, or the Ten Commandments; they live as if they were irrational creatures, and now that the Gospel has come to them, they grossly abuse their Christian liberty.

. . . In the first place; let the preacher take the utmost care to avoid all changes or variations in the text and wording of the Ten Commandments, the Lord's Prayer, the Creed, the Sacraments, etc. Let him, on the contrary, take each of the forms respectively, adhere to it, and repeat it anew, year after year. For young and inexperienced people cannot be successfully instructed, unless we adhere to the same text or the same forms of expression. They easily become confused, when the teacher at one time employs a certain form of words and expressions, and, at another, apparently with a view to make improvements, adopts a different form. The result of such a course will be, that all the time and labor which we have expended will be lost.

. . . But if any refuse to receive your instructions, tell them plainly that they deny Christ and are not Christians; such persons shall not be admitted to the Lord's Table, nor present a child for baptism, nor enjoy any of our Christian privileges, but are to be sent back to the pope and his agents, and, indeed, to Satan himself. Their parents and employers should, besides, refuse to furnish them with food and drink, and notify them that the government was disposed to banish from the country all persons of such a rude and intractable character.

For although we cannot, and should not, compel them to exercise faith, we ought, nevertheless, to instruct the great mass with all diligence, so that they may know how to distinguish between right and wrong in their conduct towards those with whom they live, or among whom they desire to earn their living. For whoever desires to reside in a city, and enjoy the rights and privileges which its laws confer, is also bound to know and obey those laws. God grant that such persons may become sincere believers! But if they remain dishonest and vicious, let them at least withhold from public view the vices of their hearts.

In the second place; when those whom you are instructing have become familiar with the words of the text, it is time to teach them to understand the meaning of those words, so that they may become acquainted with the object and purport of the lesson. Then proceed to another of the following forms, or, at your pleasure, choose any other which is brief, and adhere strictly to the same words and forms of expression in the text, without altering a single syllable; besides, allow yourself ample time for the lessons. For it is not necessary that you should, on the same occasion, proceed from the beginning to the end of the several parts; it will be more profitable if you present them separately, in regular succession. When the people have, for instance, at length correctly understood the First Commandment, you may proceed to the Second, and so continue. By neglecting to observe this mode, the people will be overburdened, and be prevented from understanding and retaining in memory any considerable part of the matter communicated to them.

In the third place; when you have thus reached the end of this short Catechism, begin anew with the Large Catechism, and by means of it furnish the people with fuller and more comprehensive explanations. Explain here at large every Commandment, every Petition, and, indeed, every part, showing the duties which they severally impose, and both the advantages which follow the performance of those duties, and also the dangers and losses which result from the neglect of them. . . .

Finally; inasmuch as the people are now relieved from the tyranny of the pope, they refuse to come to the Lord's Table, and treat it with contempt. On this point, also, it is very necessary that you should give them instructions, while, at the same time, you are to be guided by the following principles: That we are to compel no one to believe, or to receive the Lord's Supper; that we are not to establish any laws on this point, or appoint the time and place; but that we should so preach as to influence the people, without any law adopted by us, to urge, and, as it were, to compel us who are pastors, to administer the Lord's Supper to them. . . .

Now he who does not highly value the Sacrament, shows thereby that he has no sin, no flesh, no devil, no world, no death, no danger, no hell; that is to say, he does not believe that such evils exist, although he may be deeply immersed in them, and completely belong to the devil. On the other hand, he needs no grace, no life, no Paradise, no heaven, no Christ, no God, no good thing. For if he believed that he was involved in such evils, and that he was in need of such blessings, he could not refrain from receiving the Sacrament, wherein aid is afforded against such evils, and, again, such blessings are bestowed. It will not be necessary to compel him by the force of any law to approach the Lord's Table; he will hasten to it of his own accord, will compel himself to come, and indeed urge you to administer the Sacrament to him.

THE SMALL CATECHISM [10]

PART I

THE TEN COMMANDMENTS

*In the plain form in which they are to
be taught by the head of a family.*

THE FIRST COMMANDMENT

I am the Lord thy God. Thou shalt have no other gods before Me.

(Thou shalt not make unto thee any graven image or any likeness of anything that is in heaven above, or that is in the earth beneath, or that is in the water under the earth;

thou shalt not bow down thyself to them, nor serve them; for I the Lord thy God am a jealous God, visiting the iniquity of the fathers upon the children unto the third and fourth generation of them that hate Me; and showing mercy unto thousands of them that love Me, and keep My commandments.)

What is meant by this Commandment?

Answer. We should fear, love, and trust in God above all things.

(The following Commandments are explained
in a similar manner.)

PART II

THE CREED

*In the plain form in which it is to be taught
by the head of a family.*

FIRST ARTICLE—OF CREATION

I believe in God the Father Almighty, Maker of heaven and earth.

What is meant by this Article?

Answer. I believe that God has created me and all that exists; that He has given and still preserves to me my body and soul with all my limbs and senses, my reason and all the faculties of my mind, together with my raiment, food, home, and family, and all my property; that He daily provides me abundantly with all the necessaries of life, protects me from all danger, and preserves and guards me against all evil; all which he does out of pure, paternal and divine goodness and mercy, without any goodness and merciness in me; for all which I am in duty bound to thank, praise, serve, and obey him. This is most certainly true.

(Also here the following articles, on
Redemption and Sanctification, are
explained in a similar manner.)

The majority of our modern teachers, afraid of mechanical learning and verbal indoctrination as obstacles to the development of the learner's personality, consider the old catechisms obsolete, though they are still in use in some Catholic and Protestant schools. But whatever the differences of judgment, for several centuries the catechisms kept the members of the various Christian denominations closely aware of their creed and of its moral postulates. They formed an essential part in the formation of Western Christianity from the sixteenth up to the nineteenth centuries.

JOHN CALVIN

Calvin shares with Luther the central idea of the Reformation, the idea of the salvation of man through his faith in the mediatorship of Christ. He shares with him also the idea of an "Invisible Church" which has existed from the very beginning, which, though imperfectly, is reflected in the visible Church, and which will reveal itself in full glory at the Day of Judgment toward which all human events are directed and under the sign of which they must be understood. For Calvin, as for Luther, history is the process through which God, infinite, all-powerful, and all-transcendent, shows his glory in granting clemency to the faithful in spite of man's depravity and in manifesting his wrath to the damned. Calvin, like Luther, often visualizes the epic of humanity as the battle between God and Satan. The true Church as the "Community of the Saints" is the army chosen by the Lord for fighting the battle; and for the Frenchman, who was not allowed to live in his own country, as for the German reformer, the Bible was the absolute and never-doubted authority. And for both, education was one of the main instruments to lead the people toward unity with God.

But there are also divergences in the Lutheran and the Calvinist forms of Protestantism. They are anchored in differences rooted partly in the leaders' characters and intellectual tempers, and partly in the political constellation in which they carried through their work. Despite, or, perhaps, in consequence of, the violent contrasts in his soul, Luther was much of a mystic. He struggled with the God so near and ever present, yet so incomprehensible and often cruel in his dealings with men; but finally the conflict receded before his invincible confidence in God's loving grace.

Calvin, on the other hand, is logical and methodical. His *Institutes of the Christian Religion* (*Institutio Christianae Religionis*) makes him one of the great Christian system-builders, rightly placed by historians beside St. Augustine and Thomas Aquinas. His mind did not rest until he had carried a premise to its ultimate consequence. Disorder was for him detestable: "Disobedience and confusion conflict with the Kingdom of God" (*Regno Dei opponitur omnis ataxia et confusio*). Calvin broke from historical Catholicism, not in order to destroy, but to reestablish the sacred unity of the Church, violated by strife and corruption. His systematic mind could not tolerate diverging opinions of the same truth. "*Symmetria ecclesiae multiplici (ut ita loquar) unitate constat.*" [11] Therefore, he hated the emotional sectarianism so abundant in his time; therefore, he was also willing to join an evangelical council which Thomas Cranmer, Archbishop of Canterbury, proposed. "Thus [as a consequence of the inertia of the ecclesiastical and secular princes] the body of the Church has become lacerated. So far as I am concerned I would traverse ten oceans if it appeared that I could be of some use." [12]

As mentioned before, Luther also asserted the total dependence of man on divine dispensation. But it was Calvin who in his doctrine of predestination carried the idea of God's omnipotence, omniscience, and timelessness to its logical, though paradoxical extreme.

Luther, living under the rule and protection of absolutist princes, was also by nature inclined to render "unto Caesar the things which are Caesar's, and unto God the things that are God's." In contrast, Calvin lived his most decisive years in the free republic of Geneva which allowed him, as already had been the case in the then German city of Strasbourg, more opportunity for political action than Luther had in the realm of Saxony. It was, nevertheless, not merely a constellation of political circumstances. Calvin's activist and systematic energy compelled him to organize not only a Church, but also a political commonwealth according to the principles laid down in his *Institutes*. By no means was this an easy task; the citizens of Geneva, especially its aristocracy, were just as little inclined to bend to the puritan discipline of the foreigner as any other gay and prosperous community would have been after wresting freedom from a Catholic bishop and an absolutist duke. Only the combination in Calvin's personality of a sense of divine mission and a persuasive but, if necessary, unbending statesmanship could have made Geneva the citadel from which his creed could break through hostile walls in many parts of the world and render it the most powerful form of Protestantism.

It is characteristic of Calvin that he liked to compare himself with David who fought the giant Goliath and defeated him against all odds. The conviction of his historical *vocatio* to serve the *Regnum Dei,* which made him proud and humble at the same time, already was evident in the dedication of the *Institutes* to King Francis of France.[13]

> But it shall be yours, Sire, not to turn away your ears or thoughts from so just a defence, especially in a cause of such importance as the maintenance of God's glory unimpaired in the world, the preservation of the honour of divine truth, and the continuance of the kingdom of Christ uninjured among us. This is a cause worthy of your attention, mostly of your cognizance, mostly of your throne. This consideration constitutes true royalty, to acknowledge yourself in the government of your kingdom to be minister of God. For where the glory of God is not made the end of the government, it is not a legitimate sovereignty, but usurpation.

Our attempt to characterize Calvin's educational work would be incomplete without including a description of his organization of the Church of Geneva for the purpose of propagating the pure faith, especially since this organization had such a great influence on the Puritan society of New England. For Luther, Melanchthon, and the whole Catholic tradition, except for the period of the totalitarian claims of Pope Gregory VII and his immediate successors, secular government and ecclesiastical government were two separate authorities with the duty incumbent on the first to support the latter in its attempt to secure the stability of Christian faith and conduct. Ultimately, so they thought, the state would justify its existence only if it considered itself a member of the *Corpus Christianum,* standing under the same divine law as the Church. This obligation to help in the realization of the Kingdom of God was the reason why the *potestas civilis* deserved the respect of all other institutions. Calvin himself was careful to avoid the appearance of disobedience to the magistrate, even in periods of stress. But obviously, like the Puritans later, he had nothing against merging religious and civil government as much as possible. Thus, by giving the *ecclesia visibilis* a powerful and highly articulated structure which could enforce the obedience of its members and which, so he presumed, had already been anticipated by St. Paul, Calvin built his Geneva more or less on the pattern of a theocracy, though not exactly in the legal sense of the word.

Four offices were founded by Calvin to guarantee the Church the orderly performance of the functions (*rectus ordo*) without which, from his point of view, it could not persist.[14]

> First the pastors (*pasteurs*), entrusted with the propagation of the Gospel, the administration of the sacraments and the preservation of the purity of the dogma through conferences, sermons and the catechisation of children, second the teachers (*docteurs*), third the elders (*anciens*), who formed the *Consistoire* as the most penetrating and disciplinary authority of the Church, almost a kind of Inquisition and fourth the deacons (*diacres*), who were responsible for the works of charity.

The "Office of doctors" (*L'Office des Docteurs*) was entrusted with the task of preparing youth for secular and spiritual professions. Calvin conceived of education as that part of the spiritual order that should pervade all its activities. Hence, the appointment of teachers needed the approval of the pastors because the schools had to see to it that the sound doctrine and the purity of the Evangel be not spoiled by ignorance or false doctrine. Schools, for Calvin, were not primarily institutions for learning, but means for the realization of the *Regnum Christi*; therefore they were not merely for a privileged few, but, as for Luther, for the whole people. He established a broad elementary education at the base and Christian humanist Gymnasium on the secondary level. In his conception of the latter, he was influenced by Johannes Sturm of Strasbourg which, besides Basel, had become one of the centers of German Protestant culture. On the tertiary level he founded in 1559, in connection with the Gymnasium, the famous Academy with three full professorships for Hebrew, Greek, and the liberal arts. Just as Sturm's Gymnasium became the pattern of classical schools in many countries, so also the Academy was looked upon as a pattern for the education of reformed theologians. It was not a university or even a divinity school in the typical sense of the word, but a more or less public institution where, every week, lectures were given in theology, Hebrew, Greek, and the liberal studies including physics and mathematics.

Calvin's erudition did not prevent him from paying personal attention to fundamental Christian education. Like Luther, he drew up a Catechism for the teaching of youth, convinced that, in view of the bewildering state of Christian doctrine, a uniform exposition of the elements of the creed was of the utmost necessity. Though his image of the *civitas dei* was not fully realized, it nevertheless became one of the most powerful ideas in the development of modern Christianity. Calvinism spread from Switzerland to England and Northern Germany, and finally to the American continent. According to historians of society such as Max Weber and Troeltzsch, it spread beyond the religious domain proper into the areas of family, work, and public policy in the nations directly or indirectly influenced by its creed.[15]

IGNATIUS OF LOYOLA AND CATHOLIC EDUCATION UNDER THE INFLUENCE OF THE JESUIT ORDER

The man who more than anyone else restored the fighting spirit of the Catholic Church was a worldly soldier in his youth and a spiritual soldier as an adult, the Spaniard Ignatius of Loyola (1491–1556), founder of the Jesuit Order, confirmed by Pope Paul III by the bull *Regimini Militantis Ecclesiae* (1540). Ignatius tried to subject every phase of life to Christian discipline as he understood it; every member of his Order had to regard himself as a fighter in the service of the Church and its head, the pope; every desire for freedom outside the prescribed hierarchical framework, just as every book that might deflect the mind from the path of obedience, had to be extirpated.

In this spirit must be understood the practice of education which, besides the administration of confession, soon emerged as one of the most, if not the most, important obligation of the Order.[16]

The *Ratio Studiorum* issued in 1599 after fifteen years of cooperation among the foremost Jesuit leaders, is the most cogent and coherent educational program of the Western world. In order to achieve the aim of the Society, namely "to transmit to those about us all of the schooling consistent with our Institute in such a way that they may be brought to a knowledge and love for our Creator and Redeemer," most detailed rules are set down for the teachers as well as the students in its secondary and higher schools. The books and studies for the professors of philosophy, of scholastic and moral theology, of rhetoric, and of the humanities are carefully prescribed, and so are the regulations for admission, selection, correction, punishment, exercises, disputations, conferences, examinations, and competitions. Prayer, devotion, obedience, moderation, the avoidance of new opinions and of objectionable books should direct the minds of the professors and their disciples toward conformity in fulfilling their duties.

At the same time, the *Ratio* respects individual differences among the students, creates incentives through competition, reward and play —in short, it provides the means of conditioning the adolescent youth of the nobility and the bourgeoisie of the Catholic creed. Even Protestant parents entrusted their sons to the care of Jesuit institutions. For though, according to the rules of the Order, obedience was one of the main virtues, the discipline was certainly not harder, probably even milder than at most schools of the time.

Yet, even among good Catholics the Jesuit Order has been a subject of contention. The older Orders disliked the infiltration into their established domains, and the secular clergy disliked its tendency to undermine the few remnants of national independence left by the council of Trent. There were also differences of opinion in regard to the dogma, especially the concept of grace. Jesuits destroyed even the work of reform attempted by more liberal Catholic clergymen and educators, while the universitites regarded with suspicion the intrusion of Jesuit politics.

But the power of Loyola's Company lies not merely in the strictness of its organization with its center in Rome. All the organizational discipline could not have been effective without the individual discipline which the Order undertook to inculcate into each of its members. This was achieved by a long and rigorous training under the control of the Superior and by a prescribed sequence of exercises and contemplations with the purpose to identify the mind of the disciple with the life and suffering of Christ.

The famous work which Ignatius wrote for his own and his disciples' Christian training are the *Spiritual Exercises*.

After twenty introductory Annotations the *Spiritual Exercises* are divided into four "Weeks." The first week deals with the "Particular examination to be made daily," the "general examination of conscience" and the "general confession and communion." Then there follow five "exercises" and "Observations" with the purpose of preparing the disciple for the right inner condition and the conduct necessary to understand the mystery of salvation. The exercises, contemplations, and examinations of the second, third, and fourth week follow the life and passion of Christ. After that the disciple is lead to contemplate "the mysteries of the life of our Lord"; then there follow "Rules for Thinking with the Church." Ignatius composed also a "Directory to the Spiritual Exercises."

It is impossible to give in a few pages an adequate impression of the extent and inner urgency of the *Spiritual Exercises*.

We reproduce here the following parts: [17]

Spiritual Exercises

Whereby to conquer oneself, and order one's life, without being influenced in one's decision by any inordinate affection.

In order that he who gives as well as he who receives the spiritual Exercises may the more help and profit one another it should be presupposed that every good Christian ought to be more ready to give a good sense to the doubtful proposition of another than to condemn it; and if he cannot give a good sense to it, let him inquire how the other understands it, and if he is in error, let him correct him with charity; and if this does not suffice, let him seek all suitable means in order that being brought to a right understanding of it he may serve himself from error.

FIRST WEEK

PRINCIPLE AND FOUNDATION

Man was created to praise, reverence, and serve God our Lord, and by this means to save his soul; and the other things on the face of the earth were created for man's sake, and in order to aid him in the prosecution of the end for which he was created. Whence it follows that man ought to make use of them just so far as they help him to attain his end, and that he ought to withdraw himself from them just so far as they hinder him. It is therefore necessary that we should make ourselves indifferent to all created things in all that is left to the liberty of our free-will, and is not forbidden; in such sort that we do not for our part wish for health rather than sickness, for wealth rather than poverty, for honour rather than dishonour, for a long life rather than a short one, and so in all other things, desiring and choosing only that which leads us more directly to the end for which we were created.

THE PARTICULAR EXAMINATION

To be made daily: it includes three times, and an examination of oneself to be made twice.

The first time is the morning: Immediately on rising, the man ought to resolve to guard himself carefully against that particular sin or defect which he desires to correct and amend.

The second time is after the midday meal, when he ought to ask of God our Lord that which he desires, viz. grace to remember how often he has fallen into that particular sin or defect, and to amend in future; after which let him make the first examination, demanding an account from his soul concerning the particular matter which he desires to correct or amend, reviewing the time elapsed, hour by hour, or period by period, beginning from the time when he rose till the moment of the present examination, and let him mark on the first line of the diagram as many points as there are times when he has fallen into that particular sin or defect; and afterwards let him resolve anew to amend himself until the second examination that he will make.

The third time is after supper, when the second examination will be made in the same way going through the interval hour by hour from the first examination to the present one, and marking on the second line of the same diagram as many points as there are times he has again fallen into that same particular sin or defect.

GENERAL EXAMINATION OF CONSCIENCE

in order to purify oneself and to confess better

Of Thoughts

There are two ways of gaining merit from an evil thought which comes from without.

For example, a thought comes of committing a mortal sin, which thought I resist promptly, and it remains conquered.

The second way of gaining merit is when the same evil thought comes to me, and I resist it, and it returns time after time, and I always resist it, until it goes away conquered: and this second way is much more meritorious than the first.

A venial sin is committed when the same thought of sinning mortally comes and one gives ear to it, dwelling a few moments on it, or receiving some slight sensual delectation, or when there is some negligence in rejecting such a thought.

Of Words

One must not swear by the Creator, nor by the creature, unless it be with truth, necessity, and reverence. By necessity I do not mean every sort of case when truth is to be affirmed, but only when that truth is of real importance for the profit of the soul or body, or for the safeguarding of temporal goods. And by reverence I mean when a man, in naming his Creator and Lord, religiously reflects on the honour and reverence due to Him. . . .

Of Deeds

Taking for the subject matter the ten commandments, and the precepts of the Church, and things commended by superiors, whatever transgression is committed under any of these three heads is a greater or lesser sin, according to the greater or less importance of the matter. By things commended by superiors I mean, for example, Bulas de Cruzadas and other indulgences, e.g. those for the peace of Christians, obtainable by confessing and receiving the most holy Sacrament; for there is no little sin in acting, or in causing others to act, against such pious exhortations and recommendations of our superiors.

METHOD OF MAKING THE GENERAL EXAMINATION:
IT CONTAINS FIVE POINTS

The first point is to give thanks to our Lord God for the benefits we have received.

The second, to ask grace to know our sins and to root them out.

The third, to demand of the soul an account, hour by hour, or period by period, from the time of rising down to the present examination, first of thoughts, then of words, lastly of actions, in the same order as has been explained in the Particular Examination. . . .

Similar exercises, often combined with a special physical training, have been known in Asia for thousands of years. Also the Christian monks who interrupted their sleep for the purpose of worship and forbade speaking except at special occasions built their discipline on the formation of habits through methodically regulated and devotional procedures. Their aim was the exclusion of disturbing ideas to the degree that deviation from the prescribed course of life and thought was considered worse than death and created severe inner disturbances.

Orders of "Strict Observance" still exist today. To a degree secular organizations have also used similar forms of indoctrination. The making of a soldier or of a loyal partisan, the insistence on political rituals in totalitarian and even in democratic societies, as well as the arousal of pride in desirable, and of horror of deviant forms of conduct, are fundamental characteristics of human societies. The difference lies, first, in the degree of rigidity in the training and the punishment in the case of disobedience, and second, in the quality of the ends to be achieved. Are they, or are they not, conducive to human welfare, to man's self-understanding in his relation to himself, his society, and the natural and spiritual universe of which he is a part? In other words, do they help man to transcend the narrowness of his ego and arouse in him a sense of voluntary commitment that makes him free for ever greater purposes?

Many modern readers, among them pious Christians, will be alienated by the tendency of some devotional writers of the time to follow the medieval tradition in concentrating too much on the heavenly rewards for good men and the hellish punishment for sinners, for compensation or threat are, for us, external to the intrinsic value of religion. Even a man of the kindness of St. Francis de Sales (1567–1622), who had been a student at the Jesuit College of Clermont at Paris, invites the reader of his *Introduction to the Devout Life* [18] to imagine the sinner eternally tortured in a "city cast in darkness, burning with brimstone and noisy pitch." His dwelling on the gruesome surprises all the more when we read number five of the *Spiritual Conferences.* [19]

This conference needs to be read slowly in order to reveal its depth and wisdom, or, to use a modern term, its "existentialist" quality. Even the secularly minded person, provided he is able to transfer religious into general psychological concepts, may discover ideas worth thinking about, e.g., the mutually reinforcing polarity between humility and "generosity of spirit;" or, as we would say today, between modesty and self-confidence, the crest and trough of the moods of fervor and weariness, and the anticipation of certain insights of modern depth psychology in St. Francis' recognition of the "lower part of the soul" which remains unaffected by the higher level and still "remains troubled," so that "we are disturbed, and fancy ourselves very miserable." We may also reflect about his distinction between the "good gifts which are in us and of us and others which are in us but not of us and which we receive and maintain only by the loving grace of God." We would today use other words. But we still know of that miraculous inner power which makes men confident even amidst crises, and the absence of which throws them into constant states of anxiety.

. . . .

Conference V
On Generosity

That you may thoroughly understand the nature of that strength and generosity of spirit about which you have questioned me, I must first reply to a very frequent inquiry of yours as to the nature of true humility; for in resolving this point I shall make myself better understood when I come to speak of the second matter, namely that generosity of spirit of which you now wish me to treat.

Humility, then, is nothing else than the recognition of the fact that we are absolute nothingness, and it keeps us constant in this estimation of ourselves. . . .

But the more it makes us humble and abase ourselves so much the more, on the other hand, does it make us greatly esteem ourselves on account of the good gifts which are in us but not of us: faith, hope, the love of God (little though it be, in us), a certain capacity which God has given us of being united to Him by grace, I add, as regards ourselves, our vocation, which gives us an assurance, as far as may be in this life, of the possession of eternal glory and happiness. And this esteem in which humility holds all these good gifts, namely faith, hope, and charity, is the foundation of generosity of spirit.

It is likewise for want of this generosity that so very few acts of true contrition are made; because, after having humbled and abased ourselves before the divine Majesty, when we remember and ponder over our grievous infidelities, we do not go on to make this act of confidence, reviving our courage by the assurance which we ought to have that the divine Goodness will give us grace to be henceforth faithful to Him, and to correspond more perfectly to His love. After this act of confidence, we ought instantly to make the act of generosity, saying: "Since I am fully assured that the grace of God will never fail me, I will also believe that He will not permit me to fail in corresponding with that grace." . . .

But besides what we have said of this generosity, we must add that the soul which possesses it welcomes dryness equally with the sweetness of consolation, welcomes interior weariness, sadness, and heaviness of heart, equally with the fervour and satisfaction of a mind all filled with peace and tranquility. This is because she remembers that He Who gave her these consolations is the very same Who sends her afflictions, moved in both instances by the same tender love; and this love she acknowledges to be very great, inasmuch as through internal affliction He would draw her on to the very highest perfection, which is the abnegation of every sort of consolation, resting assured that He Who deprives her of it here below will not deprive her of it eternally in heaven.

You will ask whether, at times like these, it is better to speak to God of our trouble and misery, or of something different? I tell you that in this, as in all other temptations, it is best to divert our mind from its trouble and distress by speaking to God of something else rather than of our pain. For undoubtedly, if we do, the tenderness which we have for ourselves will be moved, and we shall only aggravate and stir up our pain afresh, our nature being such that we cannot look at our troubles without feeling great compassion for them. But you say that, if you pay no heed to your troubles you will not remember them well enough to tell them. And what does that matter? Truly we are like children who love to run to tell their mother how they have been stung by a bee, so that she may pity them, and breath upon the wound which is already healed. We too wish to go and tell our Mother that we have been in great trouble, enhancing our affliction by going into every detail, not forgetting the smallest circumstance which may excite a little pity for us. Now is not this very great childishness? If we have been guilty of any infidelity, it is quite right to tell it; if we have been faithful, we should say so too (but briefly, without exaggerating either the one or the other); for all must be told to those who have the care of our souls.

You tell me now that when you have experienced some great emotion of anger, or when any other temptation has assailed you, you always feel scruples if you do not confess it. I reply that you should mention it in your review of conscience, but not in the way of confession, and only that you may learn how to behave under such circumstances. I speak of the case when you do not clearly see that you gave some sort of consent. For if you were to say: "I accuse myself of having felt great stirrings of anger for two whole days, but I never consented to them," you would be telling your virtues instead of your faults. "But," you say, "I am doubtful whether I did not commit a fault!" Well, you must steadily consider whether this doubt has any foundation. Perhaps, for about a quarter of an hour in the course of these two days, you may have been a little careless about diverting your thoughts. Well, if this be so, say quite simply that you were a little careless for a quarter of an hour in keeping yourself from dwelling on a thought of anger. You need not add that it lasted for two days, unless you wish to get advice from your Confessor, or because it concerns your review of conscience, in which cases it is well to do so. But in ordinary confessions it would be better not to speak of it, since you would only do so for self-satisfaction; and if silence with regard to it causes you a little mortification, you must bear it as you would anything else which you could not help. Blessed be God.

The Protestant educator Johannes Sturm of Strasbourg, often called the founder of the Classical Gymnasium, as well as the Jesuits, took over much of Renaissance humanism. They regarded the classical languages as a medium not only for the study of sacred history, but also for the perfect training of the mind. Until the seventeenth and in many respects even until the eighteenth century, Latin was the

indispensable medium of scholarly discourse; and in the stormy disputations between Catholics and Protestants, eloquence was sometimes more conducive to victory than the substance of the argument.

Few documents give us a better picture of the importance of
Latin eloquence in Jesuit education than the letter with which the
Jesuit humanist Petrus Perpina introduced his treatise *On the Training of Youth in the Greek and Latin Languages* (*De ratione libe-
rorum instituendorum litteris graecis et latinis*).[20]

> Even before my journey [from Spain to Rome] I had begun
> to work on the Rhetoric of Father Cyprianus Soarez in or-
> der to complement it if necessary, or to shorten and alter it
> for a new and improved edition. . . .
>
> Then I had to criticize the orations and poems of the appli-
> cants for public prices of the first and second order, for I
> was one of the judges. I had also planned to explain [in
> the Jesuit college at Paris] the three books on rhetoric by Ari-
> stotle. . . . I considered it necessary to inspire our youth
> right at the beginning of their career for the study of elo-
> quence. In addition I had to give the daily lectures, a work
> to which I would not devote myself so extensively . . . if
> I had not done so for many years. You may guess the
> amount of this work from the fact that I write regularly ev-
> ery day for four to five hours, and that I do not dare to
> shorten the time for fear I might not live up to my office
> and its obligations, the authority of Aristotle, the expecta-
> tions of the world and the glory of the Roman Gymnasium.
> [Perpina died a year after this letter, at the age of thirty-six.]

The treatise itself begins with a paragraph "The Teacher."

> Most of all it is necessary to select a teacher who leads a
> blameless life, whose diligence never tires, whose intellect
> is sharp, and whose scholarly erudition is thorough. He should
> not be one of those who, as often is the case, have wasted
> their life with unnecessary philological trivialities. Rather he
> should know well a relatively few rules derived from the best
> authors; he should be well acquainted with those authors,
> poets, historians, and orators who excel by their manner

of style; and he should be skilled in speaking and writing the ancient languages. Two qualities should be especially looked for: whether he is thoroughly familiar with Greek literature and whether he has not been tempted by false scholarly pride to believe that philology belongs to the most important disciplines to be taught.

The most important part of teaching was, of course, the introduction of the young into the doctrines of the Church. Soon the Catholic clergy discovered that one of the main instruments of the Protestants in strengthening the new faith was not only the eloquence of the sermon, but also, and particularly the catechism. We have already mentioned the concern of the Tridentinum in this respect.

One of the main advocates of a new form of catechetical instruction was the Italian Jesuit Antonio Possevino (1533–1611), a man who after severe inner struggles became one of the most effective soldiers and diplomats of the *ecclesia militans*. He won his spurs in fighting the Waldenses and Calvinists in the Alpine districts in Italy and France and as a preacher in the larger towns. At Rouen he spoke before fourteen hundred hearers and converted many of the deserters. During this whole period he resembles St. Dominic who between 1205 and 1215 preached among the Albigensian heretics in Southern France. In a passage in his *Catechetical Letter* Possevino himself refers to the missionary activity of the saint. While in Rouen he imported the Canisian catechism from Paris; in other places too he observed the efficaciousness of catechetical instruction.

Soon he attracted the attention of his superiors in the Jesuit order and the curia. In 1573 he became secretary of the Society in Rome, and from 1577 to 1587 he was employed as papal legate in Sweden, Russia, and Poland. He devoted the last two decades of his life to his literary work and the foundation of schools for the poor and priestly seminaries in Bohemia, Prussia, and Poland. In Padua he became the teacher of St. Francis of Sales and worked as an ecclesiastical diplomat in various places in Northern Italy.[21]

Possevino's main work in the field of education is the *Selected Library* [22] which informs us excellently about Catholic educational principles and doctrine as well as about the state of Catholic secular knowledge. It shows at the same time the impact of the age of explorations on the missionary work of the Church. The sacred phrase *urbi et orbi* had now a much wider meaning than a hundred years before.

The twelve first chapters of the first book of Possevino's *Selected Library* have often been reprinted under the title *On Cultivating the Mind (Cultura Ingeniorum)*, a title that one can find among several authors of the period. The famous Madrid physician Juan Huarte de San Juan had already written his famous *Examen de Ingenios* to which Possevino refers in the title and various chapters of his book. Later on Comenius used the title *De Cultura Ingeniorum* in an Oration published in 1650.

Possevino's *Cultura Ingeniorum* was motivated by four main interests the treatment of which overlaps in the actual writing. First the author develops the outline of a philosophy of education in which he attempts to prove that the ends of education can be achieved only under the guidance of the divine spirit, represented on earth by the Catholic Church. A second part, containing some controversy with Huarte, is, to a large extent, a treatise on differential psychology. Also, in this respect Christian doctrine is, from his point of view, superior to any other approach. In the spirit of the Renaissance Possevino emphasizes the desirability of an harmonious development of all faculties. The third part deals with methods of instruction, the qualities of the teacher, and the improvement of the various institutions of learning. A special chapter is given to the University of Salamanca. Finally, Possevino tells his reader how to use and read books, how to write and judge them, and how to order and preserve these precious possessions.

Of special value for the historian of education is also the fourth book of the *Bibliotheca Selecta*, for it discusses *theologia catechetica*, the establishment of clerical seminaries, and the religious indoctrination of the lay people. In the following books the author gives recommendations for sacred orders and sodalities and for the education of princes, the nobility, and higher officials, a topic that has always been of special interest to the Jesuits. They knew that having the leaders meant having the people. Later Possevino discusses the relations of

Catholicism to the Russian and Greek Orthodox Churches, to heretical sects, and to the "atheism" of Luther, Melanchthon, Calvin, Beza a.o. He deals with the Jews, Saracens, Mohammedans, Chinese, Indians, and other pagan nations, and offers his suggestions how the Japanese might be led toward salvation.

The second part of the *Bibliotheca* could be characterized as a sixteenth-century version of medieval compendia such as Hugh of St. Victor's *Didascalicon* and Vincent's of Beauvais *Speculum*. In a way it anticipates the cyclopedias of the seventeenth century, when for the last time in history one man could make the attempt to record the whole of human knowledge. Further we learn about historical and systematic jurisprudence, about the advantages and dangers of studying ancient philosophy (a time honored subject), about medicine, mathematics, history, painting, poetry, and the style of Cicero.

Possevino wrote also a special treatise on *The Necessity, Usefulness, and Method of Catechesis*,[23] dedicated to Yves le Tartier of the cathedral of Troyes in France "who later was killed by Calvinist heretics."

> The cause of Christianity—so he says there—has never been more dangerously undermined than by the fact that youth, infected either by the sins of others or by heretical doctrines, fall with increasing age into the traps of impiety and rebellion. . . .

> The evils and calamities resulting from the neglect of the catechism can be more easily felt than corrected. For heretical boys and girls insult the most famous clergymen and defame everything sacred. Publicly in villages and hostels, even in churches, young and even older people boldly offend the name of the Lord by attending the mysteries of the altar without inner or outer reverence.

Possevino also refers in this context to Gerson's treatise *On Leading the Children to Christ* and on the amazing effect which the importing of catechisms from Paris to various French towns had on converting the deserters of the faith.

We have dwelled on the work of Possevino because it describes admirably the educational interest of his contemporaries on the Catholic side, among whom the best known are: the Cardinal Antoniano, who also wrote a treatise on the Christian education of children; Juan Bonifacio, the famous author of paedagogical orations and letters; and Jean Baptist de la Salle.

All these men, whose apologetic writings culminated in the *On the Controversies concerning Christian Faith against the Heretics of the Present (Disputations de controversiis Christiani Fidei adversus huius temporis hereticos)* [24] by the Jesuit Cardinal Bellarmino, expressed in their writings on religious education the meticulous discipline they exercised in their personal life. They knew that they could stem the flood of Protestantism not merely as controversialists—which they were to the highest degree—but still more effectively as exemplary teachers of youth and as fascinating preachers. They also knew that they had to answer the "heretical" catechisms of the Protestants by a renewal of catechesis in the spirit of their own Church. While the Jesuit Order concerned itself mainly with the youth of the privileged, a number of new orders concentrated on the instruction of the poor and on charity. St. Jean Baptist de la Salle founded the Christian Brothers *(Les Frères de la Doctrine Chréstienne)* who through the superior quality of their teachers showed what devotion, diligence, and carefully planned methods can do with neglected children. St. Vincent de Paul (1576–1660) founded the Congregation of Priests of the Mission *(Congregation de la Mission,* mostly called "Lazarites") that soon included women in its missionary work.

Many of these men were great organizers. Jesuit academies spread over large parts of the world, and more and more priests were trained by a rapidly increasing number of clerical seminaries. These institutions raised the general level and guaranteed the orthodoxy of the clergy. On the other hand, they isolated theological education from the broader streams of intellectual life. They took much talent away from the older universities, which during the first years of the Counterreformation were suspected of heretical or nationalist attitudes—both of which the papacy had decided to wipe out. After all, Paris had been the stronghold of Gallicanism for more than two centuries. But even the theological faculties of the old universities accepted more and more the role of mere interpreters and defenders of a faith they considered unalterable. Thus they fell short of the vitality they had achieved during the height of the scholastic era. However, the Spaniard Francisco Suarez (1548–1617) excelled not only as a Thomistic philosopher, but still more as a jurist. His *On Law and God as the Lawgiver,* (*Tractatus de legibus ac Deo legislatore*) was highly praised by the great Dutchman Hugo Grotius who, as a theological writer of Protestant faith, searched for the common ground of Christian piety and who as the author of the work *De Jure Belli et Pacis* provided the foundation for the modern concept of natural law.

Seen from a world perspective, the Catholic Church had been, before the Renaissance, a European power, hemmed in by the Orthodox Churches and by the Muslims, who twice, in 1529 and even in 1683, appeared before the walls of Vienna. But now the Catholic countries, Spain and Portugal, conquered large empires in the new world, and the men of the Church went with the men of the army. There is much shame, sadness, and hypocrisy in the history of white colonization, and the missionaries cannot have been unaware of the cruelty involved in the process of civilizing the pagans. However, much must be understood in the perspective of the time. Giving the heathens souls with which to come to Christ meant to save them for salvation and to earn oneself a place in heaven. One of the motives of Columbus' travels, so historians tell us, and one of the reasons why they were supported, was the fear that the end of the world might come before all the world had been taught the gospel. Despite their firm belief in the superiority of their own faith and civilization, some missionaries have given us descriptions of the old Aztec culture that are landmarks of early anthropology. Also, we should not forget that Cortez was able to defeat the empire of Montezuma only with the help of native tribes tortured by the annual forays made by their rulers in order to herd together thousands of victims who were to be slaughtered on the altars of the war god Huitzilopochtli.

But many of the missionaries went into foreign lands without the protection of armies. St. Francis Xavier worked in Japan and India; Ricci and Shall, in China. And it was, to a large degree, the Jesuits who stirred up the European conscience by telling of the existence of great religious teachers even before the time of Christ. It was now the Sorbonne that condemned the Jesuits because curious people in Europe began to speak of Confucius with the same admiration as of the Christian prophets. The new picture of the *bon savage* led to a somewhat unwelcome relativism with regard to the moral uniqueness of Christianity.[25]

With its new missionary activities followed in the seventeenth century by the Protestant John Eliot's converting the Indians around Boston,[26] the Catholic Church extended the radius of its influence over the whole globe. But despite this dilatation it proved unable to disentangle itself from national diplomacies. Some of the great cardinals, such as Mazarin and Richelieu, became masters in the art of political intrigue. With the frontiers between the great denominations settled before 1700 (though cruel persecutions lasted considerably longer), the era of the fighting saints of the Counter Reformation gave way to an era of relative quietude, if not of fatigue. Catholic nations had fought on the side of Protestant nations during the Thirty Years War. Some orders, the least of all the Jesuits, became too much entangled in earthly affairs, and too many of the abbés became too much interested in the intellectual pleasantries of the "salons" to present to an increasing number of critics the symbol of a supernatural order. With the dissatisfaction mounting, Pope Clement XIV was forced to suppress the order. Finally, the French revolution in 1789 reminded the Church once more that power gained for immediate political profit may end in the loss of moral and spiritual prestige. We will speak briefly about the recovery of this prestige in one of the following chapters.

CONCLUDING REMARKS ON THE REFORMATION AND COUNTER REFORMATION

We are not yet far enough, and probably will never be, to arrive at some consensus in regard to the significance of the Reformation and the Counter Reformation. For there are involved differences in the interpretation of Christ's message that reflect on man's innermost relation to God, to himself, on the role and organisation of the Church, and on the structure of society. Even the growing mutual tolerance between the denominations, as it now emerges at last in some countries, will not create complete agreement. However, the rise of divergent creeds during and after the Reformation has forced Christendom to recognize the existence of a variety of standpoints and has made impossible, so we hope, the old forms of un-Christian persecutions in the name of Christianity.

Gradually, we may become ready for a kind of religious life that both Protestants and Catholics would have considered sinful in past centuries. We may realize that the concepts and symbols created by historical institutions at certain periods of mankind's development flow out of a profound transcendent urge of humanity. When freed from the accidents and hatreds of earlier generations, this transcendent urge may ally the souls of men more closely to each other than political machineries will ever do. Without agreement in depth, institutions will never work.

There is also reason for another hope. We have already touched upon it in our summary of the section on the Renaissance. More and more people now travel and work in countries and continents outside their parental homes. Unless we destroy each other, this fact will have its impact also on the travel and work of religious ideas. It already has.

But such contemplations lead us far beyond the scope of this chapter. If we look at the character and role of religious education during the Reformation and the Counter Reformation, one fact cannot be doubted. The conflicts of the period forced upon the leaders of the time a thorough reexamination of the premises and conditions of the Christian upbringing of youth. Always the shock of revolution impels the policy makers to ask themselves what they want to achieve in the long run, and how they can direct the minds of the younger generation into desirable channels. The progressive will have to formulate the new so that it can root, and the conservative the old so that it can stay alive.

One can hardly deny that the Protestant regions of Europe showed in the course of time a greater political and intellectual vitality than the Catholic parts. This was due to the fact that Protestantism, especially Calvinism, developed a more positive appreciation of the discipline and the economic value of work. Furthermore, it profited from the change of trade routes after the period of the explorations. But the main stimulus for the Protestants came from their insistence on the layman's personal acquaintance with the Word of God. This attitude led to their emphasis on reading. Furthermore, the daily dialogue of the common man with such a tremendously rich and imaginative book as the Holy Bible meant an enormous challenge to his brain, heart, and conscience. In many minds it meant confusion. Under these circumstances the new faculties of divinity had to provide the theological and philosophical equipment necessary for the continual interpretation of the great document and of the patristic literature. As we know, the equally necessary philological training in the ancient tongues had already been made possible by the humanists.

Furthermore, the Protestant pastor was more a preacher than was the case in the Catholic world. His sermons lasted sometimes not less than two hours. Certainly, the burden placed upon the Protestant minister as a teacher and preacher, who should work out of the fullness of his heart and the depth of his erudition, proved often too heavy. Already some years after the beginning of the Reformation, Luther's devoted friend Philipp Melanchthon, called by Protestants the *praeceptor Germaniae,* suggested a return to Aristotle, until then despised by the reformers. Melanchthon felt it necessary to correct the excesses of the new enthusiasts by means of an old and established logical framework. Indeed, it took not more than a generation before the Protestant theologians competed with those of any other denomination in the art, and often the vices, of argument. They created an atmosphere of semischolarly rigidity that soon led to discontentment. And, as the persecution of Jakob Boehme of the Saxon town of Goerlitz revealed, the Protestant divines disliked independent speculation of the mystical kind just as much as the Catholics at the time of Master Eckhart. To be sure, there was no longer the power of the old Inquisition, but as we all know, there are many ways to make the life of a dissenter miserable. Some of them were even hanged and tortured.

Yet, despite all attempts at enforcement of the "right faith," it was in the nature of a Church that was based on an individualist relation of man to God and on the interpretation of such a complicated book as the Bible that Protestantism split into an increasing variety of sects. Looking at the inner life of some of them, one can hardly deny that it was often narrow and intolerant; but looking at the whole of Protestantism, one may also aver that the competition of minds and opinions became a source of continuous religious renewal, community initiative, and a spirit of democratic freedom which, with all the risks involved in any great venture, has been one of the elements of modern civilization. Even Catholicism has profited from the contest.

On the Catholic side the most urgent objective was the consolidation of the Church, a formidable task which the reform councils of the preceding centuries had been unable to achieve. At the insistence of the emperor Charles V, who was determined to stem the tide of the Reformation, it was accomplished at the Council of Trent (1545–1563), though only partly and against much opposition from the papacy. However, the council proved that the Catholic Church was capable of resistance against Protestantism and against the decentralizing tendencies within its own ranks.

From the point of view of religious education, the Tridentinum was of decisive importance. It used the work of medieval Scholasticism for a clear formulation of the creed and thus gave the clergy a firm hold in its disputes with the Protestants. It defined not only the meaning and observance of the sacraments, but went even into such details as food habits and fasting. Some attempts were made to get Protestants, especially the English bishops and Elizabeth I, to the Council. But even if there had been more mutual willingness to cooperate, they would have been doomed to fail because the Church could not discuss dogmatic differences merely on the basis of the Bible.

The council initiated also the compilation of a catechism. In 1554 there had already appeared the *Summa Doctrinae et Institutionis Christianae* by the Jesuit Peter Canisius and two years later his shorter and often translated catechism under the title *Institutiones Christianae sive Catechismus Catholicus*. The Catechism resulting from the suggestions of the Council of Trent was the *Catechismus Romanus* or *Roman Catechism* (1570), prepared by a committee of eminent priests under the spiritual guidance of Cardinal Carlo Borromeo. Since, despite its tendency toward centralization, the Church was wise enough not to insist on a universal catechism, some of the great theologians such as Bellarmine and Bossuet could compile widely used works of this kind, and many catechisms—e.g. the Baltimore Catechism for the United States—have been adapted to specific regional conditions.

Besides a catechism, the Council of Trent initiated also a catalogue of the forbidden books (*Index Librorum Prohibitorum*), intended to give the Church control over the publishing and reading of books touching on matters religious and moral. Among the authors *primae classis* were not only the reformers, but several works of Erasmus were condemned as well. The pope forbade also commentaries on the council's decisions without his approval and claimed for the curia the sole right of their interpretation. As all censorship, the Index had only a limited success. One of the most famous of the antiecclesiastical works, the *Encyclopedie Francaise,* was read even in the Latin American countries.

Whereas Protestantism distinguished between the *ecclesia invisibilis* as the inner union of the souls under the grace of God and the *ecclesia visibilis* as the organisational embodiment, the Council of Trent strongly affirmed the holy character of the Roman Church as the indispensable mediator between man and God. Catholic youths were to be taught that the Catholic Church was instituted by Jesus himself, that it has the duty to guard, teach, and maintain the truth coming from Christ, and to preach it to the whole world without any interference of human power. It is both supernatural and visible, and the condition of salvation. According to the Tridentinum, the Catholic Church has the right to demand submission and obedience of all those who are aware of its existence. Its supreme head and authority is the pope as the successor of St. Peter and the Vicar of Christ. Consequently, matters of doctrine must not be decided by individual interpretations of Holy Writ and tradition.

Within the new framework secured by the Tridentinum there developed an amazingly rich work of education and charity, the two often combined. But there also grew the danger of inner stagnation, of intolerance, end of alienation from new spiritual and intellectual developments, recognized by Pope John XXIII when he convoked the second Ecumenical Council.

Chapter 8

New England Puritanism

Puritanism was in no way confined to New England, as the title of this chapter may suggest. About 1564, the name Puritan was first applied to people in old England who, influenced by Protestant refugees from Switzerland, objected to the hierarchical and ornamental tendencies of the Elizabethan Church as signs of spiritual laxness.

However, New England, unhampered by the weight of old institutions, gave the Puritans the opportunity to try their doctrines about man, church and state in actual practice. And one of the main instruments for establishing the new community of saints was, according to their Protestant tradition, the proper education of youth.

In various synods between 1646 and the middle of the nineteenth century, New England Calvinsim or Puritanism reaffirmed the points laid down at the Synod of Dort in 1618 and 1619, all stemming from Calvin's rigorous assertion of God's absolute sovereignty which cannot allow anything to happen, neither in time nor space, that is not foreknown and foreordained by divine will. Calvin's theory of predestination, or of unconditional election, is the only logically cogent deduction from the basic Christian assumption of an omnipotent, omniscient, omnipresent, only and eternal God. But, as every theory that tries to grasp the ultimate depth by human logic, it creates new riddles. Nevertheless, it is the most uncompromising, and the absence of compromise was the divine foolishness and the greatness of the Puritans without which they could not have founded a new culture on a threatening continent. Combined with a similarly severe belief in man's total depravity as a consequence of the fall of the first couple, the doctrine of predestination explains the three other of the "Five Points of Calvinism" set down at Dort: limited atonement, irresistibility of grace, and final perseverance of the saints in the state of grace eventuating in the state of glory.

From these theological premises, argued for and partly against in the Calvinist camps with the same vehemence as the Catholic doctrines were argued at the Council of Trent, there follow certain general and educational practices among the Puritans.

Since man is powerless before God, who has already decided whether in His infinite grace or according to His rightful wrath He will consider the sinner saved or unsaved, it is not in the will of man whether he will be converted. He is helplessly ensnared in his wretchedness, but God in His overwhelming majesty may create a crushing sudden conviction. Cotton Mather, together with several of his relatives, one of the leaders of the early Boston theocracy, and Jonathan Edwards, the profoundest theologian among the Puritans and also one of the most powerful figures in the "Awakenings" which from time to time rolled over the New England communities, describe the experience of conversion in many places.

It begins with a traumatic sense of being "the chief of sinners," of living in "a miserable condition," and of facing the "danger of damnation." [1]

The God-smitten person weeps, compares himself with snakes and toads, feels himself in everlasting fire, and looks at the bottom of hell. Jonathan Edwards' famous sermon "Sinners in the Hands of an Angry God," delivered at the height of the "Great Awakening" is, together with other sermons on divine wrath, the torments of the wicked (which will be "no occasion of grief to the saints in heaven") and the inevitability of justice, the true expression of the mentality of strict Puritanism.

In the middle of the seventeenth century Shepard in "The Sincere Convert" tells the faithful: [2]

If Christ had shed seas of blood, set thine heart at rest; there is not one drop of it for thee until thou comest to see, and feel, and groan under this miserable estate.

From this abyss of abjectness the sinner is rescued by his unreserved surrender to God's will. Even eternal damnation will be accepted as a sign of God's justice. Cotton Mather, in *His Early Piety, Exemplified in the Life and Death of Nathanael Mather* (London, 1689), records the following diary entry of young Nathanael (February 19, 1682).

O that God would help me to seek him while I am young! O that would He would give unto me his grace! However, I will lay myself down at his feet. If he save me, I shall be happy forever; if he damn me, I must justify him.

The final conversion, and the acceptance by God as one of the elect, announces itself by the experience of divine light, bliss, and peace. Thus a woman writes in the *Massachusetts Missionary Magazine* [3] on "The Experience of a Young Woman at the Age of Nineteen":

Oh, what a transition then took place in my mind from distress and anguish, in which I thought I could not long exist, to a joy and sweetness that I cannot describe. This was enjoyment entirely new. . . . The face of things was now altered and all things appeared new. And everything seemed to be praising God.

The result of this waiting for the answer of the Lord not only in conversion, but also in prayer and practically every daily occurrence, was a continual process of self-examination with the purpose of finding out whether one was able to hear and live in harmony with the divine voice. One could never be sure, because no ruse of Satan was more deceiving than his lulling the reprobate into the feeling of regenerateness.

We gain the deepest insight into this life of continual dialogue with God, sometimes enthusiastic and ecstatic, sometimes depressed and fearful, from the diaries of Cotton Mather (1663–1728), son of the equally famous Boston minister Increase Mather.[4] Joy of achievement may create the sin of pride, prayer may be followed by a feeling of Hallelujah or by threatening silence. The whole personality transports itself into a sense of importance that constantly oscillates between the height of elevation and the abyss of debasement.

We give here only some of many possible quotations.[5]

12 d. lm. *Friday* [March 1702–03]
While I am thus feeble and sore broken, I have no remedy but Prayer, and Patience, and profound Submission to the awful sovereignty of God.

The Spirit of the Lord sometimes does visit me, with Raptures of Assurance, that He has loved me, and that I shall glorify Him. I am sometimes even ready to faint away, with the rapturous Praelibations of the Heavenly World; it makes me even faint and sick, to enjoy such Beginnings of my being swallowed up with God, and with His Will, World without End.

As one can also observe in the life of famous saints, no one can hold himself in this unnatural state of mine without causing the rebellion of the natural man within himself. Cotton Mather cries out at the age of forty (April, 1703):

Was ever man more tempted than miserable *Mather?* Should I tell, in how many Forms the devil has assaulted me, and with what Subtility and Energy, his Assaults have been carried on, it would strike my Friends with Horror.

Sometimes Temptations to *Impurities*; and sometimes to Blasphemy and Atheism and the Abandonment of all Religion as a mere Delusion; and sometimes to self-Destruction itself. These, even these, O miserable *Mather,* do follow thee, with an astonishing Fury. But I fall down into the Dust, on my Study-floor, with Tears before the Lord; and then they quickly vanish; tis fair Weather again. *Lord! What wilt Thou do with me?*

Also children, without regard of age, were thrown into the religious excitement. They were praised for having the marks of "aged

Christianity" upon them and for being already old though young, "full of grace, though not full of days." [6] The fact that several revivals began with prayer meetings of hyperexcited youth in the ages between five and twenty indicates that many of them fully responded to the "divine call." But if it is true that the witch-hunting of Salem also began with the hallucinations and accusations of children, then we may well imagine what the effect of this living in the presence of a threatening God and this continual vision of a burning inferno had on young minds.

Naturally, parents who loved their children exercised an extremely severe discipline in order to free them from the state of depravity. The admonition of Proverbs not to spare the rod was thoroughly followed. Perhaps nowhere in later Christianity were the spirit of the Old Testament and the idea of the Covenant so vivid as among the Puritans. But even the rod, or the most obedient conduct of a child, provided no assurance.

Thus Cotton Mather, according to his diary entry of November 7, 1697, took his little daughter, Kati, into his study. [7]

> And there I told my Child that I am to dy shortly, and she must, when I am *Dead,* Remember every Thing, that I said unto her. I sett before her, the sinful and woeful Condition of her *Nature,* and charg'd her to pray in *secret places every Day* without ceasing, that God for the Sake of Jesus Christ could give her a New Heart, and *pardon* Her sins, and make her a *servant* of His.

> I gave her to understand, that when I am taken from her, she must look to meet with more humbling Afflictions than she does, now she has a careful and tender *Father* to provide for her; . . .

> I signified unto her, That the People of God, would much observe how she carried herself, and that I had written a Book, about *Ungodly Children,* in the *Conclusion* whereof I say, that this Book will be a terrible Witness against my own Children if any of them should not be Godly. At length, with many Tears, both on my Part and hers, I told

my Child, that God had from Heaven assured me . . .
*that shee shall be brought home unto the Lord Jesus Christ,
and be one of His forever.* . . .

I thereupon made the Child kneel down by mee, and I poured
out my Cries unto the Lord, that Hee would: bless her,
and save her and make her a Temple of His Glory. It
will be so! It will be so! [Cotton Mather had fifteen children; all but six died young and only two lived to his
death.]

The identification of every inner emotion with the divine will often
lead into the realm of the ludicrous and blasphemous, though Calvin's
conception of God should have created exactly the contrary.

The following story in Sewall's diary [8] reveals the confusion in
a young mind.

Tim Dwight, a young gentleman from Dedham, fell one
day after prayers in a swoon, and for a good space was as
if he perceived not what was done to him, recovering in a
most incoherent condition lamented that his day of grace
was out.

Even Sewall could not comfort him with the reproach that it
was "sin for anyone to conclude themselves Reprobate." "Not with-
standing all this semblance [and much more than is written] of com-
punction for sin," so Sewall continues, "tis to be feared that his
trouble arose from a maid whom he passionately loved." At least, when
he was permitted to go to her "he aftsoons grew well." A fortnight
later, Sewall asked him

whether his convictions were off. He answered, no. I told
him how dangerous it was to make the convictions wrought
by God's spirit a stalking horse to any other thing. Broke
off, he being called away by Sam. [August 25, 1676]

Often the Puritans have been singled out as a group of particularly intense religiosity. And intense they were, with much arrogance
and vanity in their humility, much dogmatism in their antipapalism,

much hypocrisy in their piety, and much cruelty and self-deception in their wresting the New Jerusalem from the devil-dominated land of the redskins.

It is only human that in the war against "King Philip's" Indians they preferred to kill rather than to be killed, together with wives and children. But it is painful to read in one of the missionary sermons of Cotton Mather the following sentences.[9]

> But infinitely greater was the compassion of the great God in moving the English, thus to *shew you the Kindness* of the Lord. . . .

> Since you have the Gospel, *The people which Sat in Darkness, See a Great Light, and unto them which sat in the Region and shadow of Death. Light is sprung up.* Let this goodness of God cause you to cry out: How Good is God! and let it lead you to Repentance.

One is tempted to compare the New Englanders with the Spanish conquistadores of Mexico and the priests who followed them. For both, the pagans were in the claws of the devil and therefore their lives were not worth much unless they yielded to conversion. In all likelihood, the Spanish soldiers were more ruthless than the Pilgrims. But there is nothing in the literature of New England that, in terms of genuine interest in a foreign culture, could be compared with some of the codices and other documents by the Spanish missionaries.[10] Of course, the Spanish priests found themselves confronted with a highly developed civilization. They even discovered in it some religious rituals which—in spite of the horrors of human sacrifices—had certain similarities with Christianity, whereas the Indians of Eastern North America lived on a rather primitive level. Nevertheless, the comparison between the English and the Spanish early missionaries is by no means in favor of the first.

On the other hand, we gain a false picture of both if we judge them from a modern point of view. They reflected the spirit of their period, which, full of sweeping energy, made little use of the religious humanism of an Erasmus of Rotterdam. Much of what has been held to be especially Puritan is not so when seen under a comparative aspect. The extremes of self-humiliation and the fear and trembling before the wrath of God were part of the whole tradition—Catholic and Protestant. The devil and hellfire were realities also for Dionysius and his confrères. The arousal of sin feelings and religious anxiety was a customary means of education, and some of the greatest men of the time believed in sorcery. Witches were burned in Spain up to the nineteenth century; they haunt the minds of people even today.

We shudder at the sadism in a Puritan product such as Michael Wigglesworth's *The Day of Doom,* published in Boston in 1662. Yet, it was reprinted up to 1828, and many Christians believe still today that children who die before baptism are doomed to damnation, a superstition that Calvin himself repudiated in his *Institutions.*[11]

We would consider religious precociousness in a child a sign of anormality rather than a sign of divine favor. But men thought differently as early as in the Middle Ages. For example, Beda Venerabilis (673–735) says of Abbot Benedict of Weremouth that he had an old heart *(cor gerens senile)*[12] even in his youth. And when we frown at the continual self-inspections of the Puritans, what else are they but the Calvinist version of the Jesuit *Spiritual Exercises,* the meditations, conferences, and thought control of the religious Orders? In many countries an observer could have reported what an English traveller[13] told about the New England of his time, that every one's religious experience

> . . . must be broken in, to the prescribed measure and form. Everyone is asking, not, in his simple and solitary thoughts, how he should feel, but how his neighbor feels. Everyone must believe certain things, and do certain things, and pass through a certain process; or he is lost. And the things that they speak of are not the essential things of virtue and devotion, but the technical things of Revival.

In addition, one must not overestimate the number of the strict in Boston and its environs. There were a lot of adventurers around as in any new colonial enterprise, and even among the decent people not everyone obeyed the Mathers. Otherwise they and their colleagues would not have constantly complained about the thriving godlessness in the New Jerusalem. And when in 1707 John Leverett (instead of Cotton Mather) was elected president of Harvard and the Enlightenment of Europe slowly but steadily invaded the Puritan stronghold, the rule of the old orthodoxy was broken.

But the advent of rationalism was not merely an invasion from outside. Puritan Calvinism still left room for religious individualism, for it did not intend to separate the faithful from the Bible with all its questions and diversities. It was not a sacramental mystery cult, neither did it have a centralized hierarchy, and it worked within a social environment which still carried the memories of suppression in the old homeland. Though by no means democratic in the modern sense of the word, it consisted of independent communities of proud settlers who could express their opinions at town meetings because according to the Massachusetts law of 1638, everyone was "liable to contribute to all charges, both in church and commonwealth, whereof he doth or may receive benefit."

Furthermore, in New as in Old England the clergy was generally not hostile to the progress of science, despite all orthodoxy and witch-hunting. Rather it believed that scientific discovery was but another way of understanding God's creation. Cotton Mather fought "the cursed clamour of a [his] people fiercely possessed by the devil" which tried to prevent him from using "transplantation" against smallpox on his own stricken children. A grenade was thrown into the room of his house where his relative, the minister of Roxbury, lay in order to undergo the inoculation. The people were more backward than their ministers.

Immediate access to the Word of God, decentralization and a sense of independent cooperation in a new country still to be conquered—all these circumstances explain the emphasis of the New England colonies on a common educational system of elementary, secondary, and tertiary character. The basis, of course, was religious. To read and understand the Bible was essential for keeping off the devil, popery in religion, and despotism in politics—all three still concrete realities in the minds of the immigrants. Of the many laws concerning education issued during the early decades of the history of Massachusetts and Connecticut, the most well known is "The Old deluder, Satan

Act" of 1647 which, in order to defeat the "one cheife project of ye ould deluder, Satan, to keepe men from the knowledge of ye Scriptures, as in former times by keeping them in an unknown tongue," solemnly orders that any town of fifty householders and more "shall then forthwith appoint one within their towne to teach all such children as shall resort to him to write and read," and any town of hundred and more set up a grammar school in order "to instruct youth so farr as they shall be fited for ye university."

Such a "new colledge" was founded in 1636 and soon given the name of its first benefactor, Harvard, its main purpose being "to advance learning, and perpetuate it to posterity; dreading to leave an illiterate ministry to the churches, when our present ministers shall lie in the dust." [14]

Education began with the "Horn Books" of the seventeenth century, with the Prayer of the Lord being one of the main texts inserted beneath a sheet of transparent horn. After 1690 the New England Primer was introduced, becoming for one hundred and twenty-five years the main reading book among the Congregationalists and Lutherans. "In Adam's Fall We sinned all," began the alphabet of the Primer. The pupil was taught to offer praises to the Lord, and the reading matter emphasized the same theme: [15]

> That I was brought to know
> The danger I was in,
> By Nature and by Practice too
> A wretched slave to Sin:
>
> That I was led to see
> I can do nothing well;
> And whether shall a Sinner flee
> To save himself from hell?

Besides the Primer there was the Catechism which, in the form of questions and answers, repeated the story of man's sin and salvation.

Nevertheless, the New Englanders did not lack in the sense of the practical. The children were instructed also in the proper use of English, in arithmetic, and the early laws of Connecticut and Plymouth laid value on the readiness of youth to understand the "capital laws" of the country. Furthermore, a New England household was very different from a modern one. Every greater household was more or less self-sustaining and had apprentices, either on the farm or in the work-shop. Since this apprenticeship began at a rather early age, often at twelve, there was a continual interflow of verbal and practical learn-ing, the loss of which is one of the major problems in our modern schooling for the majority of youth. No description of education in the early colonies could be complete without mentioning the various apprenticeship laws which demanded not only a Christian education, but also the teaching and learning of a craft.

In the secondary and higher schools of New England we discover the influence of the humanism that in the fifteenth and sixteenth cen-turies had entered Cambridge University from which many of the early spiritual leaders of New England had graduated. Otherwise the rules of admission to Harvard of 1642 could not have had the following en-trance requirements: [16]

> When any Scholar is able to understand Tully, or such like classical Latine author extempore, and make and speake true Latine in verse and prose, *suo ut aiunt Marte*; and decline perfectly the paradigm's of nounes and verbes in the Greek tongue: Let him then and not before be capable of admission into the Colledge.

And in the "Requirements for Degrees" the candidate is en-joined not only to read the Old and New Testaments in the original and to interpret them logically in the Latin tongue, but also to have some knowledge of logic, natural and moral philosophy, arithmetic, geometry, and astronomy. There was even a summer course on the nature of plants.

CONCLUDING REMARKS

Today the Puritans and especially their educational practices are strangers to us. We may admire their courage, their persistence within a world of hostility, their unwavering faith in an all-powerful God though they did not know whether, in his infinite foresight and wisdom, he might already have decreed their eternal damnation. There was something grandiose in these radical determinists, willing to go to hell for the glory of God, something from which Thomas Aquinas and Luther and Calvin shrank away. But they were, at the same time, the most extreme individualists, proud and imperturbable in their conviction of having the answer for the mysterious existence of good and evil.

From their supernaturalist point of view these men were logical to the degree of inhumanity, and at the same time romantic, sentimental, adventurous, and morbidly concerned about themselves. This was one of the great spectacles of human history, a weltering of seeming absurdities and contradictions, all united in one central idea: God, the Almighty.

Nevertheless, we do not like children subjected to such a combination of the logical and the cruel. We know that the Salem witch trials were partly the results of hallucinations of disturbed young minds. However—if this is an excuse—fear of the world beyond was then part of religious education all over the Christian world. And witches were burned at many other places without anyone repenting publicly, as did the Puritans.

Forget for a while the dark clouds of superstition which then cast their shadows over all humanity, and there remains an heroic generation, hard-working, dutiful, and fearless before the world because they are anchored in the grounds of religious certainty. Whether or not we believe in their doctrine—most will not—it is still worthwhile to study them, for they express more deeply the terrific anxieties and great hopes of humanity than so many people of today whose platitudes go under the name of truth.

In their personal lives the Puritans often confused the trifling with the important. But perhaps there is nothing trifling to people who feel that the eye of God watches every one of their steps, or, that every one of their steps tells them whether they belong to the saints or the damned. Though pedantic and bigoted, they also knew of the great and transcendant, and this makes the decisive difference between their education and the education that so many of our youth receive today in their families and their schools, and even on higher levels.

Chapter 9

Pietism and the Reaction Against Protestant Ecclesiasticism

JOHN AMOS COMENIUS

The largest part of Comenius' life coincided with the period when the countries of Europe to which he was most attached were tortured by the cruelties of the Thirty Years War (1618–1648) and its impact on the political and religious life of Europe. Comenius himself, born in 1592 in Moravia, became, after the theological studies at German universities, a minister and teacher in the communities of his homeland. Later appointed bishop of the already scattered Moravian brethren, he was a refugee during most of his life, living—always for only a few years—in Poland, Germany, Sweden, England, and Holland. Several of his most precious manuscripts and many of his beloved books were lost in burning cities. Yet, as with the early Christian martyrs, his suffering but reinforced the idea of the coming salvation; the greater the first, the nearer the second—although for him the concept of salvation was not merely transcendental but also, as we will see later, extended into man's earthly existence. Actually, Comenius' thoughts about Christian life and education pointed prophetically toward the future.

But, as all harbingers of a new era, he, too, was full of contradictions. Though aware of a new science, he confused mere analogies with natural causes to such a degree that Roger Bacon of the thirteenth century would have smiled at him. And though his idea of a universal application of religious and rational insight to the totality of the human race made him more tolerant than his Christian brethren, he was still unable to look at Christianity in historical and comparative perspective. It was for him absolute; but so it is for many Christians today.

Nevertheless, rather than being narrow and dogmatic as so many theologians of the seventeenth century, Comenius was a Christian of the prophetic, enthusiastic type, not without mystical-pantheistic leanings. Every event in the great cosmos of mind and nature was for him a message from God; even the most horrible disappointments could not shatter his hope that the divine principle would finally be victorious. As one of its manifestations he interpreted the growing knowledge of the time. In spite of disagreement in certain metaphysical aspects, he welcomed the work of philosophers such as Francis Bacon and Descartes. Though he never studied them thoroughly, he admired the works of science. They gave him the courage to believe that the human mind would finally understand the laws of the universe, discover the essential identity between the natural and spiritual aspects of the creation, provide a scientific method for education, and help God and the good in their endeavor to bring about peace among the troubled nations of the world.

In this spirit he addressed one of his most touching works, *The Way of Light* (*Via Lucis*, 1668) "to the torch bearers of this enlightened age, members of the Royal Society of London, now bringing real philosophy to a happy birth." [1] One paragraph of the "Dedication" contains the following words:

> But what do you purpose in England now that halcyon days are returned, I mean, now that the upheavals of civil war are subsiding? That something has been achieved and that in a glorious manner is attested by the splendid establishment of the Royal Society in London for the investigation of the mysteries of Nature and by the publication already of so many admirable inquiries and discoveries. Blessings upon your heroic enterprises, illustrious Sirs! We have no envy towards you; rather we congratulate you and applaud

you, and assure you of the applause of mankind. Throughout the world the news will be trumpeted that you are engaged in labours the purpose of which is to secure that human knowledge and the empire of the human mind over
matter shall not for ever continue to be a feeble and uncertain thing. It will be proclaimed abroad that thanks to your
industry the confident hope may now be entertained that
Philosophy brought to perfection can exhibit the true and
distinctive qualities of things, their scope, their means,
their uses for the attainment and for the constantly progressive increase of all that makes for good to mind, body and
(as the saying is) estate. We salute you, and we encourage
you by your own example to confirm what your illustrious
countryman, Lord Bacon, wrote: "That all things are possible which can be done by some persons, though not indeed
by anybody and everybody; and by a number of persons
united, though not by a single person; and in a series of
ages though not in the same epoch, and finally by public effort and at public expense, though not by the resources and
toil of individuals."

And in two other paragraphs (27–28) he continued his praise of
the "priests in the realm of nature":

We bid you, then, who are priests in the realm of nature,
to press on your labours with all vigour. See to it that mankind is not for ever mocked by a Philosophy empty, superficial, false, uselessly subtle. Your heritage is a fair Sparta,
enrich her with fair equipment, and by making a strict examination both of facts and of opinions concerning them,
set an example, as you properly may, to politicians and theologians. He was right who said that a contentious philosophy is the parent of a contentious theology: we must therefore say at once and plainly about Politics that the main political theories on which the present rulers of the world support themselves are treacherous quagmires and the real causes
of the generally tottering and indeed collapsing condition of
the world. It is for you to show that errors are no more to be
tolerated, even though they have the authority of long tradition and are drawn from Adam himself: you must show,
not only to theologians, but to the politicians themselves,

that everything must be called back to Urim and Thummim, I mean, to Light and Truth. (*Exod.* xxviii. 30.)

Let your researches into Natural objects be so well established, let them bear upon their face so complete an assurance of trustworthiness, that if a man desires not merely to contemplate your work as long as he likes with his unaided eyes, but even to try its accuracy by the most exacting tests of his own device, he shall be certain to find that the facts are precisely what you have shown them to be. It will be an admirable precedent: and will encourage those who are at the helm of human society in the State, or of the consciences of men in the Church to act in the same way, following indeed the example of the Apostles who did not fear to submit all their doctrines to the scrutiny and judgment of the world. (I *Cor.* iv. 3, 4)

A large part of the *Via Lucis* is given to the analysis of "Light"; there are three kinds of it: (1) "Eternal light," or the glory that cannot be approached by the human senses; for God alone dwells in it. (2) "The External light"—it is "a brightness which our bodily eyes can perceive: by it God had illumined every part of this his theatre of the physical world. It is conveyed to the world by the stars of heaven, and principally by the sun." (3) "The internal light"— it is "the brightness kindled in the minds of rational creatures, illuminating them in every part and directing them upon their ways."

In a long discussion (Chapter X) the author ventures to "set forth in theorems and demonstrate in the manner of mathematicians and that as concisely as possible" his own theory of "the ways of light by which it comes forth and spreads itself."

Luckily, the Fellows of the Royal Society did not take Comenius' theory of light seriously. Probably they never read it. Four years after the publication of *The Way of Light,* Issac Newton sent his color experiments to the Society. Acknowledging his election as a Fellow, he wrote to its secretary Oldenburg on January 6, 1671: "I shall endeavour to show my gratitude by communicating what my poor and solitary endeavors can effect towards the promoting of philosophical design." And in later years the great scientist wrote: [2]

I do not know what I may appear to the world; but to myself I seem to have been only like a boy playing on the sea-
shore and diverting myself in now and then finding a
smoother pebble or prettier shell than ordinary, whilst the
great ocean of truth lay all undiscovered before me.

Hardly can one imagine a greater difference of an approach to
the same problem as that between Newton's *New Theory of Light
and Colours,* or *Huygen's Traité de la Lumière,* and the speculations
of Comenius who did not even know the optical discoveries of his
contemporaries Snell and Fermat. Instead, Comenius' "science" represents a curious mixture of Pythagorean, Platonic, medieval, and mystical ideas with a conception of nature as being divinely endowed with
qualities and purposes similar to those of man.

Yet, there remains a philosophical idea upon which modern
science is also built, namely the unity of the universe, for the understanding of which there should also exist a unified method of approach.
This idea which made the seventeenth century one of the greatest in
the history of the human intellect, led the Moravian bishop logically
to the second intuition we have found in his thought, namely the universality and essential identity of the minds of men.

All men, he believes, are children of the same divine creation;
God has helped them to develop methods by which to understand
His work and thus themselves. Should it then not be possible—yea,
it may even be God's ultimate design—to harmonize the existing differences in the human race by showing men that there is a truth in
which they all can participate if only they are taught to learn, and
willing to learn?

Thus we find in Comenius' *Way of Light,* so backward from
the point of view of empirical science, certain ideas that point toward
a future still desired by modern man, yet still distant. According to
Comenius, it is man's greatest mission on earth, to help the "universal light" shine over all humanity. This should be done by means of
the art and science of *Pansophia,* as the attempt to bring "fullness, order, and truth" into the already bewildering mass of human knowledge.

In his desire for a new intellectual order Comenius was not

alone. Several of his friends were also engaged in pansophic endeavors; and like him, they also were in danger of confusing the mere amassing of information with real harmonization, though they desired much more than to compose mere cyclopedias. Like us, they were torn between the joy over the expansion of knowledge and the threatening sense of segmentation and frustration that comes with it.

Subordinated to *Pansophia,* which should contain "the very marrow of eternal truth," Comenius wanted a *Panhistorica* that should reveal "all the variety of particular things and actions" and a *Pandogmatica* which should "review the various theories or opinions which have been held about things." For the propagation of these plans he suggested a "Universal College" that would assemble men "from the whole world, men of quick and industrious temper, of piety, warmly devoted to the welfare of the people, taken indifferently from laymen engaged in public affairs and of ecclesiastics." Furthermore, he wished that as a requisite for "the reform of the whole world" and as an "antidote to confusion of thought" some common language be established. "Hence it is that the peoples of the world are all of them still building a Babylon, and never properly understand themselves and each other in their conduct of their speech." In several paragraphs he deals extensively with the principles of the new language—and here, in contrast to his pseudoscientific excursions, he shows himself as a linquist of considerable acumen. Unfortunately, one of his greatest works, a comparative dictionary of the Latin, Czech, and German languages, was burned at one of the many fires which, during the Thirty Years War, devastated the cities of Central Europe.

From the point of view of cultural history, the whole pansophistic movement of the seventeenth century is a part of the utopianism that flowered at the same time. Thomas More's *Utopia,* which set the pattern, was written in 1516, about a hundred years before Comenius became known. In the seventeenth century Bacon wrote the *New Atlantis* (1624–1629) with the view that science would become the door to universal happiness. The Italian monk Tommaso Campanella pictured in his *Civitas Solis* (1623) a planned communistic society. A few decades later, in 1648, there appear two Christian utopias, namely Johann Valentine Andreae's *Christianopolis* and St. Golt's *Nova Solyma.*

At the same time James Harrington's *Oceana* was published. This work simplified the problem of political power by basing it almost exclusively on landed property. It had nevertheless a considerable influence upon American political thought.

All these utopias suggest the idea that we find also in Comenius and which had such a decisive influence on the future of religious education; namely, that man may have available the means by which to plant the heavenly millennium right here on earth. In romantic form, there appear here the germs of the Enlightenment and of secular optimism. As in all periods of overwhelming changes (Comenius' contemporaries experienced the dawn of modern science and the breakdown of the biblical concept of the universe, the final dissolution of the Holy Roman Empire and the rise of a new system of national states), the tensions between the old and the new were felt but not yet fully understood. Almost all the great men of the time harbored in their souls the most inconsistent views about God, nature, and man, as well as about science and religion. Comenius himself made some of his most dangerous decisions under the spell of a false prophetess. The French political philosopher Jean Bodin (1530–1596), one of the first to conceive of the fundamental political changes of his era and to base sovereignty on natural grounds instead of divine right, wrote a terrifying, widely-read and translated book on sorcery; [3] and Cotton Mather, proud member of the Royal Society, was a witch-hunter. The third book of Newton's *Principia Mathematica,* which he himself first intended to suppress, was in no way consistent with his research, while another great contemporary of Comenius, Spinoza, who claimed in his *Ethics* to proceed "more mathematico," was dogmatic and presumptuous about Harvey's discoveries of the circulation of the blood, as appears in his correspondence with Henry Oldenburg, first secretary of the Royal Society of England. But heaven knows what kind of incongruences later generations may discover in our own enlightened age.

Whenever Comenius wrote about his hopes for the establishment of a new and universal commonwealth, he returned to the theme to which he devoted, among other books, his *Great Didactic (Didactica Magna,* 1632),[4] aimed at bringing about a school reform so that "All the young shall be educated [except those to whom God has denied understanding] . . . in all those subjects which are able to make a man wise, virtuous, and pious" (Chapter XII).

Again, the underlying idea of this, the most methodical treatise on education written up to Comenius' time, is cosmic unity, or the congruity of the laws that work in nature with the laws that work in the mind. As a consequence of this unity, Comenius believed that it should be possible to develop an educational theory and practice no longer based on more or less haphazard observations, but on firm scientific principles of such validity that—this was also Descartes' and Bacon's opinion—differences of talent (*differentiae ingenii*) would become negligible. Exposed to the right method, everybody would be able to learn as much as everybody else, for if a method is right, it must also be universal.

But here also Comenius moves strangely on two levels, one of an ecstatic vision as to what science might be able to do for man, and the other of a primitive conception of what science really is. The great and exceedingly practical ideas on educational method developed in the *Great Didactic* result from the author's experiences and psychological intuitions. His scientific proofs are mainly analogies taken from nature, but in no way causal categories.

Chapter XIV may be used as an example. It begins with the following paragraphs:

THE EXACT ORDER OF INSTRUCTION MUST BE BORROWED FROM NATURE, AND MUST BE OF SUCH A KIND THAT NO OBSTACLE CAN HINDER IT.

Let us then commence to seek out, in God's name, the principles on which, as on an immovable rock, the method of teaching and of learning can be grounded. If we wish to find a remedy for the defects of nature, it is in nature herself that we must look for it, since it is certain that art can do nothing unless it imitate nature.

A few examples will make this clear. We see a fish swimming in the water; it is its natural mode of progression. If a man wish to imitate it, it is necessary for him to use in a similar manner the limbs that are at his disposal; instead of fins he must employ his arms, and instead of a tail, his feet, moving them as a fish moves its fins. Even ships are constructed on this plan; in the place of fins they must employ oars or sails, and in the place of a tail, the rudder. We see a bird flying through the air; it is its natural mode of progression. When Daedalus wished to imitate it, he had to make wings (large enough to carry such a heavy body) and set them in motion. . . .

It is now quite clear that the order, which is the dominating principle in the art of teaching all things to all men, should be, and can be, borrowed from no other source but the operations of nature. As soon as this principle is thoroughly secured, the processes of art will proceed as easily and as spontaneously as those of nature. Very aptly does Cicero say: "If we take nature as our guide, she will never lead us astray," and also: "Under the guidance of nature it is impossible to go astray." This is our belief, and our advice is to watch the operations of nature carefully and to imitate them.

Nor is it "taken from nature"—though it is profound—when in Chapter XXIV he describes "the method of instilling piety."

The Method of Instilling Piety

Piety is the gift of God, and is given us from on high by our counsellor and guide, the Holy Spirit. But, since the Holy Spirit usually employs natural agencies, and has chosen parents, teachers, and ministers who should faithfully plant and water the grafts of Paradise (I *Cor.* iii. 6–8), it is right that these should appreciate the extent of their duties.

We have already explained what we mean by piety, namely, that (after we have thoroughly grasped the conceptions of faith and of religion) our hearts should learn to seek God everywhere (since He has concealed Himself with His works with a curtain, and, invisibly present in all visible things, directs all, though unseen), and that when we have found Him we should follow Him, and when we have attained Him should enjoy Him. The first we do through our understanding, the second through our will, and the third through the joy arising from the consciousness of our union with God.

We seek God by noticing the signs of His divinity in all things created. We follow God by giving ourselves up completely to His will, both to do and to suffer whatever shall have seemed good to Him. We enjoy God by so acquiescing in His love and favour that nothing in heaven or on earth appears to us more to be desired than God himself, that nothing appears pleasanter to think of, and nothing sweeter than to sing His praises; thus our hearts are joined to His in love.

The sources from which we can draw this exaltation are three, and the manner in which we can draw from them is threefold.

These sources are Holy Writ, the world, and ourselves. The first is the Word of God, the second is His handiwork, and the third is inspired by Him. . . .

The manner of drawing piety from these sources is threefold: meditation, prayer, and examination.

These three [says Luther] make a theologian; but indeed they are essential to make a true Christian.

Meditation is the constant, attentive, and devoted consideration of the works, the words, and the goodness of God; the thoughtful acknowledgment that it is from the good-will of God alone (either active or permissive) that all things come, and that all the counsels of the divine will attain their end in the most marvelous ways.

Prayer is the frequent, or rather the continual, yearning after God, and the supplication that He may sustain us in His mercy and guide us with His Spirit.

Examination is the continual testing of our progress in piety, and may come from ourselves or from others. Under this head come human, devilish, and divine temptations. For men should examine themselves to see if they are faithful, and do the will of God; and it is necessary that we should be tested by other men, by our friends, and by our enemies. This is the case when those who are set over others are vigilant and attentive, and, by open or by secret scrutiny, try to find out what progress has been made; or when God places an adversary by our side to teach us to find our refuge in Him, and to show us how strong our faith is. Finally, Satan himself is sent by God, or comes against us of his own accord, that the state of our hearts may be made evident.

These three modes, therefore, must be instilled into the Christian youth, that they may learn to raise their hearts to Him who is the first and the last of all things, and may seek rest for their souls in Him alone.

The twenty-one rules which then follow as special devices for instilling piety are all sound and partly derived from human nature most broadly understood, as, for example, the importance of early religious influence; but they are circular, as is the whole thought of Comenius. For while they try to prove God through nature, they presuppose God as the beginning and end of all nature and the Christian revelation as the Alpha and Omega of all knowledge. They are based on the conviction that the Cross "is the safest path of life," and they end with the statement that "we have finally placed . . . our salvation in safety, when we have laid the burden on Christ, the cornerstone." This is good and profound Christian tradition, but this tradition is not "natural."

Fundamentally, education in its wholeness cannot be based on strictly inductive methods, for it is not only psychology of learning (even that, so far as human beings are concerned, cannot be totally "scientific"), but also a form of social philosophy and ethics with all their transcendent implications. Yet, there was productivity also in Comenius' confused system of education. Despite his Christian supernaturalism, he pointed more clearly than others at the great possibilities inherent in the empirical and inductive study of the human mind and its development, and he recognized the necessity of basing concepts on experience. From Comenius, though not always in the form of direct influence, a line can be drawn to Rousseau, the German philanthropists, Pestalozzi, Froebel, and finally to Herbart, the first who spoke about the logic of education with real clarity. But despite all progress, the study of education—and especially of religious education—is still today beset with methodological problems. Can we wonder that the first builder of a pedagogical system was not clear about his own procedure?

Compared with Newton who had an admirable mixture of modesty and scientific greatness, Comenius might almost appear as a highly talented, but confused intuitionist. Indeed, in some respects he was. Yet, those who study his work within its historical context will discover not only the spirit of the seventeenth century with its amazing mixture of supposedly self-evident transcendentalism and empiricism, stubborn superstition and concern with method, realistic insight and utopianism. They will also realize, how near, despite all distance in time and language, many of Comenius' problems are to those of our own period. The struggle over religious education in our schools reflects the still existing split between the religious and the scientific interpretation of the world. Our political prejudices may turn the potential blessings of nuclear physics into a gigantic process of destruction in comparison to which the Thirty Years War was a minor conflict; and, often in the same mind, otherworldliness goes together with the belief that man will be able to transplant the millennium of eternal justice and happiness from the spheres beyond into our early society. If all this is modern humanity, then Comenius is one of its greatest prophets.

THE QUAKERS

Whereas the German Reformation of the sixteenth century was one great and decisive act, dividing forever the country into Catholics and Protestants besides whom no sects of major influence could assert themselves, England, as it were, had several reformations and developed a number of denominations of historical importance. Decentralization, so characteristic of England's administrative and educational system, determined also the nation's religious development. One may even dispute whether the establishment of the Anglican Church, had a greater effect on the religious life of the English-speaking world than the religious excitements starting at the time of Wycliff and reaching to such eminent figures as Cromwell and Wesley. Certainly, the period of the greatest religious ebullience was that of Cromwell. Then the conflicts of the minds were by no means merely those of Puritanism against religious and political feudalism. Presbyterianism already existed, and there were religious movements as much opposed to the Puritan doctrine of predestination as to the Anglican ecclesiasticism of Archbishop Laud. "Seekers" were all around the country; some of them not unlike the Russian Dokhobortsy or Ranters, felt God so deeply implanted in their souls that they regarded themselves beyond good and evil, with the result that soon they were in the grip of the latter, repeating the story of the Münster Anabaptists at the time of Luther. But there were also Anabaptists, or "Baptists" of the serious type, the ancestors of the present Baptist churches, and there was the imposing figure of George Fox, father of Quakerism or the "Society of Friends."

Fox's *Journal* is one of the great autobiographical documents in the history of religion. We refer here to the abridged edition by Rufus M. Jones which contains such an excellent introduction to the reformer's ideas and their influence on Quakerism that it would be difficult to say something better in a few pages.[5]

George Fox is one of those historical figures who feel themselves to be spokesmen of divine providence, mystics, from the modern point of view, but, in their own conscience and consciousness, vessels of universal truth. In order to use words that frequently occur in his works, the Lord had "opened him" so that he "clearly saw that all was done and to be done in and by Christ"; [6] he and his followers were "preserved in the Lord's everlasting seed"; [7] and they had the "light" and saw "the principle." Consequently, the Quakers were for him not "a sect." [8]

Whereas he (Major Porter of King Charles II army) calleth me "A chief upholder of the Quakers' sect" I answer: The quakers are not a sect, but are in the power of God, which was before sects were, and witness the election before the world began, and are come to live in the life in which the prophets and apostles lived, who gave forth the Scriptures; therefore are we hated by envious, wrathful, wicked, persecuting men. But God is the upholder of us all by His mighty power and preserves us from the wrath of the wicked that would swallow us up.

This sense of unity gave Fox the power to bear all kinds of persecution and radiated even to his enemies. They could not escape the penetrating glance of his eyes; often he "overturned" [9] meetings of undisciplined religious sectarians by the gripping power of his words, and people believed that he had the power of healing. Naturally, the theology of the Church of England and of Oxford and Cambridge was for him but one more way of alienating the faithful from the Truth.[10]

These three—the physicians, the priests, and the lawyers—ruled the world out of the wisdom, out of the faith, and out of the equity and law of God. . . . But I saw they were all out of the wisdom, out of the faith, out of the equity and perfect law of God.

Like many men of the prophetic type he had hours of revelation. One of the first and most important of Fox's friends, William Penn, gives an account in his "Preface to the Journal of George Fox," which is at the same time the most vivid description of his work.

In 1652, he being in his usual retirement to the Lord upon a very high mountain, in some of the hither parts of Yorkshire, as I take it, his mind exercised toward the Lord, he had a vision of the great work of God in the earth, and of the way he was to go forth to begin it. He saw people as thick as motes in the sun that should in time be brought home to the Lord, that there might be but one Shepard and one sheepfold in all the earth. . . .

What did Fox and his "Society of Friends" profess? Actually, nothing that could not be found somewhere in the Christian tradition. The concept of man as the dwelling place of the Divine is to be found in the Christian and non-Christian traditions. But the Quakers took this idea seriously, not only in terms of religious transcendentalism, about which they spoke actually rarely, but in terms of interhuman relations. They demanded respect for the Divine Principle in every person, whether king or laborer. Therefore the rejection of caste and empty custom, the "thee" and "thou" instead of the plural form which had been introduced to indicate distinction. Women had to have the same rights in public life and worship as men. Whereas in our modern society the concept of equality is often one of leveling down rather than of leveling up, Fox's postulate of human unity symbolizes the idea of community through divine inspiration and aspiration. Fox became a social reformer. From his work started the fight of the Quakers against war, exploitation, slavery, and the extremely cruel legal code of the time.

The conviction that the divine spark was waiting in every man, and that every day's thought and action should reflect the divine presence led to a new conception of worship. Worship could not come from outside through "priests" and elaborate cult; it could only be when and where man and his community discovered the God within.[11]

> He [Fox] threw away all crutches at the start and called upon everybody to walk in the Spirit, to live in the Light. His house of worship was bare of everything but seats. He had no shrine, for the shekinah [divine manifestation] was to be in the hearts of those who worshipped. It had no altar, for God needed no appeasing, seeing that He Himself had made the sacrifice for sin. It had no baptismal font, for baptism was in his belief nothing short of immersion into the life of the Father, Son and Holy Spirit—a going down into the significance of Christ's death and a coming up in newness of life with Him. There was no communion table, because he believed that the true communion consisted in partaking directly of the soul's spiritual bread—the living Christ. There were no confessionals, for in the silence, with the noise and din of the outer life hushed, the soul was to unveil itself to its Maker and let His light lay bare its true condition. There was no organ or choir, for each forgiven soul was to give praise in the glad notes that were natural to it.

No censer was swung, for he believed God wanted only the fragrance of sincere and prayerful spirits. There was no priestly mitre, because each member of the true Church was to be a priest unto God. No official robes were in evidence, because the entire business of life, in meeting and outside, was to be the putting on of white garments of a saintly life. From the beginning to the end worship was the immediate appreciation of God, and the appropriate activity of the whole being in response to Him.

Though the Quakers knew that the simple may be nearer to God than the learned, they—like Comenius—also knew that the Light cannot shine in a dull mind. Consequently, the education of youth and adults became one of the main Quaker concerns.

Like the early Christians, the early Quakers were convinced that their truth would convert the world; and like the early Christians, they were not frightened by ridicule and torture. They had their martyrs wherever—horrible to say—they met Christians, from the towers of England to New England's Boston. But despite all suffering, wherever there was a sufficiently large community of Quakers, they established a school in order to teach (these words of Fox were often repeated) "things civil and useful in the creation." And they meant and did what they said. They had no official theology, though Robert Barclay wrote a catechism in 1673.[12] They looked askance at fiction and the aesthetic elements of life, and more puritan than the Puritans, they had not even hymns. And since, in consequence of the pantheistic substratum in their religious outlook, the divine and the real were not separated, they had no bad conscience about being interested in the *realia*. In the many schools which spread over England and America, especially in Pennsylvania, they taught, besides the three R's in the elementary grades, the sciences, mathematics, navigation, and foreign languages in their academies. The classics never played a great role in their thinking and teaching. Though Benjamin Franklin was not a Quaker, the curriculum he recommended for his Academy should have pleased his Quaker friends. So-called "Quaker realism," and the fact that many of them became wealthy, reaffirms the seemingly paradoxical fact that high spirituality—unless it is of the definitely ascetic, withdrawing, and conflict-ridden type—often goes hand in hand with practical success. This not only because it creates sobriety of conduct, but also because the conviction of unity with higher forces creates a power of concentration and a sense of confidence that spreads from a person over into those who deal with him.

The virtues on which the Quaker schools laid prime value reinforced the development of a practical Christian character. Howard H. Brinton in his book, *Quaker Education*,[13] described the four main aims in the light of which the Friends' schools operated in the past.

First, they tried to instill in the young a sense of belonging to the Quaker community by a "religiously guarded" education and by the example of dedicated and "concerned" teachers. Second, they aimed toward "pacifism" by the application of nonviolent discipline and methods and by awakening in their pupils an inward sense of rightness. Third, they emphasized equal education of both sexes and equality of races and classes, and fourth, they insisted on "simplicity" by which they meant moderation in dress, speech, and deportment, scholastic integrity, and avoidance of empty verbalism by emphasis on practical subjects in the curriculum.

But better than by any secondary source has the spirit of early Quaker education been revealed by William Penn's *Some Fruits of Solitude In Reflections and Maxims on the Conduct of Human Life* (1693) of which we reprint here some of the maxims on "Education" and some concerning the right spirit of faith and love. Further we reprint in part his *Advice to His Children, Relating to their Civil and Religious Conduct* (1699)[14]—still today a rich source of living wisdom.

4. [Education.] We are in pain to make them scholars, but not men! To talk, rather than to know; which is true canting.

5. The first thing obvious to children, is what is sensible; and that we make no part of their rudiments.

6. We press their memory too soon, and puzzle, strain and load them with words and rules; to know grammar and rhetorick, and a strange tongue or two, that it is ten to one may never be useful to them; leaving their natural genius

to mechanical and physical, or natural knowledge unculti-
vated and neglected; which would be of exceeding use and
pleasure to them through the whole course of their life.

9. It were happy if we studied nature more in natural things;
and acted according to nature; whose rules are few, plain,
and most reasonable.

10. Let us begin where she begins, go her pace, and close
always where she ends, and we cannot miss of being good
naturalists.

11. The creation would not be longer a riddle to us: the
heavens, earth, and waters, with their respective, various,
and numerous inhabitants; their productions, natures, sea-
sons, sympathies and antipathies; their use, benefit, and
pleasure, would be better understood by us: and an eternal
wisdom, power, majesty, and goodness, very conspicuous to
us, through those sensible and passing forms: the world
wearing the mark of its Maker, whose stamp is every where
visible, and the characters very legible to the children of
wisdom.

12. And it would go a great way to caution and direct people in their use of the world, that they were better studied
and knowing in the creation of it.

13. For how could men find the conscience to abuse it, while
they should see the Great Creator look them in the face, in
all and every part thereof?

15. It is pity, therefore, that books have not been composed
for youth, by some curious and careful naturalists, and also
mechanics, in the Latin tongue to be used in schools, that they
might learn things with words: things obvious and familiar
to them, and which would make the tongue easier to
be attained by them.

17. Finally, if man be the index or epitome of the world,
as philosophers tell us, we have only to read ourselves well to be
learned in it. But because there is nothing we less regard,

than the characters of the Power that made us, which are
so clearly written upon us, and the world he has given us,
and can best tell us what we are and should be, we are
even strangers to our own genius: the glass in which we
should see that true, instructing, and agreeable variety,
which is to be observed in nature, to the admiration of
that wisdom, and adoration of that power, which made
us all.

516. The preparation of the heart, as well as answer of the
tongue, is of the Lord: and to have it, our prayers must be
powerful, and our worship grateful.

517. Let us choose, therefore, to commune where there is
the warmest sense of religion; where devotion exeeds for-
mality, and practice most corresponds with profession; and
where there is, at least, as much charity as zeal; for where this
society is to be found, there shall we find the Church of God.

518. As good, so ill men, are all of a church; and every
body knows who must be head of it.

519. The humble, meek, merciful, just, pious, and devout
souls, are every where of one religion; and when death has
taken off the mask, they will know one another, though
the diverse liveries they wear here, make them strangers.

522. It is a sad reflection, that many men hardly have any
religion at all; and most men have none of their own: for
that which is the religion of their education, and not of
their judgment, is the religion of another, and not theirs.

523. To have religion upon authority, and not upon conviction, is like a finger-watch, to be set forwards or back-
wards, as he pleases that has it in keeping.

524. It is a preposterous thing, that men can venture their
souls, where they will not venture their money: for they
will take their religion upon trust, but not trust a synod
about the goodness of half a crown.

532. When our minds exceed their just bounds, we must needs discredit what we would recommend.

533. To be furious in religion, is to be irreligiously religious.

535. It were better to be of no church, than to be bitter for any.

547. If I am even with my enemy, the debt is paid: but if I forgive it, I oblige him for ever.

548. Love is the hardest lesson in Christianity; but, for that reason, it should be most our care to learn it. Difficilia quae pulchra.

556. Love is above all; and when it prevails in us all, we shall all be lovely, and in love with God, and one with another. Amen. (*Some Fruits of Solitude.*)

From: The Advice of William Penn to his
Children
relating to their
Civil and Religious Conduct
1699

6. Having thus expressed myself to you, my dear children, as to the things of God, his truth and kingdom, I refer you to his light, grace, spirit, and truth within you, and the holy scriptures of truth without you, which from my youth I loved to read, and were ever blessed to me; and which I charge you to read daily; the OLD TESTAMENT, for history, chiefly; the PSALMS, for meditation and devotion; the PROPHETS, for comfort and hope, but especially the NEW TESTA-MENT, for doctrine, faith, and worship: for they were given forth by holy men of God in diverse ages, as they were moved by the holy Spirit. . . .

7. Cast up your income, and live on half; if you can, one third; reserving the rest for casualties, charities, portions.

8. Be plain in clothes, furniture and food, but clean; and then the coarser the better; the rest is folly, and a snare. Therefore next to sin, avoid daintiness and choiceness about your person and houses. For if it be not an evil in itself, it is a temptation to it; and may be accounted a nest for sin to brood in.

9. Avoid differences: what are not avoidable, refer; and keep awards strictly, and without grudgings. Read Prov. xviii. 17, 18. XXV. 8 Matt. V. 38 to 41. I Cor. 1. 10 to 13. It is good counsel.

19. Have but few books, but let them be well chosen, and well read, whether of religious or civil subjects. Shun fantastic opinions: measure both religion and learning by practice; reduce all to that, for that brings a real benefit to you, the rest is a thief and a snare. And, indeed, reading many books is but a taking off the mind too much from meditation. Reading yourselves and nature, in the dealings and conduct of men, is the truest human wisdom. The spirit of a man knows the things of a man; and more true knowledge comes by meditation and just reflection, than by reading; for much reading is an oppression of the mind, and extinguishes the natural candle; which is the reason of so many senseless scholars in the world.

20. Do not that which you blame in another. Do not that to another, which you would not another should do to you. But above all, do not that in God's sight, you would not man should see you do.

21. And that you may order all things profitably, divide your day; such a share of time for your retirement and worship of God; such a proportion for your business; in which remember to ply that first which is first to be done; so much time for yourselves, be it for study, walking, visit, etc. In this be first, and let your friends know it, and you will cut off many impertinencies and interruptions, and save a treasure of time to yourselves which people most unaccountably lavish away. And to be more exact, (for much lies in this) keep a short journal of your time, though a day require but a line; many advantages flow from it.

27. Love silence, even in the mind; for thoughts are to that, as words to the body, troublesome; much speaking, as much thinking, spends; and in many thoughts, as well as words, there is sin. True silence is the rest of the mind; and is to the spirit, what sleep is to the body, nourishment and refreshment. It is a great virtue; it covers folly, keeps secrets, avoids disputes, and prevents sin. See Job XIII. 5. Prov. X. 19. Chap. XII. 13, chap. XIII. 3. chap. XVIII. 6, 7. chap. XVII. 28.

28. The wisdom of nations lies in their proverbs, which are brief and pithy; collect and learn them, they are notable measures and directions for human life; you have much in little; they save time and speaking; and, upon occasion, may be the fullest and safest answers.

29. Never meddle with other folks business, and less with the public, unless called to the one by the parties concerned (in which move cautiously and uprightly) and required to the other by the Lord, in a testimony for his name and truth; remembering that old, but most true and excellent proverb, Bene qui latuit, bene vixit, "He lives happily, that lives hiddenly or privately; for he lives quietly." It is a treasure to them that have it: study it, get it, keep it; too many miss it that might have it: the world knows not the value of it. It doubles man's life, by giving him twice the time to himself, that a large acquaintance, or much business, will allow him.

It would be too narrow to judge the work of the Quakers in the field of religious education by looking mainly at the rearing of children, and at the schools, academies and the few colleges founded by them, especially since, after the middle of the nineteenth century, the expansion of these schools has been slowing down. Some of them have been absorbed in the growing public and private secular school systems that, with the progress of humane methods of discipline and realistic concepts of curriculum, have taken over much of what in earlier times had been characteristic of Quaker pedagogy. And those colleges founded by Quakers that are well known for their scholastic achievements, Haverford (1856), Swarthmore (1869), and Bryn Mawr (1885) are today no more Quaker-minded than Harvard is Puritan.

One of the reasons for this process of "secularization" is that with the growing immersion of the Quakers as a "peculiar people" in their surrounding societies, one can hardly speak of "Friends' communities" in the old sense of the term. But it was these communities which supported their schools organizationally and spiritually through their meetings in worship and council. Yet, the more the work of Quakers in regard to schools of their own has decreased, the more their influence on education outside their own group has increased. England's public school system was in a miserable state up to the last decades of the nineteenth century. It was the Quaker Joseph Lancaster who, about 1800, promoted the idea of the education of the poor, not only in England, but also in America; and on Quaker initiative was founded the British and Foreign School Society which showed the colonial peoples of the time that there were whites interested in something more than exploitation. Quakers were influential in the expansion and improvement of the Sunday-school system and in the beginnings of adult education.

When, in the twentieth century, the demon of nationalism devastated a divided world, the Society of Friends, though small in number, had previously acquired a degree of international confidence that permitted it to cross the boundaries of warring peoples and to save hundreds of thousands of hungry and tortured human beings from misery and death. And the Quaker camps of today, assemblying young and old from different continents and races for the work of reconstruction, are certainly places about which George Fox would have conceded that they instruct their members in many things "civil and useful in the creation."

CONCLUDING REMARKS
ON COMENIUS AND THE QUAKERS

There are considerable theological differences between the Moravians on the one side, and the Quakers on the other, especially if one observes their later development. The first were closer to the Lutheran tradition; they were more interested in dogma, and their history has been different. Their movement had rapidly grown in Bohemia and Moravia during the sixteenth century, but was almost destroyed by the victory of the Catholic over the Protestant forces at the Battle of the White Hill in 1620, two years after the beginning of the Thirty Years War. Comenius held the rest together when he published his *Ratio Disciplinae* and collected money for the worshippers, then mostly in Germany. Today the Moravians count less than a hundred thousand members scattered mostly over Europe and America, whereas the Society of Friends, though also small in number (slightly over two hundred thousand) is known all over the world.

Yet, there are also similarities between the Moravian bishop and the founders of the Quakers which, in spite of all the historical changes, have endured. Both were not satisfied with establishments that from their point of view had lost their inner vitality. Both dared brave them, and both went heroically through many years of suffering. Both revealed a mystical trend that connected them more with, say, Master Eckhart than with the fighting dogmatic Churches of the time. Love, in spirit and in action, was to them a surer sign of God's indwelling than doctrinal righteousness. The innermost force that connected them with the divine connected them also with their fellowmen. For—so they thought—the more deeply a person looks into his self as a creation of God, the more he discovers also his unity with all mankind, with its hopes and sorrows, its achievements and failures. The sense of certain universal qualities in all humanity and the world-mindedness that dawns in Comenius and appears more and more clearly in the Quakers did not necessarily come from traveling and comparison, though both the Moravians and the Quakers traveled widely and engaged in missions. Rather it sprang from a fundamental religious experience, just as their advocacy of democratic institutions is less political than religious.

The awareness of a uniting element in life extended over into nature. Not that the Moravians and the Quakers lacked a sense of the all-transcendent majesty of God (the latter received their originally derisive nickname from their ecstatic vision of the divine presence), but, unlike Calvin, neither Comenius nor the founders of the Society of Friends emphasized the radical dualism between God and nature, or between the spirit and the things of the earth. With a primitiveness that would make a modern high school graduate laugh, Comenius commingled material and spiritual light. He constantly confused analogy and causality. Yet, through all his naïveté there shines the image of the ultimate unity of the world. And a reason, not merely pedagogical, caused Comenius to illustrate in his *Orbis Pictus* concepts by concrete objects. For, as one can understand the universe through the contemplation of God, so one can understand it through looking at things. And it was not merely utilitarianism that motivated the Quakers to emphasize the practical arts in their schools. It was the conviction that learning and doing, thinking and building, or the inner and the outer, are but two facets by which God wants man to glorify His creation.

Finally, though both the Moravians and the Quakers laid much stress on Christian conduct—both in their ways were a "peculiar people"—less than many other educators of the time, they used fear and the vision of hell as incentives toward salvation. To be sure, for them too the fall of the first couple was a symbol of the cruel reality of man's sinfulness, but they also believed that the seed of goodness was always waiting in man to be unfolded.

AUGUST HERMANN FRANCKE

The German August Hermann Francke was born in 1663, the same year as Cotton Mather; he died just one year (1727) before his American colleague, whom he had sent a long letter with a most detailed description of his philanthropic work at Halle. Cotton Mather, always fond of writing, published a free translation of the Latin original under the following title: *"Nuncia Bona a Terra Longinqua.* A Brief Account of some Good and Great Things, a doing for the kingdom of God in the midst of Europe." [15]

August Hermann Francke is also in other ways connected with North America. Salzburgers and Moravians who settled in Georgia and Pennsylvania had been trained by him. Count Zinzendorf, Heinrich Melchior Muehlenberg, and Johann Christoph Kunze, who greatly influenced American Protestanism, were Francke's friends.

There is, however, one essential difference between the Mathers and the German Pietists of whom Francke is one of the main representatives. The Mathers were Calvinists and dogmatic theologians, convinced of predestination with all its consequences. Francke belonged to the Lutheran Church which had never worked out a precise theory about unconditional election, though also deeply influenced by the Augustinian interpretation of grace. But like his older friend, Phillipp Jakob Spener (1635–1705), who as pastor in the Lutheran church at Frankfurt am Main had founded the *Collegia Pietatis* (hence the name "Pietist"), Francke was alienated from the Lutheran clergy because of their theology, a product of brains which were erudite but not wise, thorough but not deep, and subtle but uninspiring. Neither as persons nor as preachers did they reach the hearts of the people. But this was exactly Francke's concern. He wanted to educate young ministers toward Christian inwardness which would show itself in an active life with the love and sacrifice of Christ as supreme example. Neither Spener nor Francke were responsible for the sweetish Jesus mysticism of some pietists; the manly and energetic Francke was even still farther away from sentimentality than Spener. He could not have founded his famous orphanage at Halle and developed in connection with it advanced and exemplary schools for boys and girls of the middle classes, had he not been a man of iron will and discipline. He was also one of the first to establish an institution for the training of teachers (*Seminarium Praeceptorum,* 1705); he proved his interest in good teaching and learning also by his insistence on small classes (not more than twenty-two students per teacher), though from 1695 to 1714 his institutions had grown from a small house for neglected and unruly children to 1,675 boys and 700 girls. He also appreciated the value of manual training and scientific experimentation as a means of education.

Of the many writings of Francke [16] we are here interested first in those on the preparation of the clergy and second in those on the Christian education of children.

To the first group belongs his *Idea Theologiae* where he says:

The study of theology should be a culture of the mind by virtue of which, under the guidance of the Holy Spirit and through pious and zealous prayer, it gains an accurate and vivid knowledge of the truth contained in the sacred scriptures and becomes increasingly firmer in this knowledge through assiduous application. The student who has used his study for improvement, true conversion in Jesus Christ, and daily re-creation, will be an example to others through the purity of his doctrine and the gift of his wisdom and thus help them to fight against the tyranny of Satan and for the expansion of the kingdom of God among men.

Similarly, Francke says in his *Thimoteus, Given as an Example to all Students of Theology,*[17]

Theology, rather than being mere erudition and contemplation, should aim at discipline of the will and the affections with the purpose to improve men, not merely to teach them. . . . Why do you study other books more than sacred scripture? They should serve you only as a guide to read the Bible with real profit.

Insistence on discipline is also the main theme of Francke's writings on the Christian education of children. He was an extremely severe disciplinarian, convinced that the evil will, the result of the original sin, had first to be broken before the new man could be born. A Puritan aversion to any kind of pleasure such as dancing, sports, and play reigned in his institutions. Physical exercise could well be had by such useful activities as carrying earth and handiwork; he had thirty lathes in his institutions. There were no free afternoons and Sundays.

The main purpose of all instruction—so Francke says in his main pedagogical work with the title *Brief and Simple Instruction How to Lead Children toward True Piety and Christian Wisdom* [18]—is "the glory of God."

Hence the necessity of good example on the part of teachers and parents and the importance of catechetical instruction.

Truly, children in tender age cannot be induced to learn much by heart and strain their mind. Yet, the fundamentals of Christianity must be taught, however simple and childlike. But this is not enough, otherwise they would rattle off like parrots. Rather they must be trained to be quiet and to break their will ["ihren Willen brechen"]. Also one must endeavor with all possible love, kindness and patience that they open their souls to the influx of the divine spirit which even in little children is not dormant and that they allow the light of divine love and true brotherliness to burn in their hearts.

The following chapters of the *Brief and Simple Instruction* deal with early reading of the Bible, with memorizing, with the necessity of "indefatigable, though gentle" exhortations, with such virtues as truthfulness, obedience, and industry and their contraries, with prayer, and with the avoidance of bad company.

Especially illustrative of Francke's educational ideas is Chapter 16, "On Discipline."

Some people are of the opinion that children should be corrected only through gentle admonition and be saved the rod or other severe means of punishment when words fail to make an impression. But experience, the best teacher, tells us that one cannot totally eliminate the rod especially with children already pampered, older and fortified in their self-will. Severity will be necessary until they have overcome themselves and follow loving guidance without enforcement. But if there is one occasion that more than any requires pondering and understanding on the part of the teacher, then it is punishment. For through untimely punishment the good in children may be more easily suppressed than promoted; they may begin to hate their teachers and even their parents; and they may do everything merely from fear, and become spiteful, mendacious, and perfidious. They may even acquire a strong feeling of distaste against all piety and pious studies, because they feel that they cannot achieve anything without pain and anxiety.

And here is the sentence that may explain to us why Francke, despite all his insistence on "breaking the will," was apparently dearly revered by his pupils.

And it is especially important that all punishment spring from such deep compassion that the children can well feel that one suffers himself while beating them and that one would prefer throwing away all rods and guide with words if the bitter occasion would permit otherwise.[19]

Finally, in Chapter 17, he gives us the *Summa* of his educational wisdom which is essentially the same in all great representatives of the Christian tradition.[20]

In order to educate children so that they preserve true and candid piety up to their old age, teachers as well as parents, yea, all around them, must be conscious of their Christian duty. But, indeed, that requires more than the intelligence of natural man. We need wisdom from above to seek always and everywhere the honor of the Allmighty and the glory of His name. Such wisdom does not deviate but goes the way of righteousness shown to us by the word of God; it tries to understand the great love that he has for the young . . . and it finally knows that man cannot well accomplish such a great work as education out of his own skill and virtue. Rather those endowed with Christian wisdom know that there is no power in him who plants, but the power is in God alone who must bestow his blessing.

The combination of willpower and Christian charity, expressing itself in Francke's personality and work, not only made a deep impression on his contemporaries, but also influenced educational legislation. The ravages of the Thirty Years War (1618–1648) had destroyed many of the educational achievements of the Reformation. Francke, who began his work in a period when half of the German population was still destitute and the peasants remembered the hordes of wild children who had fallen like locusts upon the villages, proved that youths of respected families and orphans could be educated together, and, in his writings, he explained to the German schoolmaster how it could be done.

Frederick William of Prussia and his son, Frederick II, the Great, then introduced the educational legislation through which Prussia became the European example of popular education. Certainly, Frederick the Great was much more an enlightened free thinker than a dogmatic Christian—an attitude which saved him from forcing religious uniformity on his widened territory and especially on the newly conquered, mostly Catholic Silesia. In his domain, so he said, everyone had the right to go to heaven according to his own fashion. On the other hand, he was wise enough to realize the value of Francke's concept of education for training an orderly and obedient citizenry—perhaps too submissive to government and the ruling classes, but industrious, God-fearing, and more literate than most of the people in the other parts of Europe, including France and England.

JOHN WESLEY

On his journey to the German Pietist—also called "Moravian"—community of Herrnhut, near the border between Saxony and Bohemia, John Wesley (1703-1791) tried to meet the son of August Hermann Francke at Halle, though without success. In his Journal he wrote: [21]

> August Hermann Francke whose name is indeed as precious ointment. Oh may I follow him, as he did Christ, and "by manifestation of the truth commend myself to every man's conscience in the sight of God."

Unless they would have had sufficient time to go into details of doctrine, particularly the doctrine of justification, the two men would have understood each other well, for they had much in common. This was partly due to character, and partly to environment.

Probably not only by training, but also by nature both were methodical and gifted organizationally; both combined a profound love for their suffering fellowmen with a talent for leadership; both possessed the kind of energy that increases with the number of obstacles because it was inspired by the feeling of a divine mission; both would have been egotistically self-centered had not their faith in Christ and the Cross instilled in them an absorbing concern for their own and their fellowmen's salvation. There was no good life for them that did

not combine individual and communal responsibility. Thus they became not only theologians and preachers, but also educators and missionaries.

In the development of their character both were supported by
their environment. Though Wesley came from a poverty-stricken par-
sonage with nineteen children—his father had even been in prison for
his debts—and Francke from a comfortable home, both enjoyed in
their early youth the education of exemplary parents and later an
academic training as good as the country could provide. They entered
their professional life with a preparation adequate to their talent. And
when they had arrived at the depth of their faith—which for both was
the same as the depth of their personality—they encountered a clergy
that could not but arouse their opposition. Official Protestantism in Germany had bogged down into a barren intellectualism that was nearer
to medieval Scholasticism in its decay than to the gospel of Luther;
while the Established Church of England, to the ministry of which
Wesley aspired in his youth, was just as void of deeper religious emotion, just as dependent on the state and the ruling classes, and, in
addition, was often morally rotten.[22]

On his voyage to America Wesley traveled with a group of Germans whose God-inspired calm during a dangerous storm convinced
him that they were truly reborn in Christ, whereas he was not, for
he had been afraid of death. When he arrived in America, the searching questions of the Moravian leader Spangenberg made him fear that
in talking about his convictions, the "Spirit of God," and Jesus Christ,
he still used "vain words." [23] In America he began to translate German hymns. And it was his listening to the reading of Luther's Preface to the Romans at a meeting of a "society in Aldersgate Street"
which decidely conrtibuted to his inner transformation.[24]

> I felt my heart strangely warmed. I felt I did trust in Christ,
> Christ alone for salvation, and an assurance was given me
> that He had taken away my sins, even *mine,* and saved *me*
> from the law of sin and death.

And as he had received inspiration from Luther's writings, so also
had his brother and co-worker Charles. Apparently, sometimes a great

man's work that has become stale at home, remains fresh abroad. Also John Bunyan felt that Luther's Commentary on the Galatians was "written out of his own heart." [25]

Thus, in spite of differences and disappointments in detail, German religiosity was closer to Wesley than his own Established Church, which, nevertheless, he never wished to desert. In addition, except when he discovered the "heathen" in a man—which he easily did—he was more tolerant than most of his contemporaries. "I would wish all to observe," so he wrote, "that the points in question between us and either the German or English Antinomians are not points of opinion, but of practice. We break with no man for his opinion. We think, and let think." [26]

Yet, as great as the similarities were between the world of Francke and the world of Wesley, the differences also were great. Francke, living in the turbulent seventeenth century, knew as much about sin, evil, and faithlessness as Wesley, but he addressed a world, or at least he could believe he did so, in which no organized philosophy had yet arisen to oppose the Christian theistic dogma. All that the scientists wanted was to be left alone instead of being burned or thrown into prison. But things were different with Wesley. He had to fight not only a hardened Church, but also a new and dangerous philosophy, namely deism. Locke's *Reasonableness of Christianity, as Delivered in the Scripture* (1695) made a deep impression even on English theologians, and in 1733 Matthew Tindal's *Christianity as Old as the Creation, or, the Gospel a Republication of the Religion of Nature,* the "Bible of Deism," had already gone through its fourth edition. And there could be no doubt that a considerable part of the Christian clergy belonged to the buyers.

The life of Wesley coincided with that of David Hume whom he called "the most insolent despiser of truth and virtue that ever appeared in the world." [27] And when in his journal entry of August 8, 1773, he speaks of certain "menders of the Bible," he accuses them that "hereby they promote the cause of infidelity more effectually than either Hume or Voltaire." [28] In France, Voltaire was busy undermining the authority of the Catholic Church, which Wesley would not have taken amiss had it not got at the very roots of Christianity. Hence

he called the French "philosopher," "a creature" who surprises him
for having given a good word to Pascal's *Thoughts*—otherwise, "certainly, never was a more consummate coxcomb." [29] His animosity
against the French free thinkers transfers even to their language. After
reading Voltaire's *Henriade* and giving him some scanty praise for his
lively writing he continues: "and by him I was more than ever convinced that the French is the poorest, meanest language of Europe;
that it is no more comparable to the German or Spanish than a bag-
pipe is to an organ." [30]

Another great document of the Age of Enlightenment, Montesquieu's *Spirit of Laws* became so popular that Wesley felt compelled
to write a review of it. He was careful in tone and even recommended
"his extremely fine imagination," his high degree of "understanding," his lively style, and his originality. Nevertheless, he could "not
greatly admire him" because in spite of all its virtues, "little less than
half" of the book was

> dry, full unaffecting and unentertaining, at least to all but
> Frenchmen. What have I or any Briton to do with the petty
> changes in the French government? . . . But what I least
> of all admire is, his laying hold on every opportunity to de-
> preciate the inspired writers—Moses in particular. Indeed
> here his ponderance and decency seem to fail him, and he
> speaks of the Jewish lawgiver with as little respect or re-
> serve, as he would of Lycurgus, Romulus, or Numa Pom-
> pilius. [31]

But the abomination of abominations was Rousseau, the author
of *Émile*. [32]

> I read with much expectation a celebrated book—Rousseau
> upon Education. But how I was disappointed! Such a more
> consummate coxcomb never saw the sun! How amazingly
> full of himself! Whatever he speaks he pronounces as ora-
> cle. But many of his oracles are as palpably false as that
> "young children love old people." . . .
>
> But I object to his temper more than to his judgment: He is
> a mere misanthrope; a cynic all over. So indeed is his broth-

er-infidel, Voltaire; and well nigh as great a coxcomb. . . .
Such discoveries I always expect from those who are too
wise to believe their Bibles.

A seventeenth-century divine as August Hermann Francke had
not yet to fight such brazen heretics. But, as already indicated, the
difference is not only one of intellectual, but also of national surround-
ings. As a consequence of the establishment of state churches in Germany, each of them as far as possible coextensive with the realm of a
particular principality, the formation of sects as independent religious
associations had become almost impossible, and at least dangerous.
To be sure, the Moravian Pietists at Herrnhut in Saxony were tolerated,
but on the whole, there was only the alternative between conformity
and emigration. Thus Francke's pietism remained, in spite of all difficulties, within the official Church and could do so all the more because both state and clergy gradually understood the value of
Francke's work. In contrast, Wesley worked within a nation that had
never completely submitted to the claims of government and Church,
that for a long time had been used to free association, had founded
a colonial empire, and had expanded its industry. Thus, England offered much more room to free initiative than the small German principalities could ever do. Consequently, when Wesley finally understood
that the opposition of his Church was unconquerable, he could cir-
cumvent it by the creation of a movement which not only held its
own against political and religious reaction, but which could develop
into the worldwide and democratic Methodist denomination.

There will always be differences of opinion as to the forces that
brought about the change from the England of the Code of Conformity, of profligate kings, and licentious cavaliers to Victorian England.
However hypocritical this Victorian England may have been in some
respects, it had nevertheless come after a profound spiritual, moral,
social, and educational revival. Certainly, political and economic liberation, humanitarian movements, the moral indignation of such men as
Dickens, Carlyle, and Ruskin, and, finally, socialism and the self-
help of labor, worked together. But, when one asks how this transformation could occur without civil war, why neither the ideas of the

French revolution nor Marxism was able to get hold of the minds of the poor, why men such as Lord Shaftesbury, Michael Sadler, William Wilberforce, Robert Raikes, and Lord Dartmouth—to mention only a few—gave their support to the emancipation of the suppressed, and why, finally, even the Established Church had to reform itself, then one will always meet the spirit of the Evangelical revival. This spirit was provided mainly by Wesley and the leaders of the small religious meetings or "classes" where the poor gathered the strength for the peaceful, yet indomitable assertion of their inalienable rights. And the reason for this influence (which, of course, the Baptists shared with the Methodists) lies in the fact that Wesley considered Christianity "essentially a social religion; . . . to turn it into a solitary one"—so he said—"is to destroy it." [33]

Certainly, Wesley agreed with Luther that [34] "neither our faith nor our works justify us, . . . [or] deserve the remission of our sins. But God himself justifies us, of his own mercy, through the merits of his Son only." More than Luther, however, he saw the mark of the Christian in his good works. "But it should also be observed, what faith is, whereby we are justified. Now, that faith which brings not forth good works, is not a living faith, but a dead and devilish one."

It was this conviction that enabled the Methodist to preach in the fields to the colliers of Newcastle, even though, with the connivance of the "gentlemen" and the clergy, they were attacked by an ignorant mob. It was this conviction that enabled them to start their crusade against the slave trade through which many Englishmen of the time grew rich. With the Quakers, the Methodists helped to lay the foundations of popular education and to humanize the penal code. And later they went as itinerant preachers to the frontiersmen of America who otherwise would have been without spiritual help and guidance.

Another comparison, besides that of Francke and the Pietists, urges itself on the historical mind—that with the American Puritans. There was, nevertheless, a decisive doctrinal difference. Calvinism was for Wesley "the very antidote of Methodism"—he spoke of it as of "the most deadly and successful enemy which I ever had." [35] However, Wesley's journal and the Puritan diaries reveal the same tendency toward introspection, the same sometimes blasphemic propensity to see the finger of God even in the most trivial event, and the same anxiety about one's heavenly ledger. But whatever one thinks about their creed, without it they would not have achieved what they did achieve.

Compared with his gigantic work of reform, Wesley's writings on education proper are merely illustrations of a greater scheme. When, in 1748, he opened Kingswood School, he gave it severe regulations, of a kind that could also have been drawn by August Hermann Francke.[36]

His letters and sermons are full of educational suggestions; he wrote several essays on the right upbringing of youth, and insisted on daily self-examination, for which he gave elaborate rules. The aim of education is for Wesley "Christian Perfection." This term is central in Wesley's theology, and one for which he was frequently attacked by the orthodox clergy. In his "Letter to the Lord Bishop of London," [37] who had accused the Methodists and Moravians of "shameful disturbance to the parochial clergy," of seducing the "lowest and most ignorant of the people by pretences to greater sanctity," Wesley writes: [38]

> To the charge of holding "sinless perfection," as your Lordship states it, I might likewise plead, Not guilty; seeing one ingredient thereof, in your Lordship's account, is freedom from temptation, Whereas I believe, "there is no such perfection in this life, as implies an entire deliverance from manifold temptations." But I will not decline the charge. I will repeat once more my coolest thoughts upon this head; and that in the very terms which I did several years ago, as I presume your Lordship cannot be ignorant.

> What, it may be asked, do you mean by "one that is perfect," or, "one that is as his Master?" We mean one in whom is "the mind which was Christ," and who "so walketh as He walked;" a man that "hath clean hands and a pure heart;" or that is "cleansed from all filthiness of flesh and spirit;" one "in whom there is no occasion of stumbling," and who, accordingly "doth not commit sin." To declare this a little more particularly: We understand by that scriptural expression, "a perfect man," one in whom God

hath fulfilled his faithful word: "From all your filthiness, and from all your idols will I cleanse you. I will also save you from all your uncleanness." We understand hereby, one whom God hath sanctified throughout, even in "body, soul, and spirit;" one who "walketh in the light, as He is in the light," in whom "is no darkness at all;" the blood of Jesus Christ his Son, having "cleansed him from all sin."

In order to achieve the state of perfection, education has to begin early in order to "break" the otherwise rampant self-will of the child; i.e., he has to learn Christian meekness, humility and self-denial. Example, especially of parents and teachers, is of utmost importance, and so is perseverance and continual self-examination, not only of one's conscience, but also of one's deeds and relations to his fellowmen.

We reprint here from "A Collection of Forms of Prayer for Every Day in the Week" the "Sunday Evening General Questions which a serious Christian may propose to himself before he begins his Evening Devotion." [39] (Similar questions are proposed for every other day in the week.)

Sunday Evening

General Questions which a serious Christian may propose to himself, before he begins his Evening Devotion.

1. With what degree of attention and fervour did I use my morning prayers, public or private?

2. Have I done any thing without a present, or at least a previous, perception of its direct or remote tendency to the glory of God?

3. Did I in the morning consider what particular virtue I was to exercise, and what business I had to do in the day?

4. Have I been zealous to undertake, and active in doing what good I could?

5. Have I interested myself any farther in the affairs of others, than charity required?

6. Have I, before I visited, or was visited, considered how I might thereby give or receive the improvement?

7. Have I mentioned any failing or fault of any man, when it was not necessary for the good of another?

8. Have I unnecessarily grieved any one by word or deed?

9. Have I before, or in every action considered how it might be a means of improving in the virtue of the day?

From the several essays on the education of children we reprint in part Wesley's "Thoughts on the Manner of Educating Children." [40]

1. A GENTLEMAN with whom I was conversing a while ago, was speaking largely on the manner of educating children. He objected strongly to the bringing them up too strictly; to the giving them more of religion than they liked; to the telling them of it too often, or pressing it upon them whether they will or not. . . .

2. As all this was perfectly new to me, I made little answer for the present; but it put me upon much thought. I knew it was quite agreeable to the sentiments of Rousseau, in his "Emilius," the most empty, silly, injudicious thing that ever a self-conceited infidel wrote. But I knew it was quite contrary to the judgment of the wisest and best men I have known. I thought, If these things are so, how much mischief have we done unawares! . . .

4. Yet I allow that what is commonly called a religious education frequently does more hurt than good; and that many of the persons who were so educated are sinners above other men, yea, and have contracted an enmity to religion, which usually continues all their lives. And this will naturally be the case, if either the religion wherein they are instructed, or the manner of instructing them, be wrong. But in most of those that are termed religious schools, there is a grand error either in the former or the latter instance.

5. With regard to the former, how few are there of those that undertake the education of children, who understand the

nature of religion, who know what true religion is! For they think they have religion, when, indeed, they have none at all; and so add pride to all their other vices.

8. In the name of God, then, and by the authority of His word, let all that have children, from the time they begin to speak or run alone, begin to train them up in the way wherein they should go; to counter-work the corruption of their nature with all possible assiduity; to do everything in their power to cure self-will, pride, and every other wrong temper. Then let them be delivered to instructors (if such can be found) that will tread in the same steps; that will watch over them as immortal spirits, who are shortly to appear before God, and who have nothing to do in this world but to prepare to meet Him in the clouds, seeing they will be eternally happy, if they are ready; if not, eternally miserable.

CONCLUDING REMARKS ON
FRANCKE AND WESLEY

Passing from the thought of Comenius and the Quakers with its wide spiritual horizons to that of Francke and Wesley, one feels as if looking along a narrowing avenue. To be sure, both were far above the typical clergyman of the time and disappointed in the ruling orthodoxy, and they had the courage to support their conscience with action. But we miss in them the profound curiosity that drove Comenius to search for the unity of religion, science, and education as an expression of the inner unity of the creation, and we miss also the broad vision of humanity which made the Quakers the symbol of a spirit that reached above the boundaries of religious institutions and the ideologies of warring nations.

As a result of the Protestant situation in Germany, the pietism of Francke and his friends became absorbed (or should we say diluted) by the Protestant state church, just as the original religious socialism of Johann Hinrich Wichern (1808–1881) became integrated into the Prussian form of religious and political conservatism. However, as

Wichern's Inner Mission remained, so also there remained Francke's example as a father of youth, a teacher of teachers, and a guide of conscientious theologians. Thus, in regard to religious education and educational philanthropy Francke was on the German side what Francis de la Salle was on the French side, though the possibility of founding a religious order gave the Catholic a far wider influence than the Protestant.

In this respect, Wesley was favored by the lesser degree of ecclesiastical centralization and, as a consequence, the greater degree of organized dissent that prevailed in England. When the Established Church remained hostile to his way of interpreting and preaching the gospel, he was able to give institutional form to his movement and thus start one of the most influential forces in Protestantism. His work and its effect on his nation and the North American States may be used as an illustration of the great advantage enjoyed by those countries which have successfully resisted the monopolistic ambitions of a state church. For in these countries room is left for a continuous reinvigoration of the religious spirit and for the possibility of holding under its influence social classes that otherwise would have expressed their opposition to the ruling system not only by political action, but through a total alienation from the religious tradition represented by this system.

Paradoxically as it may seem, decentralization and the chance for organized dissent not only in matters political, but also in matters religious has kept the people and these nations spiritually together. There have always been sects which, despite all differences in worship, expressed the Christian idea of brotherhood and human dignity. In contrast, the countries of the continent, both Catholic and Protestant, have, up to this day, not yet recovered from the fact that the politically and socially dissatisfied found themselves too often opposed by a united front of Church and political conservatism. Violent revolutions and the communism of today have resulted from this situation.

Chapter **10**

The Disintegration of the Christian Dogma (Bacon, Hobbes, and Spinoza)

One may well ask what this chapter, which leads us back to the period before Wesley and deals with the ideas of Francis Bacon (1561–1626) Thomas Hobbes (1588–1679), and Baruch Spinoza (1632–1677), has to do with religious education, for none of these men was specifically concerned with it. Yet, they, or—to say it better—the movements to which they gave expression, influenced the concept of the role of religion and of religious education more than the theologians of the time. The questions they asked were not entirely new. In a groping form they had already been asked by the scholastics of the late Middle Ages, and they had been sharpened with the appearance of men such as Machiavelli, Copernicus, and Galileo.[1] What should be the relation between the Church, faith and Christian ethics on the one hand, and society, the state and politics on the other? How can science and religion be brought into harmony? How can the various Christian denominations—to take over modern political terms—live in "peaceful coexistence" rather than in the state of "hot" or "cold" war? After the Renaissance the old problems received new urgency as a result of the development of empirical research and the new social order caused by the Reformation and by the rise of nationalist societies.

In order to illustrate the new state of Western mentality historians refer rightly to the work of Francis Bacon. He never attacked the dogma of his Church. For this he was too prudent; in addition, as his *Confession of Faith* and *Meditationes Sacrae* reveal, he had, in himself, a mystical strain and believed truly in the revelation. But certainly, the critical reader of his time could not help thinking of the credulity of the people and of the doctrinarism and quarrelsomeness of the theologians when he read the following paragraph of the *Instauratio Magna* [2]

> Man, as the minister and interpreter of nature, does and understands as much as his observations on the order of nature, either with regard to things or the mind, permit him, and neither knows nor is capable of more.

Bacon also spoke, in the *Novum Organon,* of the "idols of the human mind" in contrast to "ideas of the divine," [3] the idols being the "Idols of the Tribe," the "Idols of the Cave," the "Idols of the Marketplace," and the "Idols of the Theater."

More directly than Bacon, did Thomas Hobbes's *Leviathan* hit the central scheme of the Gospel, the necessity of divine grace and the superiority of man's relation to God over all other interests and concerns.

Thomas Hobbes has become one of the most controversial figures in the history of European philosophy, not only because of the aversions his works evoked in men of his and later epochs, but also because of the ambiguities in his own thinking. However, historians consider him one of the founders of the theory of human society as a scientific discipline, and this scientific bent is certainly due to the fascination mathematics exercised upon his mind.

When a thinker attempts to make "science," in the exclusive sense of an empirical discipline, the instrument for the understanding of humanity, he will incline toward a naturalistic and deterministic interpretation of man and society. His sociology will be an analysis of horizontal human relations; it will not have the vertical component that interprets man as related to a divine depth and height of existence.

As we can see from certain developments in the modern social, or "behavioral" sciences, society then becomes its own measure. Ethics loses its roots in the older religious and metaphysical foundations, and, since ethics is a determining factor in education, education too becomes, as we say, "secular." For the seventeenth and eighteenth centuries it was a concrete question: Should the clergy maintain the right to direct the course of education, to determine what a person had to believe, and in which faith the children were to be brought up, or should the state become the guardian of society and its schools? If confronted with different denominations as in the United States, should it leave matters spiritual to the individual's own decision? If not always in theory, at least in practice the European Churches became increasingly dependent upon the government. When the two forces conflicted and trouble arose, the end was generally compromise. This situation was already prepared during the Reformation when both faiths, Catholic and Protestant, needed the protection of the princes. But more than anyone else Hobbes provided the systematic and un-abashed theory for the dogma of *cuius regio, eius religio.*

There are few chapters in the history of great literature where one can find so much equivocation as in the following extracts from Thomas Hobbes's *The Leviathan, or the Matter, Form and Power of a Commonwealth, Ecclesiastical and Civil.*[4] There, he equates the law of nature with the law of God, and sees both incorporated in and most efficiently guaranteed by the government of the country. Hence— so he says—it is the supreme duty of the Christian to obey the com-mand of his sovereign, for thus he proves the essential identity of the secular and divine order. Inevitably, this theory renders the mon-arch absolute, even in matters of conscience. What more did the abso-lutist princes of Europe need as a moral support for their control of the minds and especially of religious education?

> There can, therefore, be no contradiction between the Laws of God and the Laws of a Christian Commonwealth. And when the Civil Sovereign is an Infidel, everyone of his own subjects that resisteth him sinneth against the Laws of God (for such are the Laws of Nature).

There are certain similarities between Thomas Hobbes and Ba-ruch Spinoza, born in 1632, almost half a century after the English-man. Both were influenced by their study of mathematics and tried to apply their conception of the "scientific method" to speculation; Spinoza believed he had developed his *Ethics* *"more mathematico."* Each of them has been named by different historians "the father of political philosophy." Both can somehow be classified as "naturalists" and both understood the necessity of power for the orderly regulation of human affairs. But, whereas Hobbes interpreted nature and man in a prevailingly materialistic sense, for Spinoza they were the embodiments of the divine principle. And whereas, for Hobbes government meant might, for Spinoza it meant the securing of liberty.[5] Both were opposed to the tyranny of the churches and their dogmas, and it was mainly for this reason that they looked for the help of governments. Hobbes wished to replace ecclesiastical tyranny by state absolutism—religion as the most intimate inner experience may not have interested him. To Spinoza any authority was objectionable that arrogated to itself the right to control the piety of men and the liberty of thought. Hobbes, living during and after the Thirty Years War that broke the last vestiges of medieval universalism of Church and empire, realistically acknowledged the plurality of sovereign and state systems and their official religions; but he was not, like Spinoza, a believer in pluralism, or in tolerance as a value in itself. He certainly was an eminent thinker, but evokes in us no feeling of warmth, whereas one can hardly learn about Spinoza's life and read his works without a profound feeling of sympathy and admiration. Hobbes was not a liberator, but Spinoza was, because to the horror of the theological world he saw the Bible as a historical document and thus broke the chains of biblical literalism; he also bridged the gap between the "natural" and the "supernatural" and thus—like the Stoic philosophers at the time of Christ—attributed to the world the quality of cosmic unity. For this reason he could become the inspirer of poets, among them Goethe, of liberal theologians, such as Schleiermacher, and of idealist philosophers, such as Schelling, whose thought was a formative element in the world view of Ralph Waldo Emerson in America, and, to a larger degree, of existentialism in Europe.

We reprint here the title and the Preface of one of the wisest and most courageous works ever written, Spinoza's *Tractatus Theologico-Politicus.*[6] So far as I know there occurs here, in the title, for the first time the phrase *"Libertas philosophandi"* (freedom of thought) which has become the central concept in the never ending struggle of the universities for unfettered research and teaching.

A Theologico-Political Treatise Containing Certain Discussions

Wherein is set forth that freedom of thought and speech not only may without prejudice to piety and the public peace, be granted; but also may not, without danger to piety and the public peace, be withheld.

Hereby know we that we dwell in Him and He in us, because He has given us of His spirit.

Men would never be superstitious, if they could govern all their circumstances by set rules, or if they were always favoured by fortune: but being frequently driven into straits where rules are useless, and being often kept fluctuating pitiably between hope and fear by the uncertainty of fortune's greedily coveted favours, they are consequently, for the most part, very prone to credulity. The human mind is readily swerved this way or that in times of doubt, especially when hope and fear are struggling for the mastery, though usually it is boastful, over-confident, and vain.

This as a general fact I suppose everyone knows, though few, I believe know their own nature; no one can have lived in the world without observing that most people, when in prosperity, are so over-brimming with wisdom (however inexperienced they may be), that they take every offer of advise as a personal insult, whereas in adversity they know not where to turn, but beg and pray for counsel from every passer-by. No plan is then too futile, too absurd, or too fatuous for their adoption; the most frivolous causes will raise them to hope, or plunge them into despair.

Thus it is brought prominently before us, that superstition's chief victims are those persons who greedily covet temporal advantages; they it is, who (especially when they are in danger, and cannot help themselves) are wont with prayers

and womanish tears to implore help from God: upbraiding
Reason as blind, because she cannot show a sure path to the
shadows they pursue, and rejecting human wisdom as vain;
but believing the phantoms of imagination, dreams, and other
childish absurdities, to be the very oracles of Heaven. As
though God had turned away from the wise, and written his
decrees not in the mind of man, but in the entrails of beasts,
or left them to be proclaimed by the inspiration and instinct
of fools, madmen, and birds. Such is the unreason to which
terror can give mankind! . . .

I have often wondered, that persons who make a boast of pro-
fessing the Christian religion, namely, love, joy, peace, temperance, and charity to all men, should quarrel with such
rancorous animosity, and display daily towards one another
such bitter hatred, that this, rather than the virtues they claim,
is the readiest criterion of their faith. Matters have long since
come to such a pass, that one can only pronounce a man
Christian, Turk, Jew, or Heathen, by his general appearance
and attire, by his frequenting this or that place of worship,
or employing the phraseology of a particular sect—as for
manner of life, it is in all cases the same. Inquiry into the cause
of this anomaly leads me unhesitatingly to ascribe it to the
fact, that the ministries of the Church are regarded by the
masses merely as dignities, her offices as posts of emblement
—in short, popular religion may be summed up as respect
for ecclesiastics. The spread of this misconception inflamed
every worthless fellow with an intense desire to enter holy
orders, and thus the love of diffusing God's religion degenerated into sordid avarice and ambition. Every church became
a theatre, where orators, instead of church teachers, ha-
rangued, caring not to instruct the people, but striving to attract admiration, to bring opponents to public scorn, and to
preach only novelties and paradoxes, such as would tickle
the ears of their congregation. This state of things necessarily
stirred up an amount of controversy, envy, and hatred, which
no lapse of time could appease; so that we can scarcely wonder that of the old religion nothing survives but its outward
forms (even these, in the mouth of the multitude, seem rather
adulation than adoration of the Deity), and that faith has
become a mere compound of credulity and prejudices—aye,

prejudices too, which degrade man from rational being to beast, which completely stifle the power of judgment between true and false, which seem, in fact, carefully fostered for the purpose of extinguishing the last spark of reason!

As I pondered over the facts that the light of reason is not only despised, but by many even execrated as a source of impiety, that human commentaries are accepted as divine records, and that credulity is extolled as faith; as I marked the fierce controversies of philosophers raging in Church and State, the source of bitter hatred and dissension, the ready instruments of sedition and other ills innumerable, I determined to examine the Bible afresh in a careful, impartial, and unfettered spirit, making no assumptions concerning it, and attributing to it no doctrines, which I do not find clearly therein set down. With these precautions I constructed a method of Scriptural interpretation, and thus equipped proceeded to inquire—What is prophecy? in what sense did God reveal Himself to the prophets, and why were these particular men chosen by Him? Was it on account of the sublimity of their thoughts about the Deity and nature, or was it solely on account of their piety? These questions being answered, I was easily able to conclude, that the authority of the prophets has weight only in matters of morality, and that their speculative doctrines affect us little.

Next I inquired, why the Hebrews were called God's chosen people, and discovering that it was only because God had chosen for them a certain strip of territory, where they might live peaceably and at ease, I learnt that the Law revealed by God to Moses was merely the law of the individual Hebrew State, therefore that it was binding on none but Hebrews, and not even on Hebrews after the downfall of their nation. Further, in order to ascertain, whether it could be concluded from Scripture, that the human understanding is naturally corrupt, I inquired whether the Universal Religion, the Divine Law revealed through the Prophets and Apostles to the whole human race, differs from that which is taught by the light of natural reason, whether miracles can take place in violation of the laws of nature, and if so, whether they imply the existence of God more surely and clearly than events, which we understand plainly and distinctly through their immediate natural causes.

Now, as in the whole course of my investigation I found nothing taught expressly by Scripture, which does not agree with our understanding, or which is repugnant thereto, and as I saw that the prophets taught nothing, which is not very simply and easily to be grasped by all, and further, that they clothed their teaching in the style, and confirmed it with the reasons, which would most deeply move the mind of the masses to devotion towards God, I became thoroughly convinced, that the Bible leaves reason absolutely free, that it has nothing in common with philosophy, in fact, that Revelation and Philosophy stand on totally different footings.

Furthermore, as man's habits of mind differ, so that some more readily embrace one form of faith, some another, for what one moves one to pray may move another only to scoff, I conclude, in accordance with what has gone before, that everyone should be free to choose for himself the foundation of his creed, and that faith should be judged only by its fruits; each would then obey God freely with his own heart, while nothing would be publicly honored save justice and charity. . . .

In order to establish my point, I start from the natural rights of the individual, which are co-extensive with his desires and power, and from the fact that no one is bound to live as another pleases, but is the guardian of his own liberty. I show that these rights can only be transferred to those whom we depute to defend us, who acquire with the duties of defence the power of ordering our lives, and I thence infer that rulers possess rights only limited by their power, that they are the sole guardians of justice and liberty, and that their subjects should act in all things as they dictate; nevertheless, since no one can so utterly abdicate his own power of self-defence as to cease to be a man, I conclude that no one can be deprived of his natural rights absolutely, but that subjects, either by tacit agreement, or by social contract, retain a certain number, which cannot be taken from them without great danger to the state. . . .

Chapter 11

The Enlightenment and the Idea of Tolerance

One never feels so much the inadequacy of generalizations as when one is trying to press the work of great minds into general, historical and philosophical categories. Neither Bacon, Hobbes, or Spinoza, living between 1561 and 1677, belong to the "Enlightenment," or the era of "Rationalism," its main representatives being *"les philosophes"* of France (Voltaire, Diderot, Condorcet), or Hume of England, or *die Aufklärer* of Germany (Wolff, Nicolai), all living in the eighteenth century. Yet, without the first the latter could not have created the body of critical ideas that distinguished the political, intellectual and religious temper of the era after 1750 from that of earlier times.

The first characteristic of the new era was a supreme confidence in the power of human reason; the second was the victory of the inductive-empirical approach in scholarly research; the third was the intense speculation about the validity of the methods which reason uses for the understanding of reality; the fourth was the tendency to compare different cultures, the knowledge of which was spread by explorers, travelers, and by missionaries to foreign continents; the fifth was the fight against the tyranny of superstitions, especially the burning of heretics and witches; and the sixth characteristic of the Enlightenment was the application of the concept of freedom against obsolete systems of government, generally supported by the clergy.

Together with this new spirit of inquiry and comparison, of anti-dogmatism and antiobscurantism in matters of religion and politics, there developed the idea of tolerance. One learned about the depth and dignity of the non-Christian religions and ways of life, and became tired of the endless controversies of theologians about problems beyond the reach of plausible argument. Wise men understood that if there is one attitude that leads away from, rather than toward truth, it is the conviction that no one else has the truth but oneself.

Not that orthodoxy in thought and religion was definitely broken. We have it still today. But during the eighteenth century there appeared, or reappeared, too many heretical opinions to be suppressed by fire and sword; atheism, materialism, naturalism, pantheism, cynicism, sensualism, deism and its inevitable companion, "natural religion." Almost every one of the present-day "isms" already existed or emerged during the Enlightenment.

Had there not been the resistance of the European Churches against scientific and social progress, and, as a reaction to it, the sometimes blind hatred of the rationalists, there might have been possible an organic transition from the old to the new forms of man's understanding of himself and the universe. England, as a matter of fact, almost succeeded. But as things stood, the opponents stiffened. While people still lived under the shadow of the French revolution and read the anti-Christian works of Voltaire and de Volney, Châteaubriand published his romantic *Génie du Christianisme* and the Jesuit Order, dissolved by Pope Clemens XIV in 1773 at the request of the Catholic courts of Europe, returned in 1814 to take up the work of religious mission and propaganda. Everywhere the clergy tried to consolidate its strength by new alliances with the governments of Europe which, after the defeat of Napoleon, rapidly forgot that only with the help and sacrifice of the people had they rid themselves of the conqueror. As in earlier times, the governments of Europe used the public school as a medium for religious and political indoctrination; with every major political change teachers and pupils were subjected either to the claims of conservative-ecclesiastical, or of liberal-secular parties. Even in countries where church and state were separated, as in the United States as a consequence of the Constitution, and in France since 1905, or where, as in Belgium, the state equally supports public as well as "private" (i.e., mostly Catholic) schools, the conflicts have not ended.

However, though this situation of permanent controversy is unpleasant, it is also a sign of the fact that the Western nations accept cultural pluralism as the best way of living and are no longer willing to tolerate the one-sided influence of one particular creed on the political and spiritual decisions of the young and their parents—except in dictatorial countries such as Spain and Portugal, or in a prevailingly Catholic country as Italy with its strange contrast between a liberal constitution and the rule of the clergy over the schools. But in spite of all disappointments, modern man shows a greater tolerance with regard to differences of serious opinions than people of earlier times, and this is, to a large degree, the result of the Enlightenment, whatever its shortcomings in other respects.

To illustrate the kind of mentality against which the leaders of the Enlightenment directed their attacks, we need not refer to the cases of obscurantism and ecclesiastical injustice still frequent in the eighteenth century, but can quote from the works of so highly educated a person as John Wesley who, as we have seen, was regarded as an undesirable reformer by his own colleagues.

Like many other divines he did not wish to avoid truth. He just was prevented from seeing it by his literal belief in the Bible. In his way, he was even interested in science; electricity especially attracted his attention. In an amateurish fashion he recommended it for medical use. He also read books on science [1] though he selected those by clergymen who confirmed his own point of view. On October 9, 1765, he wrote: [2]

> I read Mr. Jones' ingenious *Essay on the Principles of Natural Philosophy*. He seems to have totally overthrown the Newtonian principles, but whether he can establish the Hutchinsonian is another question.

Certainly, Comenius, born more than a hundred years before Wesley, had a warmer relation to science than the Englishman who lived close to the great member of the Royal Society. As we have seen, the Moravian bishop failed to understand scientific procedure; nevertheless, he had a vision of its greatness, and he tried to profit from it. In contrast, three decades after Newton's death, Wesley was still so confused about the law of causality that in one essay, he—together with many other clergymen—ascribed the great earthquake of Lisbon on August 15th, 1765, to the wrath of God over the immorality of the Portuguese people, especially the supposed avarice of its king and the wealthy. He also gave as a cause of the Lisbon catastrophe "that scandal not only of all religion, but even of human nature," the Catholic Inquisition,[3] as if divine justice could have been interested in destroying the houses of the poorest of the Portuguese who lived near the harbor, while the wealthy, who lived higher up, mostly survived.[4]

That which Wesley hoped to achieve by leading men back to the Bible, the men of the Enlightenment hoped to accomplish by leading people to clear thinking and by providing better schools and, through them, a better understanding of nature and the nature of the child. The general condition of the mind they asked for was, besides the appreciation of free inquiry, already demanded by Spinoza, the attitude of respect for other people's serious opinion.

John Locke (1632–1704), to whom the fathers of the American Constitution felt deeply indebted, emphasized, in the *Letter concerning Toleration* (1666), that people learn to distinguish "exactly the business of civil government from that of religion, and to settle the just bonds that lie between one and the other." This letter is of such admirable quality and clarity that there is no reason for further comment.[5]

A Letter Concerning Toleration

The toleration of those who differ from others in matters of religion, is so agreeable to the gospel of Jesus Christ, and to the genuine reason of mankind, that it seems monstrous to man to be so blind, as not to perceive the necessity and advantage of it, in so clear a light. . . .

I esteem it above all things necessary to distinguish exactly the business of civil government from that of religion, and to settle the just bounds that lie between the one and the other. If this be not done, there can be no end put to the controversies that will be always arising between those that have, or at least pretend to have, on the one side, a concernment for the interest of men's souls, and, on the other side, a care of the commonwealth.

The commonwealth seems to be a society of men constituted only for the procuring, preserving, and advancing their own civil interests.

Civil interest I call life, liberty, health, and indolency of body; and the possession of outward things, such as money, lands, houses, furniture, and the like.

It is the duty of the civil magistrate, by the impartial execution of equal laws, to secure unto all the people in general, and to every one of his subjects in particular, the just possession of these things belonging to this life. . . .

Now that the whole jurisdiction of the magistrate reaches only to these civil concernments; and that all civil power, right, and dominion, is bounded and confined to the only care of promoting these things; and that it neither can nor ought in any manner to be extended to the salvation of souls; these following considerations seem unto me abundantly to demonstrate.

First, because the care of souls is not committed to the civil magistrate, any more than to other men. It is not committed unto him, I say, by God; because it appears not that God has ever given any such authority to one man over another, as to compel any one to his religion. . . . All the life and power of true religion consists in the inward and full persuasion of the mind; and faith is not faith without believing. . . .

In the third place, the care of the salvation of men's souls cannot belong to the magistrate; because, though the rigour of laws and the force of penalties were capable to convince and change men's minds, yet would not that help at all to the salvation of their souls. For, there being but one truth, one way to heaven, what hopes is there that more men would be led into it, if they had no other rule to follow but the religion of the court, and were put under a necessity to quit the light of their own reason, to oppose the dictates of their own consciences, and blindly to resign up themselves to the will of their governors, and to the religion which either ignorance, ambition, or superstition had chanced to establish in the countries where they were born? In the variety and contradiction of opinions in religion, wherein the princes of the world are as much divided as in their secular interests, the narrow way would be much straitened; one country alone would be in the right, and all the rest of the world put under an obligation of following their princes in the ways that lead to destruction: and that which heightens the absurdity, and very ill suits the notion of a deity, men would owe their eternal happiness or misery to the places of their nativity.

These considerations, to omit many others that might have been urged to the same purpose, seem unto me sufficient to conclude, that all the power of civil government relates only to men's civil interests, is confined to the care of the things of this world, and hath nothing to do with the world to come.

Whereas the Englishman Locke could write about tolerance without danger of imprisonment—though not without controversy—it was dangerous for a Frenchman to speak frankly about this topic. Therefore Montesquieu (1689-1755), known as the author of one of the greatest books of the eighteenth century, *The Spirit of Law* (*L'Esprit des Lois*), which greatly influenced Jefferson, preferred to express his aversion to the foolish political, social, and ecclestiastical conventions of his time in the guise of fictitious letters written by Persian travellers in Europe, *Persian Letters* (*Lettres Persanes*), printed anonymously in Amsterdam, 1721. Montesquieu was the friend of many of the enlightened men of his time and close to some of the *philosophes* and contributors to the famous *Encyclopédie*, which more than any other work of the eighteenth century spread the gospel of rationalism and utility.

The *Persian Letters,* immediately widely read, are in some ways comparable to Erasmus' *Praise of Folly,* but, in comparing the Christian with a foreign culture, they reveal the spirit of the Enlightenment. One short quotation will suffice to reveal the tenor of the work.[6]

USBEK TO RHEDI, AT VENICE

I meet here certain people who are never done discussing religion, but who seem at the same time to contend as to whom shall observe it least.

These disputants are, however, no better Christians, nor even better citizens, than others; and that is what moves me; for the principal part of any religion consists in obedience to the laws, in loving mankind, and in revering one's parents.

Indeed, ought it not be the chief aim of a religious man to please the Deity who has founded the religion which he professes? But the surest way to please God is, without doubt, to obey the laws of society, and do our duty towards men. For, whatever religion we may profess, as soon as we grant its existence, it becomes at once necessary to assume that God loves men, since He establishes a religion for their happiness: then, since He loves men, we are certain of pleasing Him in loving them too—in other words, in fulfilling all the duties of charity and humanity, and in breaking none of the laws under which men live.

We are much more certain of pleasing God in this way, than in the observance of this or that ceremony; for ceremonies have no goodness in themselves; they are only relatively good, and on the supposition that God has commanded them. But this is a subject which might be discussed endlessly; and one could easily deceive oneself regarding it, because it is necessary to choose the rites of one religion from among those of two thousand.

A man prayed to God daily in the following terms: "Lord, I do not understand any of those discussions that are carried on without end regarding Thee: I would serve Thee according to Thy will; but each man whom I consult would have me serve Thee according to his. When I desire to pray, I know not in which language to address Thee. Nor do I know what posture to adopt: one bids me pray standing; another, sitting; and another requires me to kneel. That is not all: there are some who insist that I ought to wash every morning in cold water; others maintain that Thou regardest me with horror if I do not remove a certain small portion of my flesh. I happened the other day to eat of a rabbit in a caravansary; three men who were present made me tremble: all three maintained that I had grievously offended Thee; one, (a Jew) because that animal was unclean; another (a Turk) because it had been strangled; and the third (an Armenian) because it was not a fish. A Brahmin who was passing by, and whom I asked to be our judge, said to me, "They are all wrong, for it appears that you did not kill the animal yourself." "I did, though," said I. "Ah, then, you have committed an abominable act which God will never pardon," said he to me, in a severe tone. "How do you know that the soul of your father had not passed into that beast?" All these things, O Lord, trouble me beyond expression. I cannot move my head but I am threatened with Thy wrath. Nevertheless, I would please Thee and devote to that end the life which Thou hast given me. I may be deceiving myself, but I think that the best means to accomplish this aim is to live as a good citizen in the society where Thou hast placed me, and as a good father in the family which Thou hast given me. (Letter XLVI)

Poetry joined the philosophers and satirists in the battle for a more universal concept of religion. Lessing (1729–1781), the German poet and philosopher, pictured in his drama, *Nathan the Wise* (*Nathan der Weise*), the Jew Nathan as the reconciling element between the Mohammedan Saladin and the Christian crusaders. *Nathan the Wise* is the reflection of Lessing's conflicts with Protestant orthodoxy allied with absolutist government. When the poet was ordered to discontinue the controversy and his *Fragments* were confiscated, he decided to see "whether they would let him preach undisturbed from his old pulpit, the stage." [7] *Nathan the Wise* [8] was one of the most often performed plays on the German stage until the National-socialists did what the absolutist princes had not dared to; they banned it from the theatre and, of course, from the schools, where it had been widely read.

ACT THIRD

Scene VII

Saladin and Nathan

SALADIN

I'm not returned too soon for you, I hope;
You've brought your meditations to a close?
Speak then; no soul can hear us.

NATHAN

              I am willing
The world should hear us.

SALADIN

              Nathan is so sure
Of his good cause? Ah, that I call a sage;
Never to hide the truth; to take on it
Your all; your soul and body, goods and life.

NATHAN

When necessary it shall be, and useful.

SALADIN

With right I hope henceforth to bear my title,
Reformer of the world and of the law.

NATHAN

A noble title certainly. Yet, Sultan,
Ere I bestow my perfect confidence,
Permit me to relate a story to you.

SALADIN

Why not? I ever had been fond of stories
Well told.

NATHAN

The telling well I do not promise.

SALADIN

Again so proudly modest!—Come, your story!

NATHAN

In gray antiquity there lived a man
In Eastern lands, who had received a ring
Of priceless worth from a beloved hand.
Its stone, an opal, flashed a hundred colors,
And had the secret power of giving favor,
In sight of God and man, to him who wore it
With a believing heart. What wonder then

This Eastern man would never put the ring
From off his finger, and should so provide
That to his house it be preserved forever?
Such was the case. Unto the best-beloved
Among his sons he left the ring, enjoining
That he in turn bequeath it to the son
Who should be dearest; and the dearest ever,
In virtue of the ring, without regard
To birth, be of the house the prince and head.
You understand me, Sultan?

SALADIN

Yes; go on.

NATHAN

From son to son the ring descending, came
To one, the sire of three; of whom all three
Were equally obedient; whom all three
He therefore must with equal love regard.
And yet from time to time now this, now that,
And now the third,—as each alone was by,
The others not dividing his fond heart,—
Appeared to him the worthiest of the ring;
Which then, with loving weakness, he would promise
To each in turn. Thus it continued long.
But he must die; and then the loving father
Was sore perplexed. It grieved him thus to wound
Two faithful sons who trusted in his word;
But what to do? In secrecy he calls
An artist to him, and commands of him
Two other rings, the pattern of his own;
And bids him neither cost nor pains to spare
To make them like, precisely like to that.
The artist's skill succeeds. He brings the rings,
And e'en the father cannot tell his own.
Relieved and joyful, summons he his sons,
Each by himself; to each one by himself
He gives his blessing; and his ring—and dies.—
You listen, Sultan?

SALADIN
(who, somewhat perplexed, has turned away)
Yes; I hear, I hear.
But bring your story to an end.

NATHAN

'Tis ended:
For what remains would tell itself. The father
Was scarcely dead, when each brings forth his ring
And claims the headship. Questioning ensues,
Strife, and appeal to law; but all in vain.
The genuine ring was not to be distinguished;—
    (*After a pause, in which he awaits the Sultan's answer*)
As undistinguishable as with us
The true religion.

SALADIN

That your answer to me?

NATHAN

But my apology for not presuming
Between the rings to judge, which with design
The father ordered undistinguishable.

SALADIN

The rings?—You trifle with me. The religions
I named to you are plain to be distinguished—
E'en in the dress, e'en in the food and drink.

NATHAN

In all except the grounds on which they rest.
Are they not founded all on history,
Traditional or written? History
Can be accepted only upon trust.
Whom now are we the least inclined to doubt?
Not our own people—our own blood; not those
Who from our childhood up have proved their love,
Ne'er disappointed, save when disappointment
Was wholesome to us? Shall my ancestors
Receive less faith from me, than yours from you?
Reverse it: Can I ask you to belie
Your fathers, and transfer your faith to mine?
Or yet, again, holds not the same with Christians?

SALADIN

(By heaven, the man is right! I've naught to answer.)

NATHAN

Return we to our rings. As I have said,
The sons appealed to law, and each took oath
Before the judge that from his father's hand

He had the ring,—as was indeed the truth;
And had received his promise long before,
One day the ring, with all its privileges,
Should be his own,—as was not less the truth
The father could not have been false to him,
Each one maintained; and rather than allow
Upon the memory of so dear a father
Such stain to rest, he must against his brothers,
Though gladly he would nothing but the best
Believe of them, bring charge of treachery;
Means would he find the traitors to expose,
And be revenged on them.

SALADIN

                And now the judge?
I long to hear what words you give the judge.
Go on!

NATHAN

       Thus spoke the judge; Produce your father
At once before me, else from my tribunal
Do I dismiss you. Think you I am here
To guess your riddles? Either would you wait
Until the genuine ring shall speak?—But hold!
A Magic power in the true ring resides,
As I am told, to make its wearer loved—
Pleasing to God and man. Let that decide.
For in the false can no such virtue lie.
Which one among you, then, do two love best?
Speak: Are you silent? Work the rings but
      backward,
Not outward? Loves each one himself the best?
Then cheated cheats are all of you! The rings
All three are false. The genuine ring was lost;
And to conceal, supply the loss, the father
Made three in place of one.

SALADIN

                   Oh, excellent:

NATHAN

Go, therefore, said the judge, unless my counsel
You'd have in place of sentence. It were this:
Accept the case exactly as it stands.

Had each his ring directly from his father,
Let each believe his own is genuine.
'Tis possible your father would no longer
His house to one ring's tyranny subject:
And certain that all three of you he loved,
Loved equally, since two he would not humble
That one might be exalted. Let each one
To his unbought, impartial love aspire;
Each with the other vie to bring to light
The virtue of the stone within his ring;
Let gentleness, a hearty love of peace,
Beneficence, and perfect trust in God,
Come to its help. Then if the jewel's power
Among your children's children be revealed,
I bid you in a thousand, thousand years
Again before this bar. A wiser man
Than I shall occupy this seat, and speak
Go!—Thus the modest judge dismissed them.

SALADIN

God!

NATHAN

If therefore, Saladin, you feel yourself
That promised, wiser man—

SALADIN

(rushing to him, and seizing his hand, which
he holds to the end).

I? Dust!—I? Naught!
O God!

NATHAN

What moves you, Sultan?

SALADIN

Nathan, Nathan!

Not ended are the thousand, thousand years
Your judge foretold; not mind to claim his seat.
Go, go!—But be my friend.

CONCLUDING REMARKS TO CHAPTERS 10 AND 11

One might well have combined the descriptions of the disintegration of the Christian dogma and of the Enlightenment in one chap-

ter. Those who caused the disintegration were, in a way, the harbingers of the Enlightenment; it depends whether one wants to see the whole development as one continuous process, or as two separate acts.

There are, however, essential differences. Bacon and his contemporaries of the sixteenth and seventeenth centuries still lived in a feudal climate. To be sure, they broke through some parts of the medieval walls, but the walls were still around. In contrast, in spite of initial opposition of the clergy to the spirit of Newton, the rationalist curiosity of the eighteenth century had opened new vistas of the world. Both the ecclesiastical and the political powers either yielded or compromised with the new temper. If not, they were preparing their defeat, as France proved all too clearly.

If one identifies the beginning of our Western culture—somewhat arbitrarily—with the Greeks and Romans, then Christianity would be its first revolution, the Renaissance and Reformation its second, and the period of empirical inquiry and of Enlightenment its third. In comparison with the latter, the Renaissance and the Reformation may even be called minor events, for, notwithstanding all the conflicts and changes which they brought about, they have not moulded our modern way of living and thinking so decisively as science and its application.

Yet, despite all mutations, the history of culture shows a remarkable continuity. As a matter of fact, no decisive period has ever been fully repudiated by the next. The process is less one of displacement than of accumulation and orchestration. Plato, Aristotle, and the Roman law melted into the theology and constitution of the medieval Church; medieval Catholicism survived the Renaissance and the Reformation; and our modern age of science would be an age of barbarism if all the spiritual movements of the past had stopped before it. When they were almost banned, as under Hitler and Stalin, barbarism indeed was knocking at the door.

Education especially is a preserving force; it refuses to see lost that which once helped the human race to better understand itself and the universe. Only the accidental and superficial are gradually shed, often not even these. In addition, parents do not want to experiment with their children. They first wish to see them rooted before the risk of the new is taken. But education is not only conservative; although slow, it is also evolutionary. It leads the younger generation not only into the past, but also into the present and into the future. Perhaps its very steadiness guarantees human evolution. The Copernican world picture has gradually been accepted in our schools, and even in remote areas—except the State of Arkansas—one now agrees that the theory of evolution is the most workable hypothesis we possess, though there is no certainty that one day it might become obsolete. That which is closer to truth, although it may not be *the* truth, can be silenced for a while, but not forever.

The conservative tendency in education may explain why it is difficult to find immediate reflections of the new rationalism in the field of religious instruction. Dogmatism still prevailed. Newton was born less than a hundred years after Luther's death, six years before the end of the Thirty Years War. The time of change from the period of bloody confessional conflicts to the beginning of modern science was too brief to permit contemporary understanding and absorption by the average layman.

However, those of the aristocracy and the upper bourgeoisie, especially those who had seen parts of the world either on the grand tour or as men of business, favored the modern mood. They were in no way antireligious. The Bible was for them sacred. They did not like to dwell on its internal contradictions or on its contradictions with their own experiences. Like Locke, the advocate of "natural religion," they still believed in Christ and immortality. But they wanted privacy in religion as they wanted it in their personal life.

Thus Locke, in his *Thoughts Concerning Education*, laid more value on a sound worldly upbringing than on religious indoctrination. Also in Chesterfield's famous *Letters to his Son* the supernatural played little, if any, role in comparison with the aesthetic and practical components of life. Locke and Chesterfield, like Newton, were Englishmen, and despite denominational conflicts, the English had been less exposed to the fury of religious controversy than the continent. Their ideal was that of the "gentleman" who insisted on good manners, enlightened understanding of the virtues and foibles of the human race, and on that balance of mind which comes from a sense of proportion concerning the things that make life and one's fellowmen as tolerable as they can be. Like the Earl of Shaftesbury in his *Letter Concerning Enthusiasm* and in his *Characteristics on Men, Manners, Opinions, Time,* they looked with a sense of distance, if not disgust, at the religious intolerance of the Churches and at "enthusiasts" who preferred exile and martyrdom to compromise with their faith. And they all were influenced by that most remarkable Frenchman, le Seigneur de Montaigne (1533–1592) who wrote one of the wisest essays on education. In the midst of religious wars, he was able to look at the world with a kind of optimistic scepticism as the relatively best solution he had discovered when looking at himself and the human race.[9]

Chapter 12

The Romantic Movement

JEAN JACQUES ROUSSEAU

Few writers have caused so much excitement among their contemporaries as the Swiss Jean Jacques Rousseau, and there is probably none concerning whom the exciting power goes hand in hand with so many defects in logic and empirical trustworthiness. In addition, both his social and political ideas, formulated particularly in his *Social Contract,* and his educational theories, laid down chiefly in his *Émile, or Of Education,* are not really original. They were expressed more basically, and more clearly, in the writings of Montaigne, Locke, and the English deists before him. Philosophically he is indebted, among others, to Leibnitz for his optimistic view of man and world. Yet, Rousseau's ideas spread, shortly after their publication, from France, where he lived most of his time, to the farthest West and the farthest East. South Americans, who wished to free themselves from the Spanish absolutist and ecclesiastical yoke, and Russians who thought of reform in their backward country, found in his writings the igniting words and phrases. Even today his works are still eagerly read by the intellectual youth of Asia and Africa struggling for independence. He was appreciated least of all, so it seems, in colonial America; for Jefferson and his friends he was too fantastic. But it is difficult not to be impressed by his power of formulation and the astuteness of some of his arguments. Even those ideas which he received from others became so internalized that they appear to issue from a fresh source. And it was not merely the oppressed who answered his call to "nature" (which meant freedom from obsolete and moribund customs and institutions) but also and primarily those high in rank. As a matter of fact, during all his persecutions by governments and clergy of various countries, he received more protection from the nobility and corresponded more interestingly with its members in France, Germany, and Poland, than from the people at large. Only after his death did the latter feel strong enough to carry some of Rousseau's ideas into practice, though, in regard to the French revolution, it did so with poisonous admixture of immaturity. This is the reason why he is probably nowhere as much disliked as among those parts of the French population which wish that the revolution of 1789 had never happened.

The educational idea which fascinated the more sophisticated at Rousseau's time was what we may call the notion of "negative education." They felt that not only adults, but also the young—and they perhaps even more—had been denied a "natural" development. The children of the well-to-do especially had been put into the stiff and overloaded dress in the style of their parents; the girls had been more in contact with powder and perfume than with fresh water; they all had been forced to learn what they did not understand; and their religious instruction probably did more harm than good to their souls and their opinions about religion. As a matter of fact, rarely was religion in such low prestige as at the end of the eighteenth and the beginning of the nineteenth century. Even in America only a dwindling minority of students confessed to be believers.

Therefore, the voice of Rousseau was listened to eagerly. Do away with all the impositions on the child which are mostly ideas of adults turned into prejudice. Let "nature" do its work! It is, nevertheless, a mistake to believe that Rousseau recommended "negative education" in the sense of a complete absence of authority and guidance. The tutor who stands behind Émile in order to bring him up in isolation from corrupt society guides very much. But he does so by directing the boy's experiences in such a way that they come to him naturally and that he profits from them through his own understanding, not because some authority has told him so.

But the one area of experience concerning which Rousseau recommends complete abstinence until the questioning comes from within, is religion. There is no necessity to comment on this point since Rousseau himself, in his *Émile,* just before the famous deistic confession of creed by the Savoyard priest, has given us a perfect delineation of his ideas.[1]

> The ideas of a creating and annihilating power, omnipresence, eternity, omnipotence, are those of the divine attributes, which so small a part of mankind are able to form, confused and indistinct as they are, and which nevertheless do not appear obscure at all to the common people, because they form nothing of them. How is it possible to present these ideas in all their force; that is to say, in their full obscurity, to those youthful understandings which are as yet totally occupied with the primary operations of the senses, and are hardly able to conceive anything but what they feel? . . . If we speak to them of the power of the deity, they think him almost as strong as their father. Their knowledge in all cases being to them the measure of possibilities, they judge everything that is told them to be less and inferior to what they know. Such are the conclusions natural to ignorance and weakness of understanding. . . .
>
> I foresee how much my readers will be surprised to find I have attended my pupil throughout the whole first stage of life without once speaking to him of religion. He hardly knows at fifteen years of age whether or not he has a soul, and perhaps it will not be time to inform him of it when he is eighteen; for, if he learns it too soon, he runs a risk of never knowing it at all.
>
> If I were to design a picture of the most deplorable stupidity, I would draw a pedant teaching children their catechism; and were I resolved to crack the brain of a child, I would oblige him to explain what he said when he repeated his catechism. . . .
>
> Let us beware of divulging the truth to those who are incapable of understanding it; for this is the way to substitute

error in the room of it. It were better to have no idea of God at all, than to entertain those which are mean, fantastical, injurious, and unworthy a divine object; it is a less crime to be ignorant of, than insult, him. I had much rather, says the amiable Plutarch, that people should believe there is no such person as Plutarch in the world, than that they should say, he is unjust, envious, jealous, and so tyrannical as to require of others what he has not left them power to perform.

The great evil of those preposterous images of the Deity, which we may trace in the minds of children, is, that they remain indelible during their whole life; and that when they are men, they have no better conceptions of God than they had when they were children. I once knew a very worthy and pious woman in Switzerland so well satisfied of the truth of this maxim, that she would give her son no early instructions about religion; lest he should content himself with such imperfect ideas as he was then only able to conceive, and neglect the acquisition of more perfect ones when he grew up. This child never heard the name of God pronounced but with awe and reverence; and whenever he began to speak of him, was immediately silenced, as if the subject was too great and sublime for his comprehension. This reserve excited his curiosity, and his self-love aspired after the time when it should be proper for him to be made acquainted with the mystery that was so carefully concealed from him. The less he was spoken to of God, the less he was suffered to speak of him, the more his thoughts were employed on this unknown object. He saw God in everything around him; and what I should fear most from this air of mystery carried to extremes, would be, that in overheating the imagination of a young man, it would turn his head, and that in the end it would make him a fanatic instead of a believer.

JOHANN HEINRICH PESTALOZZI

Pestalozzi (1746–1827), has sometimes been described as a "disciple of Rousseau." When, at the age of eighty, he looked back at the motivations, the struggles, the achievements and failures of his life,[2] he

wrote about Rousseau's influence on the younger revolutionary generation of Switzerland.[3]

> The writings which were recommended to us as inspirations
> in our struggle (for the reform of our fatherland) were, despite
> all the good ideas they contained, products of the artificiality
> and perilous unnaturalness of the age. . . . The influence of
> Rousseau was a special sign of the confusion into which the
> upsurge of noble patriotism had led the best of our youth.
> And soon the great and passionate events of the time raised
> this confusion to the level of radicalism, heedlessness, and
> total bewilderment [characteristic of the period of the French
> revolution]. This development was further enhanced by Vol-
> taire and his seductive betrayal of the pure, simple, and inno-
> cent sense of religion. It created a state of mind totally un-
> fitted to mould the future of our old and conservative city
> [Zürich]; it was able neither to preserve the good we had, nor
> create something better and more stable.

> The figure of Rousseau had an evil influence on me also. . . .
> As soon as his *Émile* appeared my unrealistic and dreamy
> mind was enthralled by his unrealistic dreambook. I com-
> pared the education I had received in my mother's modest
> living room and in my school with Rousseau's ideas and de-
> mands concerning the education of his *Émile*. Education in
> family and school all over the world in all social classes ap-
> peared to me to be crippled, and I thought that only in
> Rousseau's high idealism might there be found the remedy
> against its miserable condition. In addition, the new idealism
> of political liberty, so greatly enhanced by Rousseau, strength-
> ened in me the desire to find a greater and more fruitful
> sphere of action for my people.

These sentences reflect the conservatism of an old man who no
longer understood the rebellious, though not at all unproductive enthusiasm of his youth. He was much more just in his Lenzburg Address on "The Idea of Organic Education" [4] which he delivered in 1809,
as a man of sixty-three. There is perhaps no deeper recognition of
Rousseau's work and tragedy than the one contained in the following
part of the Lenzburg address.

Before Basedow [a famous German educational reformer]
Rousseau, as if coming from a higher plane, had already directed education from old into completely new ways. Power-
fully captivated by the impression of all-powerful nature,
concerned as no one else, with the alienation of his contemporaries from the natural ways of life and spirit, he burst the
fetters of the mind with herculean vigor and gave the child
back to himself by relating education to him and to human
nature. But he was in conflict with himself, in conflict with
society and its immutable needs, in conflict even with the human mind itself and the laws of its unfolding, because he
was unable to reach the point of inner unity between nature and culture, without the understanding of which we cannot understand its diversity. Hence he could not compre-
hend the means by which to secure the organic vitality and
genuine independence of childhood, nor was he able to harmonize the inner and the outer world of men. Therefore his
own period understood him only as a rebel against his time,
and the educators misunderstood him almost without exception. He found only admirers who idolized him, commen-
tators who distorted him, and adversaries who hated him,
with the result that his *Émile*, though being one of the great
documents in the history of civilization, remained a sealed
book. There was no one who could have placed it into the
right light; in this respect, it shared the fate of the great ideas
of Comenius.

As every intellectually awake person at his period, Pestalozzi read
Rousseau avidly. In addition to the Bible, it was perhaps the only book
he ever read completely. But, as we have already mentioned, by no
means were Rousseau's ideas so unique as Pestalozzi believed. The
power of his language deceived many with regard to his originality.
The rebellion of Pestalozzi's generation in the name of "nature" and
"natural law" against the unnaturalness and corruption of the dying
era of Louix XIV and the flagrant social injustices in Switzerland had
been prepared by a number of writers, French, English, German, and
Swiss. When Pestalozzi wrote his first revolutionary essays, the American Declaration of Independence had already been written. Zürich, his
birthplace, had, under the leadership of such men as Bodmer and Brei-

tinger, become the center of German progressive thought. Thus, even without Rousseau, the young Pestalozzi, in whom the excitement of a time of crisis vibrated, would not have remained within the Protestant conservatism of his early youth.

Reading the essay, "The Evening Hour of an Hermit" (1780), in which, as in an intuitive flash, Pestalozzi develops the essential ideas of his later educational thought and work, one cannot resist using the modern label of "existentialism." With all its confusing interpretations, existentialism would not have attracted such wide interest if it did not express an essential mode of man's reaction to the problems of human existence. During his whole life Pestalozzi appears to be an existentialist, attracted by the mysterious forces in the human soul, rejecting conventional definitions for fear of losing the depth of truth, and constantly exposed to emotional extremes because of his inability to see himself in a certain objective distance. If, in this respect, Pestalozzi resembles Kierkegaard, he does so even more in his final answer to the problem of existence, that only in taking seriously the gospel of Christ can man find peace and meaning.

The "Evening Hour" begins with a grand appeal:

Man who is the same whether in a palace or in a hut, what is he in his innermost nature? Why do the wise not tell us? Why are the greatest of our thinkers not concerned with knowing what their race is? Does a peasant use his ox without knowing it? Does not a shepherd care for the nature of his sheep? . . .

What man is, what his needs are, what elevates and humiliates him, what strengthens and what weakens him ought to be the most important knowledge for the rulers as well as for the humblest.

There then follow, in highly aphoristic fashion, a long series of paragraphs in which—in true existentialist fashion—man's "nature" is identified with man's "truth" or "realization of his self." The process of maturing is explained as a process of organic development from the child's instinctive urge for his mother's love and protection to the more complex and independent stages. It is one of Pestalozzi's elemental and most fruitful convictions that each successive step in the evolution of the personality must lead to insecurity and bewilderment, unless the preceding one is fully completed and mastered. And the base of all later growth is the embracing affection of the mother and the spirit of the home.

Sometimes these contemplations remind us of Freud and Adler, sometimes of modern sociology, and sometimes they sound like notes for a philosophy of personality of the humanistic version. Yet, there is a profound difference. Pestalozzi's concepts of "nature" and "natural" or "organic" development are neither naturalistic as with Freud and the modern social sciences, nor have they much in common with secular humanism. Rather, they are profoundly Christian, though undogmatic.

The religious character appears clearly when Pestalozzi, after dis-cussing in "The Evening Hour of a Hermit" the various human rela-tions necessary for sound personal growth, suddenly changes from the human "horizontal" to the "vertical" metaphysical level, and ex-claims:

God is the nearest relationship of man. . . .

Your tender, kind and feeling nature is not strong enough to suffer force and death without God.

The faith in God, the father of your house and the source of your welfare, the faith in God's fatherhood, this faith gives you solace, strength and wisdom which neither force nor death can take from you.

Faith in God is the highest accord of man's feelings; in this faith man the child faces God the father. . . .

Historically, this combination of naturalism and metaphysics in the area of education had already begun with Comenius whom Pesta-lozzi mentions several times, though in rather general terms.

Both the Moravian and the Swiss were essentially mystics. They were convinced that a divine harmony exists between the human soul and the mysterious Absolute that Ralph Waldo Emerson later called the "World Soul." Hence, they considered nothing in the educational process more important than to instill early in the child the pious reverence that sees sacredness in every phenomenon of life, in man's relation to his fellowmen, and his relation to the whole universe.

Both Pestalozzi and Comenius were so intrinsically religious that their piety shines through every one of their works. They could not speak of nature without thinking of God as its creator; they could not speak of the human being without sensing the divine in even the poorest soul. For both parental love and the good family were the reflection of the fatherly love of God on the level of human relations. There are many places in Pestalozzi's writings where God appears, almost anthropomorphically, as the father image, though they are in no way characteristic of his total religiosity. Finally, for both, education was not merely a way of teaching and learning, but the human attempt to participate in the divine plan to unfold the best in individual man and in humanity as a whole.

The evolutionary metaphysics of education, so profoundly professed in Froebel's *Education of Man,* is fully prepared in Pestalozzi.

As the seed contains the fruit, so the "Evening Hour of a Hermit," written after the breakdown of Pestalozzi's first educational experiment at the Neuhof, contains all the essential elements of the great man's later thought and labor. But the work that made him famous was his *Leonard and Gertrude,*[5] the first part of which was published in 1781. The quick popularity of this book rested on the taste of the time for idyllic moods; its intention, however, was different. It pictures the rottenness of the life in a poor Swiss village, where Gertrude, the pious wife of a mason was burdened with debts owed to a crooked inn-owner, is the only source of educational wisdom and inspiration. From her the lord of the land, who is anxious to restore a sound social life in his community, learns the essence of education. Observing how Gertrude brings up her children, he and his friends realize the interdependence between family spirit and the spirit of the community, of religion and education, and also of physical welfare and human dignity. The truth of *Leonard and Gertrude* is proved by the fact that an understanding and imaginative reader may find it just as applicable to the social problems of New York as it was two hundred years ago to the conditions of a tiny Swiss village under a feudal system. The work is so much a whole that it is impossible to represent its spirit by brief extracts; it should be read and contemplated in its totality.

Pestalozzi was not a systematic thinker. Whenever he tried he fell short of the depth of his visions and experiences, as, for example, in his *How Gertrude Teaches Her Children.*[6] Yet, he felt the constant urge to give himself an account of his thinking and doing. Out of this endeavor there arose a large number of books and essays in which, among other problems, the relation of education to religion is a recurrent scheme.

We translate here freely first a passage from his already mentioned work *On the Idea of Organic Education.*[7]

The beginning of our endeavors [toward the moral education of the child] coincides with the time of early childhood. The first condition of their success is that they correspond with human nature. How can they do so? When the child is still young, nature asks us to continue consciously that which so far it has done instinctively. It asks that we develop humanely and understandingly the loving and faithful state of mind the truth and blessing of which the innocent child has so far enjoyed unconsciously in his relation to the mother. For sooner or later this state of innocence, the faith in the mother, will weaken and vacillate. Nature then demands new means of faith. And unless we plant faith in God deeply into the child's soul we create the danger of cutting the natural links of human development.

However, in the state of early childhood, this desirable continuity can be achieved only by appeal to the child's natural sensitive faculty. The motivations of faith in God must already be provided before the child's sensuous and natural attachment to the mother is fading. Faith in God, as it were, must be melted into the maturing relation to the mother. Here is the only chance for a pure, continuous, and natural development from the innocence of childhood toward human morality, for the latter grows from the first. Only this

sacred process of growth leads to real faith and love, the lift-
ing of sensuous affection toward the level of moral and spiritual maturity.

Also in his *Swan Song* Pestalozzi discusses the psychological relation
between religion and education.[8]

The unifying vitality of the human race [Gemeinkraft des
Menshengeschlects] is impossible without a common spirit
which motivates us from within and binds the various forces
in our nature one to the other. . . . In its essence this unity
is the pure gift of divine grace from which there spring all
human powers and all human care that enable the mind to
dominate the flesh. All motivations of the human community which stem from the sensual and egotistic desires of our
flesh and blood rather than from the spirit and life of our divine nature, are neither organic nor productive.

Thus it is evident that the truth of fundamental and organic
education and the totality of its means issues from the divine
spark which is planted into human nature and harmonizes
with the spirit of Christianity. On the other hand, it is
equally evident that our present education with all its arti-
ficiality, corruption and routine does not spring from the divine spark in the depth of man, but from his brutal and
sensuous desires. Consequently, it contradicts the spirit and
essence of Christianity and can have no other effect but to
undermine it. . . .

In spite of his natural piety, or perhaps exactly because of it, Pestalozzi distinguished clearly between piety and superstition. With powerful words he contrasted the two in *Leonard and Gertrude*.[9]

Deceiver, [so Pestalozzi addresses the spirit of clerical domi-
nation] as long as the world has existed you have used man's
faith in God to steer him into superstition and idolatry. . . .

You capture the pious in their hour of deepest devotion. . . .

Deceiver, you ask the orphan: "Do you know *my* God?", and
the suppressed: "Have you learned *my* creed by heart," . . .

You wave the banners of murder as if they were the symbols of love.

You contrive to set yourself at the side of God, and your service seems to the peoples of the earth more important than the service of God.

Statements like this explain why the governments belonging to Metternich's Holy Alliance after the defeat of Napoleon watched with severe apprehension Pestalozzi's growing popularity among the teachers of Europe. The Prussian government forbade "Pestalozzianism" in the Normal Schools, called "Seminare," which formed the pattern for the modern systematic training of teachers. Yet, it is the gradual infiltration of Pestalozzi's ideas, developed later by men such as Froebel, Diesterweg, and Herbart in Germany, by Charles and Elizabeth Mayo in England, and by Edward Sheldon, Henry Barnard, and Horace Mann in the United States, which made possible a relative efficiency in teaching during the pressure of a rapidly expanding elementary school system. Unfortunately, even those who write about education in our popular journals know little or nothing about the lamentable state of elementary schooling before the time of Pestalozzi. Otherwise he would be known as one of the great liberators of humankind.

Finally, some words about Pestalozzi's ideas concerning the practical side of religious education. He wrote several essays on this subject which prove that he was not unaware of the difficulty in religious instruction and of the complexity of the Bible of which he wanted the most simple and impressive parts explained to children.[10] He was opposed to the use of catechisms and, needless to say, against all orthodoxy and denominationalism. Rather he wanted religion to become part of the total educational process, most effective perhaps when not mentioned.

The most impressive statement on the right and false role of religion in the gradual enlightenment of the people is contained in the chapter in *Leonard and Gertrude* with the title: "How Arner [the reform-minded lord of the village] Shields His People from Superstition." This chapter must be understood not as a protest against the profession of the clergy as such, but as many similar statements of Pestaloz-

zi's time, a sign of violent opposition to a priesthood that had allied itself with the reactionary and feudal forces and helped to suppress the
desire for political and mental freedom.

Here are some of the basic sentences:

Arner knew about the spirit of bigotry. He also severed the
aims of intellectual from the aims of religious education.
. . . He divorced theological erudition from those parts of
popular instruction which should foster logical drill and general knowledge. He did not intend to burden his good people
with the stuff of catechisms and the doctrines of the most
difficult of all branches of scholarship [theology], for he
knew that all the nations of the earth, from the shores of the
Indus and up and down to the two poles must necessarily
become arrogant and insipid slaves of priesthood if one tries
to achieve the goals of general intellectual knowledge and
progress by explaining religious doctrines.

In the circumstances of our time, superstition is immensely
nourished. Every day our moral climate becomes increasingly
dreamy and oscillating. . . .

The abuse of the Bible and of our creed for purposes alien
to man becomes more rampant than ever.

More and more the people's interests are directed toward the
forces of imagination than to those of reason—

More and more are their minds filled with poetic opinions
about the meaning of religion and encouraged to consider
these opinions as signs of scholarly enlightenment and objects
for scholarly investigation.

What our time needs is this:

That we think with a profound urge for truth about the
right and wise ways of governing the people, that we do not
neglect the intellectual education of men, that the natural
sense of survival be supported by the knowledge of means
and skills which give man a sense of order, peace and security in his civil life,

that wise and efficient means be found to counteract the
sources of his main natural faults, such as his lack of prudence,
of rationality, of orderliness, and education,

that in the formation of human society we do not appeal
to emotions, but to the people's intellect, its skills, and its
industriousness,

that the welfare of the citizen be not made dependent
on their creed, and still less on worthless and man-made religious institutions and thus on the influence of priesthood,

that we make people increasingly critical, though with
greatest care, wisdom and prudence,

that we establish such customs and human relationships
which prevent the contagious influence of dream-like feelings, especially the muddled sentimentality that oscillates
between the extremes of happiness and anxiety and which
makes men sublimely poetic at one moment, and miserable
at another.

In one word, we must find means which, instead of making
men weak and bewildered, elevate them to a higher state of
education and enthusiasm.

FRIEDRICH SCHLEIERMACHER

Rarely, if ever, in its long history, did traditional Christianity have
such low prestige among the educated as it did about the year 1800.
The influence of papacy on the Christian world was almost negligible.
In 1773 Pope Clement XIV had to yield to the pressure of Catholic
monarchs to suppress the Jesuit Order. In France, the writings of the
sceptical *"Philosophes,"* the materialism of Baron Holbach, de la Met-
trie, and the Count de Volny still held sway in spite of the failures of
the revolution of 1789. In England the enlightened circles and even the
clergy of the Established Church looked with undisguised aloofness at
the rich sectarianism of the people that kept genuine religion alive. And

though in Germany scepticism and materialism found no vital response, orthodox Protestantism was in retreat before the flowering philosophical idealism, the depth and beauty of the new poetry, and the growing interest in science and humanistic scholarship.

In order to survive as a cultural factor, religion had to meet the challenge. This was attempted in 1799 by a thirty-year-old Protestant chaplin in Berlin, Friedrich Schleiermacher (1768–1834) whose dormant intellectual capacity had been aroused by members of the Romantic circle in the Prussian capital. Significantly, he gave his work the title, *On Religion. Speeches to its Cultured Despisers (Ueber die Religion. Reden an die Gebildeten unter ihren Verächtern)*. Once the stream of his intellectual creativeness was released, Schleiermacher, besides producing a famous translation of Plato's dialogues, became one of Germany's leading philosophers and by far the most outstanding theologian of his time. Liberal Protestantism all over the world considers him rightly its first great spokesman, and, though he did not write expressly on religious education proper, his influence can be felt wherever people try ways of transmitting the Christian heritage to the young without leading them into conflict with our modern intellectual point of view.

Schleiermacher's *Speeches* are an extremely critical answer to both the theological orthodoxy of the past and the rationalistic trends of the eighteenth-century Enlightenment; they show the influence of Spinoza, Rousseau, Kant, Goethe, and almost every great creation of Western thought. But, in the *Speeches* as well as in his numerous other writings on theology and philosophy, the author proves that his eclecticism is not that of a compiler but of a mind capable of courageous synthesis. Otherwise, his work would not have been an answer to the past or a challenge to the future.

Without any pious illusions he scans the mentality of his cultured contemporaries.[11]

At all times but few have discerned religion itself, while millions, in various ways, have been satisfied to juggle with its trappings. Now especially the life of cultivated people is far from anything that might have even a semblance to religion. Just as little, I know, do you worship the Deity in sacred

retirement, as you visit the forsaken temples. In your orna-
mented dwellings, the only sacred things to be met with are
the sage maxims of our wise men, and the splendid com-
positions of our poets. Suavity and sociability, art and science
have so fully taken possession of your minds that no room remains for the eternal and holy Being that lies beyond the
world. I know how well you have succeeded in making your
earthly life so rich and varied, that you no longer stand in
need of an eternity. Having made a universe for yourselves,
you are above the need of thinking of the universe that made
you.

Schleiermacher attributes this situation largely to the inertness and
stagnation of the Christian Churches, to the confusion of religion with
historically conditioned dogmas, including the ideas of immortality and
a personal God, and finally "to the ill-put together fragments of metaphysics and ethics now called purified Christianity."

The sum total of religion is to feel that, in its highest unity,
all that moves us in feeling is one; to feel that ought single
and particular is only possible by means of this unity; to
feel, that is to say, that our feeling and living is a being and
living in and through God. But it is not necessary that the
Deity should be presented as also one distinct object. To
many this view is necessary, and to all it is welcome, yet it
is always hazardous and fruitful of difficulties. . . . But to
treat this objective conception of God just as it were a perception, as if apart from His operation upon us through the
world the existence of God before the world, and outside of
the world, though for the world, were either by or in religion
exhibited as science, is, so far as religion is concerned, vain
mythology. What is only a help for presentation is treated
as a reality.

The defenders of Christianity have alienated thinking persons also
by the assertion that there could be neither law nor social order without
religion.

If, Schleiermacher says,

general jurisdiction is only possible when religion is combined
with law, none but persons skilled to infuse the spirit of re-

ligion into the human soul should be statesmen. And in what dark barbarousness of evil times would that land us.

Just as little can morality be in need of religion. A weak, tempted heart must take refuge in the thought of a future world. But it is folly to make a distinction between this world and the next. Religious persons at least know only one. If the desire for happiness is foreign to morality, later happiness can be no more valid than earlier; if it should be quite independent of praise, dread of the eternal can be no more valid than dread of a wise man.

Nor should religion be mingled with art, science, and philosophy. But, though distorted when subordinated to and mixed with alien elements, religion is nevertheless as inherent and active in all worthwhile human activities as the sap in a tree, the sound in a melody, or the air in our breath. Without religion, life becomes dull and empty. Religion is paradoxical; it is "a peculiar sphere," yet it is a reflection upon us of "the whole" of which we are a part.

In order that you may understand what I mean by this unity and difference of religion, science, and art, we shall endeavor to descend into the inmost sanctuary of life. There, perhaps, we may find ourselves agreed. There alone you discover the original relation of intuition and feeling from which alone this identity and difference is to be understood.

This is the peculiar sphere which I would assign to religion— the whole of it, and nothing more. Unless you grant it, you must either prefer the old confusion to clear analysis, or produce something else, I know not what, new and quite wonderful. Your feeling is piety, in so far as it expresses, in the manner described, the being and life common to you and to the All. Your feeling is piety, in so far as it is the operation of God in you by means of the operation of the world upon you.

As a consequence of these definitions, Schleiermacher can say with a good conscience: "Religion is the natural and sworn foe of all narrowmindedness, and of all onesidedness."

Later he continues:

> The only remedy is for each man, while he is definitely active
> in some one department, to allow himself, without definite
> activity, to be affected by the infinite. . . .

> Religion takes the form of some peculiar receptivity and taste
> for art, philosophy and morality, and is consequently often
> mistaken. Oftener, I say, it appears thus than freed from all
> participation in one-sidedness, than completed, all embrac-
> ing. Yet this complete form of religion remains the highest,
> and it is only by it that, with satisfactory result, man sets
> alongside of the finite that he specially concentrates on, an
> Infinite; alongside of the contracting endeavor of something
> definite and complete, expansive soaring in the Whole and the
> Inexhaustible.

Thus, at the end of the section on "the nature of religion" Schleiermacher affirms that every original insight and "every new communication of the universe to man" is a "revelation." All life, lived deeply
and consciously, is a series of revelations, a continuous dialogue between the individual and the Divine.

Schleiermacher's *Speeches on Religion* are the most stirring expression of faith made by a Protestant clergyman after Luther. As in all
great works written at a turning point of history we find in them a revealing dialectic.

Just because he takes the criteria of rational inquiry, developed
during the era of the Enlightenment as seriously as he takes religion,
he concludes that it can lead only to logical ambiguities and depleted
symbolism, if not to cynicism, if theologians try to meet and to convert
the scholarly mind by the use of rationalistic methods. In doing so they
confuse two essentially different forms of man's reaction to the wonder
of existence. But rather than admitting the defeat of religion, Schleiermacher resurrects it by ascribing to it a separate domain of feeling and
intuition. By virtue of religion, man experiences a certainty that science
cannot give. He experiences his individual being within the universal
Being, or his essential unity with nature, man and Cosmos.

But though we may agree that much of what Schleiermacher says is profound, the question will be raised whether he says enough, or whether, in eliminating some ambiguities, he does not create others. What, if we follow the mood of the first edition of the *Speeches on Religion,* is the difference between Christianity and other faiths? Some may hope that mankind will eventually become spiritually united and that the divisive claims of the various religions will disappear. But many religious people will argue that a religion cannot survive that has only intuitions that float like gossamer in the air of transcendental realms. Is such a religion more than aestheticism? Schleiermacher would answer that people who ask this question have misunderstood him. For he emphasizes that the intuitions of which he speaks are of universal value and thus provide the most powerful impetus to all human creativeness. He also admits the necessity of dogma and of historical religions, but only in a relative sense.

Yes, so the critics would say, but in making faith relative, one destroys it. And in depriving a tradition of the symbolic structure that holds it together, one contributes to its collapse. People, so the critics would continue, need certainty, concreteness, a personal God, and the hope for salvation and immortality. They cannot receive the strength for a morally productive, and therefore strenuous life from a romantic and cosmic pantheism, and that is exactly the world view of the *Speeches.* With growing pastoral experience and systematic thinking (or should we say, with growing willingness to compromise?) Schleiermacher himself modified his early conception of religion according to more conservative principles. In his *Lectures on Philosophy of Education,*[12] delivered in the twenties of the nineteenth century, little is left of the religion of feeling, so characteristic of the *Speeches.*

To be sure, some of the tenor of the early Schleiermacher remains also in the mature educational philosophy of the *Lectures on Education.* There also one feels the influence of Rousseau, so clearly discernible in the *Speeches.* Although not so radical as Rousseau in his insistence on the postponement of religious influence, he too is of the opinion that the young child is incapable of true religious experience because of his lack of knowledge of the world. To force religion on him can produce nothing but the mere show of piety.

Schleiermacher rejects the idea that the public schools should give religious instruction. This practice, he says, is a useless leftover from the period when education was under the control of the Churches, whereas now it is under the control of the state. Youth should be taught religion by special appointees of the Church as a supplement to family education. The recent tendency, he avers, at a time of political reaction to restore the old alliance between government and Church must lead to one-sided interpretations of the Christian faith, to intolerance and conflict. If the family and the Church are unable to provide a Christian upbringing, the state, as examples prove, cannot do it either.[13] In a more conventional mood the *Lectures* deplore the general lack of acquaintance with the religious tradition and emphasize the necessity of explaining the Bible and the meaning of cult as basic to the life of a Christian community.[14]

However, the difference between the more romantic *Speeches* and the more conservative *Lectures on Philosophy of Education* should not deceive us with regard to the quality of the latter. Like Kant's lectures on education,[15] they were posthumously edited from notes. Consequently, they are not attractive in terms of style. But the reason why they have received so little attention lies deeper. It stems from the fact that, generally speaking, theologians are not interested in education and educators not interested in theology. This, together with the aloofness of philosophy departments, has created a deplorable gap in our knowledge of the history of educational thought. If this were not the case, Schleiermacher's *Lectures* would be esteemed as a great attempt at a comprehensive system of education, together with Plato's *Republic* and the writings of Comenius, Herbart, and Dewey.

The value of Schleiermacher's educational system results from his exhaustive thinking about the ethical problem. In his various writings on this topic, especially in his *Outline of an Ethical System (Entwurf eines Systems der Sittenlehre)* [16] he develops further Schelling's "philosophy of identity" which, in contrast to Kant's ethical dualism, is a bold attempt at the reconciliation of the old contrast between mind and nature, or freedom and determinism. He explains the moral endeavor of man as a reflection of the interaction between these two poles of being, thus adding a new and important chapter to the philosophy of education.

Schleiermacher's ethics and his *Lectures on Philosophy of Education*, in addition to the customary psychological and pedagogical dimension, established a social dimension, the latter being concerned with the clarification of the relation between the person and his human environment. The plenitude and harmony of man's existence, according to the author, rests not only on a feeling of belonging to a universe of meaning, but also on the healthy interaction between the person and his family, his country, and finally the whole of humanity.

CONCLUDING REMARKS

It is a matter of definition whether one should include Rousseau and Pestalozzi in the Enlightenment or in Romanticism. Historians would agree that Schleiermacher does not belong to the first. Yet, the three have so much in common that, at least in the context of this book, they form a unit. For, in all three we find the intellectual endeavor to liberate mankind from obsolete ideas combined with the Romantic tendency to give feelings and emotions their proper place in man's religious life.

We will speak first of Rousseau and Pestalozzi. Their sensitiveness to the transrational and their optimism with regard to man's inner freedom certainly sets them apart from the kind of rationality and still more from the scepticism and materialism that we find among some representatives of the rationalist era. Yet, one could hardly hear a more trenchant criticism of the theology without religion and the religious instruction without meaning than in the utterances of the two Swiss. They bitterly attacked the unholy alliances between the clergy and oppressive governments as well as the cult of empty words used for the preservation of social injustice and ignorant passivity on the part of the people. And, like the rationalists, they too were convinced that good and straight thinking is the indispensable means of progress in religion.

On the other hand, one has to read only the first lines of the *Émile* with their battle cry of *"retournez à la nature,"* in order to understand why the sophisticated Voltaire ridiculed Rousseau. Or one may read any one of Pestalozzi's writings in order to learn why he had more sympathy with a peasant's simple piety and groping for his rights as a human being than with the problems of an erudite in his study. This also Voltaire might not have understood. But neither Rousseau nor Pestalozzi possessed the humor and the delight in satire as a weapon against reaction as did Montesquieu and Voltaire in France, Swift in England, and Lichtenberg in Germany. For this they were too much involved. Humor needs perspective.

When, after freeing his curious mind from early Pietist influences, the young Schleiermacher had wandered through the rich fields of civilization, from Plato to Spinoza, Kant, and Goethe, the climate of the time had changed. Although only twenty-two years separated Pestalozzi's birthday from his own, and Rousseau's preceded it by only fifty-six years, Schleiermacher's concern was no longer primarily with the power of orthodoxy. As the result of the Enlightenment and the general disillusion in the life of the Churches, he cared more about the growing apathy of the educated to all things religious, a greater danger to the future of the faith than the dissent of heretics.

Of course, the influence of the conservative group was still great in Schleiermacher's time. As it had threatened Lessing, it also threatened Kant and Fichte. But more and more people turned toward the new idealistic philosophy, the new poetry, the romantic movement, and toward historical and scientific research. There they believed they could find what the clergy could not give.

Furthermore, in contrast to Rousseau and Pestalozzi, Schleiermacher was, despite deep inner conflicts, endowed with a sense of inner harmony. Unlike Pestalozzi, whom nature had destined for loneliness, he was happy in the company of interesting men and women of whom he found many in Berlin, the capital of resurging Prussia and one of the centers of the new German bourgeois culture.

Finally, whereas neither Rousseau nor Pestalozzi were scholars, Schleiermacher learned to like the regularity of the life of a thinker and preacher. To be sure, in the literary and educational world of today he is less known than the two citizens of Switzerland—as often is the case with men in whom the desire for proportion and synthesis operates as a brake on the rush of exaggerating and, therefore, striking emotions. Nevertheless, it was entirely in the line of Rousseau and Pestalozzi that Schleiermacher became the greatest exponent of a new Protestant *"Innerlichkeit"* (inwardness), and also the greatest exponent of the liberation of Protestantism from the dogmatic dualism of traditional Christianity. As such he had, directly and indirectly, a decisive influence on Protestant religious education. But he also compelled the Protestants to pay the price for freedom in the realm of religion. This price is the tension between the desire for stability on the one hand, and the urge to be open to the ever-growing wealth and conflict of ideas on the other.

As we will see later, the Catholic Church has tried to avoid this dilemma by affirming its tradition, while Protestantism, divided into fundamentalist and liberal groups, finds itself in a battle with constantly moving and often dangerously uncertain frontiers. We will speak about this in the concluding chapters.

Chapter 13

Horace Bushnell and The Changing American Scene

Horace Bushnell (1802–1875), who served for most of his career as Congregational minister in Hartford, Connecticut, was not one of the very great; but he was, nevertheless, an influential theologian and religious educator. He was a heretic in the eyes of the American Protestant orthodoxy which suppressed one of his books, and a reactionary to the worshippers of science and the cult of industrial progress. Actually, he was more a man of compromise than a bold actor. But in trying to understand the nature of science and by recognizing more than others the signs of the changing American attitude toward dogmatic creeds, especially the Calvinist doctrine of total depravity and predestination, he became one of the leaders of liberal theology and of a new religious education.

The influences which worked on him reflect the turbulent intellectual weather of the nineteenth century. He admired Jonathan Edwards, but was nevertheless on the side of the reformers. Coleridge made a deep impression on him; and, directly or indirectly, Kant, John Frederic Denison Maurice, one of the leaders of Christian socialism in England, and Emerson influenced his thought. Humanitarianism and the idea of social evolution, political conservatism, and progressivism molded his social outlook, though as a preacher to the prosperous classes of Hartford, he remained amazingly unaffected by the plight of the indigent and the many Catholic immigrants who at his time entered the industrial cities of New England. They, not to speak of the Negroes, were for him nothing but human material that would and should be absorbed into the superior Anglo-Saxon civilization.

Eventually he struggled out of the dilemmas of theological eclecticism to arrive at the interpretation of divine revelation as a process of continuing inspiration, by which he could keep the old relatively intact and at the same time be open to the new. In his *Nature and the Supernatural* (1858) he tried to convince his readers that, rather than being embarrassed and bewildered by the evolutionary sciences, the Christian should see the "hand of God" in the successive stages of the earth's development, without at the same time falling into the traps of naturalism, pantheist transcendentalism, and a concept of progress that considered the sovereignty of Christian ideas reinforced by the "grand commercial apostleship of steam and telegraph." [1] The "supernaturalness of man" was, in his opinion, confirmed and by no means refuted by science. Finally, in his work *The Vicarious Sacrifice* (1866) he tried to reconcile his religious optimism with the tragical depth of Christianity. He interpreted the Cross as the symbol of the Divine martyrdom by which God, as the center of love, revealed his mercy to humanity, though being the God of love, he really required no sacrifice to reconcile himself with man. Apparently, the idea of an avenging God and the story of Christ, which would have been a story of humiliation, suffering, defeat, and death save the victory of the resurrection, was the paradox which troubled and at the same time spurred the New England theologian's mind, as it still is the dark and frightful "mysterium" for thousands of thinking Christians.

Bushnell, like Schleiermacher, tried to solve the dilemma by asserting that the depth of the Christian religion could not be understood by logical discourse, but only through the consent of the heart and the emotions. Only through intuition could the depth of Christianity be grasped. Logically, he objected to the confusion of faith and dogma and to "confounding things to be spiritually discerned with things logically reasoned." [2] And, as with Schleiermacher and the whole Romantic movement, there was a strong aesthetic component in Bushnell's religion. Religion, he thought, has to do with taste and requires "responsive sensibility." He introduced his lectures *God in Christ* by an essay on language where he praised "eloquence" as "a power sublime above all others possible to man," and he ventured deep into the areas of pantheist symbolism by declaring: [3]

> Thus, if God is to be himself revealed, He has already thrown out symbols for it, filling the creation full of them, and these will all be played into metaphor. . . . And if we do not take the word in some light, frivolous, merely rhetorician way, we can say nothing of Christ so comprehensively adequate as to call him the metaphor of God: God's last metaphor! And when we have gotten all the metaphoric meanings of his life and death, all that is expressed and bodied in his person of God's saving help and new-creating, sin-forgiving, reconciling love, the sooner we dismiss all speculations on the literalities of his incarnate miracles, his derivation, the composition of his person, his suffering—plainly transcendent as regards our possible understanding—the wiser shall we be in our discipleship. We shall have him as the express image of God's person. We shall have the light of the knowledge of the glory of God, in the face of Jesus Christ. Beholding in him as in a glass the glory of the Lord, we shall be changed into the same image. The metaphoric contents are ours, and beyond that nothing is given.

This point of view, far removed as it is from Calvinist theology, is equally distant from his spiritual ancestors' educational theory and practice. To illustrate this point, we present here some extracts from his main work on education, *Christian Nurture*,[4] in which he collected essays dating back to 1848. The ideas contained in this book, which remind us of Pestalozzi, originated in a period when the author had not yet written his *Nature and the Supernatural* with its distinction between the created and the creation, which comes from Jonathan Edwards, or his *Vicarious Sacrifice* with its insight into the tragical aspect of Christianity. Rather there prevails in *Christian Nurture* a monistic optimism with regard to the nature of childhood and the possibilities of Christian preparation inherent in a pious family. It represents the best of the American middle-class spirit with its belief in the reforming powers of good men; it is a book of a humanist grounded in a religious conception of the unity of the universe, and so full of general educational wisdom that it may be quoted here in some length.[5]

Assuming then the question above stated, What is the true idea of Christian education?—I answer in the following proposition, which it will be the aim of my argument to establish, viz:

That the child is to grow up a Christian, and never know himself as being otherwise.

In other words, the aim, effort, and expectation should be, not, as is commonly assumed, that the child is to grow up in sin, to be converted after he comes to a mature age; but that he is to open on the world as one that is spiritually renewed, not remembering the time when he went through a technical experience, but seeming rather to have loved what is good from his earliest years.

This doctrine is not a novelty, now rashly and for the first time propounded, as some of you may be tempted to suppose. I shall show you, before I have done with the argument, that it is as old as the Christian Church, and prevails extensively at the present day in other parts of the world. Neither let your own experience raise a prejudice against it. If you have endeavored to realize the very truth I here affirm, but find that your children do not exhibit the character you have looked for; if they seem to be intractable to religious influences, and sometimes to display an apparent aversion to the very subject of religion itself, you are not of course to conclude that the doctrine I here maintain is untrue or impracticable. You may be unreasonable in your expectations of your children.

One of the reasons why children cause trouble is that

we do not make a Christian atmosphere about us—do not produce the conviction that we are living unto God. There is a marvelous want of savor in our piety. It is a flower of autumn, colored as highly as it need be to the eye, but destitute of fragrance. It is too much to hope that, with such an instrument, we can fulfill the true idea of Christian education. . . .

However, this confidence in the educability of the child does not warrant an easy optimism.

There are many who assume the radical goodness of human nature, and the work of Christian education is, in their view, only to educate or educe the good that is in us. Let no one be disturbed by the suspicion of a coincidence between what I have here said and such a theory. The natural depravity of man is plainly asserted in the Scriptures, and, if it were not, the familiar laws of physiology would require us to believe, what amounts to the same thing. And if neither Scripture nor physiology taught us the doctrine, if the child was born as clear of natural prejudice or damage, as Adam before his sin, spiritual education, or, what is the same, probation, that which trains a being for a stable, intelligent virtue hereafter, would still involve an experiment of evil, therefore a fall and a bondage under the laws of evil; so that, view the matter as we will, there is no so unreasonable assumption, none so wide of all just philosophy, as that which proposes to form a child to virtue, by simply educing or drawing out what is in him.

The declarations of Scripture, and the laws of physiology, I have already intimated, compel the belief that a child's nature is somehow depravated by descent from parents, who are under the corrupting effects of sin. But this, taken as a question relating to the mere *punctum temporis*, or precise point of birth, is not a question of any so grave import as is generally supposed; for the child, after birth, is still within the matrix of the parental life, and will be, more or less, for many years. And the parental life will be flowing into him all that time, just as naturally, and by a law as truly organic, as when the sap of the trunk flows into a limb. . . .

A perfectly uniform demonstration in religion is not possible or desirable. Nothing is thus uniform but death. Our exercise varies every year and day from childhood onward. Society is going through new modes of exercise in the same manner, excited by new subjects, running into new types of feeling, and struggling with new combinations of thought. Quite as necessary is it that all holy principle should have a varied exercise—now in one duty, now in another; now in public aims and efforts, now in bosom struggles; now in social methods, now in those which are solitary and private; now in high emotion, now in deliberative thought and study. Accordingly, the Christian Church began with a scene of extraordinary social demonstration, and the like, in one form or another, may be traced in every period of its history since that day. . . .

In matters of religion, we have burst the bonds of Church authority and erected the individual mind into a tribunal of judgment within itself; we have asserted free will as the ground of all proper responsibility, and framed our theories of religion so as to justify the incommunicable nature of persons as distinct units. While thus engaged, we have well nigh lost, as was to be expected, the idea of organic powers and relations. The State, the Church, the family, have ceased to be regarded as such, according to their proper idea, and become mere collections of units. A national life, a church life, a family life, is no longer conceived, or perhaps conceivable, by many. Instead of being wrought in together and penetrated, to some extent, by historic laws and forces common to all the members, we only seem to lie as seeds piled together, without any terms of connection, save the accident of proximity, or the fact that we all belong to the heap. And thus, the three great forms of organic existence, which God has appointed for the race, are in fact lost out of mental recognition. The conception is so far gone that, when the fact of such an organic relation is asserted, our enlightened public will stare at the strange conceit, and wonder what can be meant by a paradox so absurd.

My design, at the present time, is to restore, if possible, the conception of one of these organic forms, viz: the family. For though we have gained immense advantages, in a civil, ecclesiastical, and religious point of view, by our modern development of individualism, we have yet run ourselves into many hurtful misapprehensions on all these subjects, which, if they are not rectified, will assuredly bring disastrous consequences. . . .

In the course of his further deliberations Horace Bushnell gives a number of pedagogical suggestions which were not only "progressive" for his time but are still today so sound and applicable that many parents could learn much from them—to their own and their children's happiness.

Children are also discouraged and hardened to good by too much of prohibition. There is a monotony of continuous, ever sounding, prohibition, which is really awful. . . .

Again, it is a great discouragement of piety in children, when they are governed in a hard, unfeeling way or in a manner of force and overbearing absolutism. Anything which puts the child aloof from the parent, or takes away the confidence of love and sympathy, will as certainly be a wall to shut him off from God. If his Christian father is felt only as a tyrant, he will have a tyrant in God's name to bear; and that will be enough to create a sullen prejudice against all sacred things. . . .

Another and even more common way of discouraging children in matters of piety is by an overexacting manner, or by an extreme difficulty of being pleased. Children love approbation, and are especially disappointed, when they fail of it in their meritorious endeavors. . . .

Closely akin to this, is the fault of holding displeasures too long, and yielding it with too great difficulty. It is right that children, doing wrong, should encounter some kind of treatment that indicates displeasure. But the displeasure should not take the manner of a grudge, and hold on after the wrong is visibly felt and repented of. On the contrary, there should even be a hastening toward the child, in glad recognitions and cordial greetings, when the tokens only of relenting begin to appear; even as the prodigal's father is represented, in the parable, as discovering him, in his return, when he is yet a great way off, and advancing to meet and embrace him. . . .

Again, it will be found that piety is very commonly discouraged in children, by giving them tests of character that are inappropriate to their age. There is an immense cruelty put upon children here, by parents who have really no design but simply to be faithful. Their child, for example, loses his temper in some manner in which he is crossed; and the conclusion is forthwith sprung upon him that he has a bad heart, and is certainly no Christian child. Whereupon he ceases to pray; or, if he is put to it as a form, does it with an averted and reluctant feeling, as if the wrong were conclusive against his prayers. It is only necessary to ask how the father, how the mother would themselves fare, tested by the same rule? If irritation, passion, any loss of temper, is conclusive against the little being who has scarcely began to be practiced in self-government, how is it with them who ought by this time to be immovably fixed in their serenity? . . .

The sum of all I would say here is, let children be judged as children, and let them not be cruelly discouraged in all thoughts of love to God, because they falter, as older people do; only in a different manner.

I must also speak of another and more general mode of discouragement, in what may be called the holding back, or holding aloof system, by which children are denied an early recognition of their membership in the Church, and an admission to the Lord's table. I have spoken of this membership already, in another place, and shall also speak, hereafter, of the supper in its more positive uses. What I now refer to, more especially, is the negatively bad or discouraging effect thrown upon their piety, by these methods of detention, or exclusion. The child giving evidence, however beautiful, of his piety, is still kept back from the fellowship and table of Christ, for the simple defect of years. As if years were one of the Scripture evidences of grace. Sometimes the difficulty is that he can speak of no experience, or change, such as we call conversion; and sometimes, if he can, that he is yet too young to be confided in. And so it turns out, after all that is said of the membership initiated in baptism, that nothing is practically made of it, or allowed to be made of it. . . .

CONCLUDING REMARKS

Horace Bushnell tried to reconcile the secular trends of his period with the religious heritage and realized that thereby he had to change some dogmatic elements of the Calvinist tradition, especially its pessimism about human nature. The trends of the time, represented by the rising middle class were scientific, empirical, industrial, and humanitarian. As a preacher and writer he addressed men and women who were optimistic, had faith in progress, and were disinclined to believe that the majority of them, including their children, were condemned to hell before they were even born. They wanted to have common sense also in matters religious, and they wanted to have their children encouraged rather than discouraged.

Horace Bushnell's life almost coincided with that of the "father of the American common school," Horace Mann, though he survived the great educator by sixteen years. Horace Mann, too, had to struggle with the Calvinist orthodoxy of New England, and his recommendation to abolish the rod as one of the main instruments of education met the stubborn opposition of the old guard among teachers and parents.

To be sure, in his theology the Hartford minister was not original, but no one could express himself so soundly with regard to the upbringing of youth without possessing a refined personal understanding for the life of children and of humanity as a whole.

The Present

THE RISE OF CATHOLIC EDUCATION

There is no field of learning where convictions assert themselves as vigorously as they do in religious education. For religious education does not intend to acquaint the pupil with the ever-changing aspects of secular knowledge but to give him a perception of a truth believed by the faithful to be eternal and to involve his salvation. Therefore we have fundamentalists who insist on the literal truth of the Bible, and sects that want to renew the spirit of the early Christian communities. We have with us the doctrines of medieval Scholasticism and of the reformers. Even religious liberals cannot discuss the concepts of Christianity in the same spirit as that in which a scientist discusses an experiment, for they, too, believe that values are at stake that should form the whole personality and its relation to the universe. Like the conservatives they envision the divine at the end of their search for truth; therefore they are often as zealous in their ways as their adversaries are in theirs.

However, labels such as "conservative" or "orthodox" versus "liberal" or "progressive" have to be qualified if attached to complex cultural phenomena; otherwise they may confuse more than they clarify. Pestalozzi, for example, was "liberal" only in his protest against the social injustice and ecclesiasticism of his time and in his insistence on "organic" as against verbal and artificial education. But, in his Christ-centered religiosity he remained in the "orthodox" tradition. It would also be misleading to believe that all religious conservatives will use inflexibly authoritarian methods of indoctrination. Religious educators, whether conservative or liberal in their creed, are today just as much interested in progressive techniques for motivating the child's participation as our teachers in public and private schools, some of them even more so. Priests and nuns study in our modern schools of education with the same eagerness to learn as secular teachers, though logically they reject any "naturalist" interpretation and application of educational and psychological methods.

However, because of its strongly hierarchical structure and system of control, one has to separate Catholic religious education from that of other Church groups. Its underlying principles are laid down in the famous encyclical proclaimed by Pope Pius XI on the "Christian Education of Youth." But, in a broad sense, the encyclical issued by Leo XIII on "The Conditions of Labor" (1891) and Pope Pius XI encyclicals on "Christian Marriage" (1930), on "Reconstructing the Social Order" (1931), and on "Atheistic Communism" (1937) also deal with the issue of education in a changing world.

In order to appreciate the significance of these encyclicals, we must understand them in their historical context. As we saw in an earlier chapter, compared with the victory of the Curia at the council of Trent over the centrifugal forces of the late Middle Ages and the remarkable resurgence of Catholicism during and after the Counter Reformation, the eighteenth century was a period of relaxation and decline.

Yet, the French revolution, in one way a defeat, at the same time stimulated a recovery. The clergy showed strength in a period of suffering, and the monarchial and conservative powers of Europe found themselves united with the Churches, Catholic and Protestant, in their opposition to the French republic and Napoleon. Even the liberals who originally had sympathized with the French people and its revolt against oppression were disappointed at the unsuspected turning of the goddess of reason into a fury of hatred. The Romantic movement was a search for new moorings in old harbors, and the Catholic Church became regarded as one of the bays where the ship of mankind could find some safety before the storms of history.

In France, Francois René de Chateaubriand wrote *Le Génie du Christianisme, ou Beauté de la Religion Chrétienne* (1802). While this work was welcomed by Napoleon as an ideological support for his version of monarchy, a later publication by the same author, which recommended a return to the older legitimate monarchy of the Bourbons, (*De Bonaparte, des Bourbons, et de la nécessité de se rallier à nos princes légitimes,* 1814) was praised by Louis XVIII as being worth a hundred thousand soldiers to him.

The reaction against the one-sidedness of the era of rationalism and against the cruelties of the French revolution was violent. Typical of this reaction, proof also of the fact that people believe what they like to believe was the fact that the writings of the Comte de Maistre, particularly his work *On the Pope* (*Du Pape*), could attract a wide audience. Especially the reactionary circles of Europe considered it a scholarly and spiritual support for the Catholic Church and the papacy. This was certainly de Maistre's intention. But the erudition displayed in his book is spurious, its arguments twisted, and its religious bias more exclusively Catholic even than Metternich's Holy Alliance which, besides orthodox Russia, included Protestant Prussia.[1] De Maistre's contempt for the people and his praise of poverty and ignorance were cynical despite their religious disguise,[2] and his defense of the Spanish and Portuguese Inquisition which he ventured in his *Lettres à un Gentilhomme Russe sur L'Inquisition Espagnole*[3] were both ethically and logically an offense to Christianity. If the Church had not separated its claim to spiritual authority from the hateful absolutism of de Maistre and the European nobility, for whom he considered himself a spokesman, it would have maneuvered itself into a corner of darkness, and Leo XIII's encyclical *On the Conditions of Labor* of 1891 could not have been written. As a matter of fact, its publication aroused even then bitter criticism by wealthy landowners and industrialists all over Europe.

In Germany, Joseph Görres turned from an advocate of revolution and nationalism into a supporter of papacy and became one of the foremost interpreters of Catholic mysticism in his *Christliche Mystik* (1836–

1842). The Görres Society of Germany to this day devotes itself to the promotion of Catholic culture.

Priests who had fled from the French revolution to England were well received and made a deep impression on the generally anti-Catholic population by their sacrificial devotion to religious and social causes. Catholicism then established itself firmly with increasing influence in England, Cardinal Newman (1801–1890) being one of its most influential defenders, and steadily gained, partly as a result of large immigrations, in the United States also.

Poets and artists of Protestant nations evoked in their admirers a new feeling for the aesthetic, if not always for the spiritual and ethical, values in Catholicism. In the course of the century the Holy See disengaged itself more and more from the tangle of national politics in which it had been fatally involved in earlier times. To be sure, the Curia protested violently against the final abolition in 1870 of its secular power by the new Savoy monarchy which, with the exception of Venice and the *Patrimonium Petri*, had already succeeded in fulfilling the old dream of Italian patriots since the time of Petrarch and Machiavelli, i.e., the unification of the nation.

But, in the long run, this deprivation only strengthened the spiritual role of the papacy. Even before the abolition of the last of the papal states, it had already felt strong enough to convoke (1869) a Vatican council and to proclaim, one year later, the dogma of papal infallibility, against the original resistance of a number of high-ranking clergymen, especially from Germany. This proclamation was the ultimate fulfillment of the intention of the council of Trent, making Rome the absolute spiritual and organizational center of the Catholic world. Without this centralization, the encyclical on the "Christian Education of Youth" [4] could not have its profound and enduring effect.

This encyclical emphasizes the claim of the Catholic Church derived from the double title "conferred exclusively on her by God himself." . . .

The first title is founded upon the express mission and supreme authority to teach given her by her Divine Founder. . . . The second title is in the supernatural motherhood, in virtue of which the Church, spotless spouse of Christ, generates, nurtures and educates souls in the divine life of grace, with her Sacraments and her doctrine.

On the following pages we are quoting some of the most pertinent paragraphs from the encyclical on "Christian Education."

(STATE RIGHTS) . . . Accordingly in the matter of education, it is the right, or to speak more correctly, it is the duty of the State to protect in its legislation, the prior rights, already described, of the family as regards the Christian education of its offspring, and consequently also to respect the supernatural rights of the Church in this same realm of Christian education.

(TRUE HARMONY) . . . These facts moreover present a most striking confirmation of the Catholic doctrine defined by the Vatican Council: "Not only is it impossible for faith and reason to be at variance with each other, they are on the contrary of mutual help. For while right reason establishes the foundations of faith, and, by the help of its light, develops a knowledge of the things of God, faith on the other hand frees and preserves reason from error and enriches it with varied knowledge. The Church therefore, far from hindering the pursuit of the arts and sciences, fosters and promotes them in many ways. For she is neither ignorant nor un-appreciative of the many advantages which flow from them to mankind. On the contrary she admits that just as they come from God, Lord of all knowledge, so too, if rightly used, with the help of His grace they lead to God. Nor does she prevent sciences, each in its own sphere, from making use of principles and methods of their own. Only while acknowledging the freedom due to them, she takes every precaution to prevent them from falling into error by opposition to divine doctrine, or from overstepping their proper limits, and thus invading and disturbing the domain of faith.

This norm of a just freedom in things scientific, serves also as an inviolable norm of a just freedom in things didactic, or for rightly understood liberty in teaching; it should be observed therefore in whatever instruction is imparted to others. Its obligation is all the more binding in justice when there is question of instructing youth. For in this work the teacher, whether public or private, has no absolute right of his own, but only such as has been communicated to him by others. Besides every Christian child or youth has a strict right to instruction in harmony with the teaching of the Church, the pillar and ground of truth. And whoever disturbs the pupil's faith in any way, does him grave wrong, inasmuch as he abuses the trust which children place in their teachers, and takes unfair advantage of their inexperience and of their natural craving for unrestrained liberty, at once illusory and false.

(SUBJECT OF EDUCATION) In fact it must never be forgotten that the subject of Christian education is man whole and entire, soul united to body in unity of nature, with all his faculties natural and supernatural, such as right reason and revelation show him to be; man, therefore, fallen from his original estate, but redeemed by Christ and restored to the supernatural condition of adopted son of God, though without the preternatural privileges of bodily immortality or perfect control of appetite. There remain, therefore, in human nature the effects of original sin, the chief of which are weakness of will and disorderly inclinations.

"Folly is bound up in the heart of a child and the rod of correction shall drive it away." (*Prov. xxii*. 15: *Stultitia colligata est in corde pueri: et virga disciplinae fugabit eam.*) Disorderly inclinations then must be corrected, good tendencies encouraged and regulated from tender childhood, and above all the mind must be enlightened and the will strengthened by supernatural truth and by the means of grace, without which it is impossible to control evil impulses, impossible to attain to the full and complete perfection of education intended by the Church, which Christ has endowed so rightly with divine doctrine and with the Sacraments, the efficacious means of grace.

(FALSE NATURALISM) Hence every form of pedagogic naturalism which in any way excludes or weakens supernatural Christian formation in the teaching of youth, is false.

Every method of education founded, wholly or in part, on the denial or forgetfulness of original sin and of grace, and relying on the sole powers of human nature, is unsound. Such generally speaking, are those modern systems bearing various names which appeal to a pretended self-government and unrestrained freedom on the part of the child, and which diminish or even suppress the teacher's authority and action, attributing to the child an exclusive primacy of initiative, and an activity independent of any higher law, natural or divine, in the work of his education.

If any of these terms are used, less properly to denote the necessity of a gradually more active cooperation on the part of the pupil in his own education, if the intention is to banish from education despotism and violence, which, by the way, just punishment is not, this would be correct, but in no way new. It would mean only what has been taught and reduced to practice by the Church in traditional Christian education, in imitation of the method employed by God Himself towards His creatures, of whom He demands active cooperation according to the nature of each; for His Wisdom "reacheth from end to end mightily and ordereth all things sweetly."

But alas! It is clear from the obvious meaning of the words and from experience, that what is intended by not a few, is the withdrawal of education from every sort of dependence on the divine law. So today we see, strange sight indeed, educators and philosophers who spend their lives in searching for a universal moral code of education, as if there existed no decalogue, no gospel law, no law even of nature stamped by God on the heart of man, promulgated by right reason, and codified in positive revelation by God Himself in the ten commandments. These innovators are wont to refer contemptuously to Christian education as "heteronomous," "passive," "obsolete," because founded upon the authority of God and His holy law.

Such men are miserably deluded in their claim to emancipate, as they say, the child, while in reality they are making him the slave of his own blind pride and of his disorderly affections, which, as a logical consequence of this false system, come to be justified as legitimate demands of a so-called autonomous nature.

But what is worse, is the claim, not only vain but false, irreverent and dangerous, to submit to research, experiment and conclusions of a purely natural and profane order, those matters of education which belong to the supernatural order; as for example questions of priestly or religious vocation, and in general the secret workings of grace which indeed elevate the natural powers but are infinitely superior to them, and may nowise be subjected to physical laws, for "the spirit breatheth where He will." (*Io., iii,* 8: *Spiritus ubi vult spirat.*)

(SEX INSTRUCTION) Another grave danger is that naturalism which nowadays invades the field of education in that most delicate matter of purity of morals. Far too common is the error of those who with dangerous assurance and under an ugly term propagate a so-called sex-education, falsely imagining they can forearm youth against the dangers of sensuality by means purely natural, such as a foolhardy initiation and precautionary instruction for all indiscriminately, even in public; and, worse still, by exposing them at an early age to the occasions, in order to accustom them, so it is argued, and as it were to harden them against such dangers.

Such persons grievously err in refusing to recognize the inborn weakness of human nature, and the law of which the Apostle speaks, fighting against the law of mind (*Rom.* vii, 23.); and also in ignoring the experience of facts, from which it is clear that, particularly in young people, evil practices are the effect not so much of ignorance of intellect as of weakness of a will exposed to dangerous occasions, and unsupported by the means of grace.

(CO-EDUCATION) False also and harmful to Christian education is the so-called method of "co-education." This, too, by many of its supporters, is founded upon naturalism and the denial of original sin; but by all, upon a de-

plorable confusion of ideas that mistakes a leveling promiscuity and equality for the legitimate association of the sexes.
The Creator has ordained and disposed perfect union of
the sexes only in matrimony, and, with various degrees of
contact, in the family and in society. Besides there is not in
nature itself, which fashions the two quite different in organ-
ism, in temperament, in abilities, anything to suggest that
there can be, or ought to be, promiscuity, and much less
equality, in the training of the two sexes. These in keeping
with the wonderful designs of the Creator are destined to
complement each other in the family and in society, precisely because of their differences, which therefore ought to
be maintained and encouraged during their years of formation, with the necessary distinction and corresponding separation, according to age and circumstances. These principles,
with due regard to time and place, must in accordance
with Christian prudence, be applied to all schools, particularly in the most delicate and decisive period of formation,
that, namely of adolescence; and in gymnastic exercises and
deportment, special care must be had of Christian modesty in
young women and girls, which is so gravely impaired by any
kind of exhibition in public. . . .

(THE SCHOOL) Since, however, the younger generation
must be trained in the arts and sciences for the advantage and
prosperity of civil society, and since the family itself is un-
equal to this task, it was necessary to create that social institution, the school. But let it be borne in mind that this
institution owes its existence to the initiative of the family
and of the Church, long before it was undertaken by the
state. Hence, considered in its historical origin, the school is
by its very nature an institution subsidiary and complemen-
tary to the family and to the Church. It follows logically and
necessarily that it must not be in opposition to, but in positive
accord with, those other two elements, and form with them
a perfect moral union, constituting one sanctuary of education, as it were, with the family and the Church. Otherwise,
it is doomed to fail of its purpose, and to become instead an
agent of destruction. . . .

From this it follows that the so-called "neutral" or "lay"
school, from which religion is excluded, is contrary to the

fundamental principles of education. Such a school moreover cannot exist in practice; it is bound to become irreligious. There is no need to repeat what our predecessors have declared on this point, especially Pius XI and Leo XIII, at the time when laicism was beginning in a special manner to infest the public school.

We renew and confirm their declarations, as well as the Sacred Canons in which the frequenting of non-Catholic schools, whether neutral or mixed, those namely, which are open to Catholics and non-Catholics alike, is forbidden for Catholic children, and can be at most tolerated, on the approval of the ordinary alone, under determined circumstances of place and time, and with special precautions. Neither can Catholics admit that other type of mixed school (least of all the so-called "*école unique*", obligatory on all), in which the students are provided with separate religious instruction, but receive other lessons in common with non-Catholic pupils from non-Catholic teachers.

(THE CATHOLIC SCHOOL) For the mere fact that a school gives some religious instruction (often extremely stinted), does not bring it into accord with the rights of the Church and the Christian family, or make it a fit place for Catholic students. To be this, it is necessary that all the teaching and the organization of the school, and its teachers, syllabus, and textbooks in every branch, be regulated by the Christian spirit, under the direction and maternal supervision of the Church; so that religion may be in very truth the foundation and crown of the youth's entire training; and this in every grade of school, not only the elementary, but the intermediate and higher institutions of learning as well. . . .

And let no one say that in a nation where there are different religious beliefs, it is impossible to provide for public instruction otherwise than by neutral or mixed schools. In such a case it becomes the duty of the state, indeed it is the easier and more reasonable method of procedure, to leave free scope to the initiative of the Church and family, while giving them such assistance as justice demands. That this can be done to the full satisfaction of families, and to the advantage of education and of public peace and tranquility, is clear from the actual experience of some countries comprising different religious denominations. There the school legislation respects the rights of the family, and Catholics are free to follow their own system of teaching in schools that are entirely Catholic. Nor is distributive justice lost sight of, as is evidenced by the financial aid granted by the state to the several schools demanded by the families.

In other countries of mixed creeds, things are otherwise, and a heavy burden weighs upon Catholics, who under the guidance of their Bishops and with the indefatigable cooperation of the clergy, secular and regular, support Catholic schools for their children entirely at their own expense; to this they feel obliged in conscience, and with a generosity and constancy worthy of all praise, they are firmly determined to make adequate provision for what they openly profess as their motto: "Catholic education in Catholic schools for all the Catholic youth." If such education is not aided from public funds, as distributive justice requires, certainly it may not be opposed by any civil authority ready to recognize the rights of the family, and the irreducible claims of legitimate liberty.

Where this fundamental liberty is thwarted or interfered with, Catholics will never feel, whatever may have been the sacrifices already made, that they have done enough, for the support and defense of their schools and for the securing of laws that will do them justice.

The five great encyclicals form such a coherent whole that an extract such as the preceding cannot provide their full meaning. It should be noted that the words "Christian" and "Christianity" are used synonymously with the Catholic Church. There is no sign of a recognition of other forms of Christianity. Where the word "liberty" occurs it denotes, according to Catholic tradition, only "legitimate" liberty, i.e., "liberty" within the theological, intellectual, and organizational framework of the Church. There is a wide difference between this concept and the democratic meaning of liberty or freedom of conscience as used by Roger Williams and Thomas Jefferson. At no place does the encyclical on "Christian Education" acknowledge the conflict between

Christian dogmatism and advancing science that has divided the souls of men since the times of Copernicus and Galileo and forced official Christianity into what Whitehead calls the "shameful retreat" before progressing empirical knowledge. The encyclical accepts without questioning the Thomistic position of the divine harmony between right faith and right reason and acknowledges, therefore, the scientists' freedom to "make use of principles and methods of their own." However, even in its relation to scientists the Church assumes the role of the supreme arbiter, for it feels entitled to "take every precaution to prevent them from falling into error by opposition to divine doctrine."

A certain practical pluralism of educational institutions is acknowledged with regard to countries with a religiously mixed population. Nevertheless, no doubt is left that this is merely a matter of contingency and expediency, for, in such countries, Catholic parents must send their children to Catholic schools where they exist, and it is demanded that these schools be supported by the state on an equal basis with the public school system.

When reading the various encyclicals one arrives at the conclusion that—save for the political claims of the medieval popes—no essential principle has been changed since the thirteenth and fourteenth centuries. The Church reigns at the top of a pyramid in a patriarchally structured society. It is superior to the state as the divine is superior to the human, it is infallible, and it has the right and duty to control the knowledge of men and the spirit of the schools.

It would, however, be a serious mistake to conclude that the stability, order, and authority of the Catholic Church are detrimental to the vitality and self-criticism of its educators. This appears with particular clarity from an article in one of the leading Catholic journals. *The Commonweal,*[5] by Philip Sharper, which begins as follows:

> Contemporary Catholic educators seem to exhibit not only a capacity but an enthusiasm for merciless self-scrutiny, and at their meetings Catholic deans and dons now belabor Catholic education with that unfettered glee formerly reserved for Catholic attacks on Horace Mann, John Dewey, and "progressive education." Underlying such a change are at least two important intuitions: one, that honest criticism

is a sign, not of disaffection, but of love; and second, that the educational process, almost by definition, calls for constant re-examination and revision.

These critiques prove the wisdom of trying to shape the Christian message in a new way. The "new way" which is emphasized in each chapter of this present book is, of course, actually the recovery of a very ancient way. It consists in attempting to have religious education do for each student what was done for each of those whom Christ in his life on earth invited to participate in the fulness of life.

Religious education, in other words, cannot feel that its primary purpose is to enable the student to "defend his faith" against all objections. The purpose of religious education is to make the student live his faith, to make him aware that the Christian education is an encounter with Christ, and the surrender which this encounter demands is made less difficult by the questioning of a skeptical world than it is by the rebellion of the self against the invasion of a loving, but demanding God.

A new way of religious education is also demanded by F. J. Sheed in his book *Are We Really Teaching Religion?* [6] The author sets up four criteria for religious education. One: does it give the pupil a real understanding of Christian doctrine? Two: does it motivate him to think seriously about his life after death? Three: do Catholics prefer Christian literature to an interesting novel? Four: do they live "in anguish" that others also receive the benefit of grace? The author concludes: "We do not measure up very well to those four tests." And frequently one finds in Catholic journals the complaint that too many Catholics are not sufficiently conscious of the secular threat. Instead of demanding concerted action, they emphasize the problems of teaching Catholic religion in public schools.[7] Catholic educators are also concerned, as are most other religious educators, with the problem of retention of religious knowledge.[8]

During the nineteenth century and the first decades of the twentieth Catholic educators, as well as Protestants, had become increasingly skeptical about the efficiency of the older methods of catechetical instruction. Of course, Peter Canisius' famous Catechism, dating back to the time of the Council of Trent, had always been used in somewhat modified versions. But it was left to the German Catholics to initiate a movement for modern catechetical progress. About 1900, Heinrich Stieglitz and the Munich Catechetical Society adopted Herbart's "five steps" to catechetical instruction and thus "replaced the text-exposition method which dates to the late middle-ages." A further development "came in 1936 with the publication of the small volume of J. A. Jungmann, S.J., which triggered a revolution, or more accurately a restoration, in the *content* of Catholic teaching." [9]

Naturally, after the moral catastrophe of the Hitler period and in face of the spread of communism, Catholic educators in many countries emphasized the necessity of grounding youth in the basic tenets of the doctrine. Out of this concern has arisen a new and apparently world-wide catechetical literature that deviates from the traditional catechism not only in its psychological approach, but also in its stronger emphasis on the Bible which up to our time the majority of Catholic laymen all over the world did not know first hand. One of the catechisms coming from Germany has been translated into the most important Western languages and is used widely in the United States. The German original bears the title *Katholischer Katechismus der Bistümer Deutschlands* [10] and went through its ninth impression in 1957; [11] (no author's name). The American title is simply *A Catholic Catechism*.[12] Part One, following a general introduction that explains the reasons for the glory and guardianship of the Catholic Church, deals with "God and our Redemption," Part Two with "The Church and the Sacraments," Part Three with "Life in Accordance with God's Commandments," and Part Four with "The Four Last Things" (death and personal judgment, heaven, purgatory, hell, christian burial, and the end of the world and the completion of God's design).

In spite of a degree of adaptation to modern pedagogical approaches there is, naturally, no divergence of the dogma. Of Mary it is said:

> After our Lord had gone up into heaven, Mary remained with the group of disciples, prayed with them in the Up-

per Room in Jerusalem, and on Pentecost received with them the outpouring of the Holy Spirit. Both in joy and sorrow she took part in the life of the infant Church. She is the Mother of Christians.

One of the main American spokesmen of the kerygmatic-catechetical method is the Reverend Joseph B. Collins. In his *Teaching Religion, An Introduction to Catechetics* [13] he deals with the history of catechetics, the principles and methods of teaching religion, with teaching techniques, and with the special methods and problems of religious instruction. The Appendix contains several papal utterances concerning the teaching of religious doctrine.

Catholic educators hope that the catechetical method will also help to improve the teaching of religion during release-time and in Sunday schools of communities without parochial schools. Such communities are generally considered to be inadequate with respect to the task of keeping the young close to the Church in our modern secular environment. Problems also emerge in Catholic higher education, not unlike those which bother Protestant denominational institutions. The more Catholic colleges become a part of American higher education, competing with nondenominational establishments on the scholarly level, the more they are compelled to appoint teachers whose primary interest is not religious, but scholarly and scientific. These teachers insist on the objective exposition of their subjects and are inclined to leave the preservation of the Catholic spirit to the administration and the chapel. This happens at a time when the staffs of some of the most prominent nondenominational colleges and universities in the United States become increasingly concerned with the totality of the cultural situation which, of course, includes the religious problem.

Nevertheless, despite the increasing involvement of the Catholic tradition in the troubles of the present, one fact remains, i.e., the firmness of the core of doctrine and dogma wherever the continuation of the faith is at stake.

So far the description of Catholic education referred to the period before the second Ecumenical Council (1962–1965). The question, therefore, arises to what degree the initiative of Pope John XXIII will affect the religious education of Catholic youth, and, indirectly, also that of other denominations.

The Council has stirred up the Christian world by causing surprising changes in the official attitude of the Catholic Church to non-Catholic Christian and even non-Christian religions. Since then Catholics and Protestants worship together at special occasions, the Catholic mass is celebrated in the vernacular, interdenominational conferences abound, and laymen are encouraged to participate more boldly—though not too boldly—in the affairs of their religious community. Under the auspices of the Church and of Catholic universities, theological institutes are founded to which even non-Christians are admitted, as had already been done by earlier Protestant centers of research. A great step forward was made by the Roman Catholic Archbishop of Munich, Cardinal Doepfner, and the German Evangelical Church's Bishop of Bavaria, Hermann Dietzfelbinger, who in 1968 published a joint pamphlet, "Leading Principles for Instruction and Education According to Common Premises of the Christian Faith." The principles discussed do not conceal the differences between the doctrines of the two Churches, but, going beyond mere instructional questions, emphasize the common theological basis on which a school with pupils belonging to either Church can operate. Teachers of both denominations must learn to leave certain topics untouched or they otherwise would offend children from the other denomination.

The pope has cut the powers and changed the name of the old heresy court, "The Sacred Congregation of the Holy Office," and the dominance of Italian prelates in the curia will be retrenched. A new interdenominational literature emerges with the purpose of engaging members of different denominations in fruitful conversations and thus overcoming the barriers built by a long tradition of suspicion and hostility.

The bishops will enjoy more freedom in the administration of their dioceses, and the clergy already expresses its criticism of ecclesiastical authoritarianism in a form that in the first decades of this century would have invited the penalty of excommunication. So many hitherto untouchable points of doctrine have been discussed at the Second

Council and so much diplomacy has been revealed that it will be difficult in the future to convince people of the dogma of the divine inspiration of the Councils of the Church which caused the persecution of the reformers Huss and Luther. Probably a whole number of obsolete tenets of faith will disappear in an aura of respectful silence.

But despite certain steps toward decentralization, the hierarchical structure of the Catholic Church will remain because centralization belongs to its very essence. Furthermore, Pope Paul VI has already warned several times against reformistic excesses, laxity in doctrine, and premature hopes for unification.

Thus, after the first enthusiasm of *"aggiornamento"* (updating), both sides seem to feel that they might lose more than gain if the spirit of friendliness endangered the sense of identity with their own peculiar historical faith. The spirit of Alfredo Ottaviani, the symbol of conservatism, is still alive in spite of the recent retirement of the Cardinal, and under the leadership of the Reverend Gomar de Pauw, a movement has emerged against the supposed profanization of the Holy Mass by the use of the vernacular as one of the signs of the Church's yielding to Protestantism.

Protestants too agree with the pope that "true ecumenism" should not come from unconcern with respect to matters of faith and point at decisive differences between the Churches of Luther and Calvin and the Roman tradition, especially with regard to the role of the Church as an institution, to such concepts as sin, grace, salvation, and the administration of the Eucharist. Arthur Michael Ramsay, the Archbishop of Canterbury, was called a "traitor" by some Anglican clergymen when at the end of March, 1966, he traveled to his historic meeting with the head of the Church of Rome. And amicable though the meeting was as the beginning of a "serious dialogue," the archbishop nevertheless spoke of "formidable difficulties of doctrine" which would have to be discussed between Roman Catholic, Anglican, and other denominations.

Nevertheless, a new spirit seems to blow through the houses of Christendom; each side tries to better understand the other. The future will tell us whether the new spirit will eventually affect the grass roots of Christian life, not only in countries traditionally inclined toward reform, but also in such countries as Spain, Portugal, and certain states of South America.

Much value was laid by the prelates of the Ecumenical Council on education as the best means of planting the right seeds of the Catholic future into the right soil.

In its Decree on Christian Education the Sacred Synod "proclaims anew what has already been taught in several documents of the Magisterium, namely; the right of the Church freely to establish and to conduct schools of every type and level." There is a certain difference from earlier manifestos in that the council recognizes the pluralistic character of modern society, the importance of sex education, of "new experiments," of "the latest advances in psychology and the art and science of teaching," and of more individualized forms and aims of instruction. All these modern endeavors, however, can only do harm if they forget the overarching aim of education, which is "the formation of the human person in the pursuit of his ultimate end and of the societies of which, as man, he is a member, and in whose obligations, as an adult, he will share."

> Since all Christians have become by rebirth of water and the Holy Spirit a new creature, so that they should be called and should be children of God, they have the right to a Christian education. A Christian education does not merely strive for the maturing of a human person . . . but has as its principal purpose this goal: that the baptized, while they are gradually introduced to the knowledge of the mystery of salvation, become ever more aware of the gift of faith they have received, and that they learn in addition how to worship God the Father in spirit and truth (cf. Jn. 4:23) especially in liturgical action, and be conformed in their personal lives according to the new man created in justice and holiness of truth (Eph. 4:22–24); also that they develop into perfect manhood, to the mature measure of the fullness of Christ (cf. Eph. 4:13) and strive for the growth of the Mystical Body; moreover, that aware of their calling, they learn not only how to bear witness to the hope that is in them (cf. Peter 3:15) but also how to help in the Christian formation of the world that takes place when natural pow-

ers viewed in the full consideration of man redeemed by Christ contribute to the good of the whole society.

Nowhere else can this education toward salvation be carried out but in the Catholic School. The States (which can play but a subsidiary role with regard to the final ends of man and his education) are nevertheless urged to use their power for aiding the purposes of the Church to observe "distributive justice," wherever there is a plurality of denominations, and to provide direct or indirect subsidy of Catholic schools. Hence the Church is critical of any system that "deprives" youth of their right to moral and Christian instruction as the Catholic Church perceives it.

This, of course, implies criticism of both the persecution of religious schools as we have it in Communist countries, and the exclusion of religious education from public schools, as it exists in France and has recently been confirmed by the decision of the Supreme Court of the United States.

Reading about the religious justification of a separate Catholic education as it is contained in the preceding quotations, one may ask himself the question: to what degree will the children of our secular era be capable of experiencing in themselves the emergence of a "new creature" due to the "rebirth of water and the Holy Spirit" and the ensuing participation in the "mystery of salvation"? However, the problem of the meaning of meaning is shared by all denominations which cherish the traditional language of Christendom.

Certainly, Catholics are right in believing with other Christians that an early indoctrination will hold a person close to his religious community. This is not merely a matter of doctrine, but also a matter of organisational influence and survival in a world of competing ideologies. Education, as has also been recognized by communist countries and to some degree by all political systems, is the most important strategic point in the battle for the souls of man. The Catholic Church has shown this realism about the interconnection of ideas and practical situations also in its decisions about two problems which will continually affect the religious attitude and the number of Catholics in the modern world: one of them is the handling of mixed marriages, and the other its attitude toward birth control.

THE PROTESTANT DILEMMA

In contrast to the hierarchical control of the Catholic Church developed by councils and papal decrees, the richly varied denominational life of Protestantism gives at first glance the impression of disunity. However strongly some Churches of the Reformation tended toward centralization—especially when they enjoyed the support of the state—they never succeeded in fully suppressing Luther's original idea of the freedom of the Christian conscience. The range of views among Protestant ministers has constantly widened, even within the same denomination. It reaches from fundamentalism to a degree of liberalism that, even with the widest stretch of imagination, cannot be reconciled with the genuine Christian creed.

The large span of opinions is represented by the literature on Christian education. Besides authors who are comfortably unaffected by the critical problems of our time, there are others who reveal a most-serious concern with the future of Protestantism. These authors know that it cannot rely on the authoritarian means available to the Catholic Church, but that it must try to awaken religious interest by means of persuasion at a time when this has become increasingly difficult.

Of the large number of books we select two which, though not of most recent origin, indicate best the trend of thought among American nonfundamentalist clergymen because they are representative of the problems existing in other countries also.

One of the most outspoken writers on the progressive side is George Albert Coe. His early work, *A Social Theory of Religious Education*,[14] shows throughout the influence of John Dewey and the pragmatic movement. He insists on the *social* interpretation of religious education and the *social* role of Christianity which require, as their starting point, individual experience and personal motivation. Consequently he wishes Christian education to abandon old methods of indoctrination and to adopt the principles of modern psychology and methodology. Three ideals should be recognized: first, "the ideal of freely unfolding individuality," second, "the aspiration for political freedom that came to partial expression in the French Revolution and in the early stages of the American experiment in popular government," and third, the incorporation of the "scientific movement" into the educational process. ("Regulated observation and experiment; the resultant discovery of laws; new control of natural forces as an end result—these are the marks of the scientific movement.") In congruence with Dewey's *Democracy and Education* George A. Coe asks also for a recognition of "the social significance of the modern secular state" as a principal educational agency.

> . . . the secularization of the state, and therefore of state schools, has been necessitated chiefly by the social inadequacy of ecclesiastical traditions and practices. The state, not the Church, has been the decisive defender and guarantor of fundamental liberties, such as the right to think, to speak, to associate with one's fellows, and to stand before courts of law as the equal of any citizen. . . . The free state, moreover, rather than any Church, has been the chief practical realization of the unity and the solidarity of men.

Inevitably, the prime need of a new religious education is the reorganization of the curriculum. "To make the Bible the practically exclusive source of material is to keep the attention of pupils fixed upon pre-democratic social conditions," although "the crude social conditions of early Hebrew history and legend" may "yield nuggets of gold for the religious teacher." Instead of the Bible as an infallible document, "the spirit of Jesus with its emphasis on brotherly love, faith and hope must be emphasized. The most daring and the most unflinching social teaching will never cease to look back to Jesus."

In his later work *What is Christian Education?*, Mr. Coe does not change his position. He says in the Preface:

> Much that calls itself Christian is survival, and it is becoming anachronistic. The education that expresses it is consciously or unconsciously feeble. Meantime, the world's need of religious enlightenment, quickening, and spiritual discipline mounts higher and higher.

> The whole situation, ecclesiastical and extra-ecclesiastical, is here confronted with a principle, already within historical

Christianity, that could recreate Christian education, and by doing so make an indispensable contribution to the healing of our sick society.

This dynamic principle takes the Christian Gospel "most intimately personal, and therefore most intensely social. . . . In short, the radicalism that has been implicit in Christianity from its beginning is here applied to Christian education."

If we look at the present practice in Protestant religious education, it is difficult to contradict Coe's opinion that it is in a critical situation. Nor can one raise against Coe the same objection that often has been raised against pragmatic philosophies; namely, that in their emphasis on the social and the dynamic, they forget to ask and to answer the question as to the ground and goal of the process; for Coe has the spirit of Christ as his guiding principle.

Nevertheless, says the more conservative Randolph Crump Miller in his *The Clue to Christian Education,* the "so-called life-centered or progressive teaching" (a term that would apply to Coe's methodological approach) has caused as much dissatisfaction among ministers, teachers, and parents as the older "catechetical or ungraded, or Bible centered, with no thought for the religious needs and experiences of the pupils." In order to fulfill its major task, to "discover and impart the relevance of Christian truth," the curriculum must be *both* "God-centered and experience-centered. Theology must be prior to the curriculum! Theology is 'truth-about-God-in-relation-to-man'." In other words, Mr. Randolph C. Miller is searching for a synthesis of progressive methodology and motivational psychology, on the one hand, and adherence to the creed on the other hand.

For example it would be possible to work out a sound curriculum based on the Apostles' creed (assuming that the creed is true in so far as it may be proved by Scripture and made meaningful in experience). But the creed would be placed *back* of the curriculum rather than in it. It would be introduced into the curriculum in terms of the relevance of Christian truth to the experiences and capacities of learners, until at the proper level it could be studied as a summary of truths which are relevant to Christian living today.

With this principle in mind one could go far in the elastic application of Christian teaching to the individual and social postulates of our age without the danger of spreading a merely pragmatic social gospel, for there is a center—the creed.

The difference between Coe, the progressive, and Miller, the moderate conservative, is not so great as it may appear at first glance. Both reflect the general development of education in modern nations. After World War I educators hoped that through a combination of individualization and socialization education would help bring about a better world. Then, especially after World War II, there came disappointment and the desire for a balance between progress and tradition.

The Protestant denominations, like the Catholic Church, have expanded their missionary work in foreign countries, not only for purposes of conversion, but also for improving the education, the social conditions, and the health of struggling peoples. Innumerable men and women have risked their lives to bear witness to Christ's gospel of love. Also, Protestantism now has its "liturgical renaissance," a reaction against the verbalism and intellectualism that so often invaded its services, and there exists, in addition, a number of journals, an overwhelming mass of books, pamphlets, and manuals for Protestant teachers and parents. Many of them are carefully done and reveal the desire to utilize modern child psychology and methodology of teaching. The more recent publications also reveal a definite tendency to understand religious life not only in terms of creed and worship, but also as a responsibility of the Christian in his daily life and in his community. Many authors try to arouse the child's sense of religious awe by directing his attention to the wonders of nature.

Unfortunately, too many of the guides and manuals for the Sunday school teachers make a pedantic impression. Even though the majority of these teachers are laymen, must they really be exposed to dozens of course outlines, materials, suggestions as to the beginning, the middle, and the end of a course, recommendations about grouping the children and about handling audio-visual aid, appendices, and bibliographies? All these mental crutches may cripple the teacher's enthusiasm, just as the pedagogy of the old seminaries and normal schools frightened many a young talent away from the teaching profession.

In many publications there prevails an atmosphere of sweetness and comfortable middle-class mentality. The gruesome social problems of our time such as war, exploitation, and class and race hatred are rarely exposed in their challenging seriousness, not even in the guides for older grades. Often the story of Jesus is not the story of Christ who dared offend the Pharisees and died for his testimony, but the story of a kind man liked by everybody in the pleasant suburb. The shuddering works of a Matthias Grünewald and other great masters, for whom the cross was still a reality, are apparently forgotten.

But are those psychologically minded teachers really right in believing that youth should not be exposed to the tragical in life? Certainly not the young child, but the thinking adolescents of our days read or hear about Hitler, world wars, forced migrations, and atomic explosions. They may fully understand why suffering and death are included in all great world religions. And they may have a greater sense of the depth of existence if the tragical retains its unyielding dignity, instead of being distorted by adults into the language of "these strange, unpredictable, lovable youngsters of ours." [15]

Indeed, youth, and especially our academic youth, are waiting. More than their parents and grandparents, they ask questions of a fundamentally religious nature. During the past decades the number of young members of the Protestant denominations has increased, probably more than the increase of population explains.

With adults, mere convention often plays a role. The answers which even educated people give with regard to their church affiliations sometimes contain nothing but superficialities. One wants to belong "somewhere," one is afraid of prejudices within one's community that may affect one's business and status, and one wants to participate in the fight against atheism, materialism, communism, and delinquency. Just as vague is the conviction that democracy and the capitalist system need the support of Christianity.

But there are also profounder interests. People know that they will have to live in trying times. They are longing for that encounter with the holy that helps man take root, decide, even endanger his life for the constructive, and to resist the destructive. They want to have symbols for the belief that, as human beings, they participate in a higher order of things. While some revert to the more conventional Churches, others feel that they cannot reconcile the symbols and meanings offered by them with their intellectual conscience, which they rightly consider something very precious.[16]

Thus a feeling of loneliness and pessimism has invaded the mind of modern man. The two world wars and the failures to achieve peace have shaken his belief in the perfectibility of the human race. We know that the wheels of machines are not necessarily the wheels of progress. The more of them we invent, the more they threaten our liberty and even our physical survival. All nations want peace, yet they do not dare disarm. This has always been so, and it is, therefore, false to believe that we are morally inferior to earlier generations. Only our task is greater, and, with the enormity and urgency of the task, there grows the sense of failure.

Rarely has the challenge to the Protestant Churches been so immense as it is today. The answer they give to this challenge will depend partly on the depth, courage, and freedom of spirit with which they educate their youth.

POSTSCRIPTUM

The reader of this book will probably stand in admiration before some of the spiritual vistas which the history of religious education reveals to his eyes, but he will also feel alienated by others. He will find love and understanding, but also dogmatism, though Christ himself said that in his Father's house are many rooms. Christendom has hurt itself and its gospel of love by elevating the conditional to the rank of the unconditional, by mistaking means for ends, by establishing false absolutes, and by idolizing merely human interests and institutions.

Some of the predicaments in the Christian tradition increase in the instruction of the young. It was not lack of interest in religion, but concern for the purity and depth of the religious that caused some thinkers to recommend the postponement of religious education until a degree of maturity had been achieved.

Religious education could not remain unaffected by changing interpretations of the nature of learning. Few teachers would be satisfied today with the child's memorizing the catechism before he has entered into its meaning. But not always, as we saw, were the changes for the better; they also lead to dilution and distortion of the Christian substance.

Even more radically than by psychological considerations, religious education has also been affected by the changes of the image which man has had about himself. The early Christians, the men of the Middle Ages, the Renaissance, the Reformation, the Enlightenment, and our scientific era thought differently about the nature of the human person and his destiny. Today we would no longer emphasize the dogma of man's total depravity above everything else and use fear and threat instead of conviction and conversion. But we have also become superficial and unimaginative with regard to ourselves and our role in the universe, whereas in earlier times there was more sincerity.

The situation has become immensely aggravated by the revolutionary transformation of our whole civilization. In comparison with it, the earlier upheavals in Western mentality may seem to be minor. The adolescent of today lives under an avalanche of impressions that no one anticipated at the beginning of this century. He hears about the conquest of space, of nuclear weapons, international interaction and hostility, democracy and communism and is expected to harmonize all these impressions with his spiritual heritage. Our expanding knowledge about ancient and foreign cultures leads to more and more comparisons between the Judao-Christian and other religions. The number of biological and philosophical interpretations of life increases to a similar degree, with many of them being sceptical about, if not hostile to, the Christian conception. The intellectual globe grows and grows, and the sector left for religion becomes smaller and smaller.

No organization, political or spiritual, can hope to avoid the danger of bewilderment by enforcing a uniformity of answers. Totalitarian systems may have the power of terror, but they have not the power of persuasion and endurance. As the history of Christianity itself proves, oppression oppresses itself.

It would be strange and even a sign of decay if in the much lamented "crisis of our time" religion and religious education were the only untouched parts of our culture. Those who refuse to participate in the historical process will sooner or later be left out by it. But then, one fundamental question emerges: From which deeper source will man receive the strength to resist conformity? What is the enduring element that so far has saved human civilization from total degradation? There can be no other answer than that there is in man an inner drive toward self-transcendence, a drive for reaching toward the ever-greater—call it man's sense for freedom and dignity. As John Amos Comenius said in his *Way of Light*: [1]

> For there is inborn in human nature a love of liberty—for liberty man's mind was convinced that it was made—and this love can by no means be driven out; so that wherever and by whatever means it feels that it is hemmed in and impeded, it cannot but seek a way out and declare its own liberty.

To be sure, religion is not the only way through which this sense expresses itself. If a matter of conventionality, it may even block the way of man to himself and the sources that nourish his mind and body. "Religion," says Martin Buber, one of the most pious men of our time, "can hide from us as nothing else can the face of God." [2] Great literature and art, devoted scholarship, good citizenship, a humane education, and above all self-discipline are also means toward self-improvement and inner contact with the creative center. But I dare say that all these achievements, in order to develop their finest potentialities, must be inspired by a religious element, or the sense of the sacred. Without it literature and art may become aestheticism; scholarship may narrow into mere specialization and intellectual aloofness; citizenship may degenerate into chauvinism, education into morally neutral information, and self-discipline into self-idolatry.

To constantly create and recreate the saving sense for the sacredness of life within a freedom-loving society: this is the noblest and most necessary task of religious education. But it will be a truly formidable task. The severe crisis of Christianity at a time of political and technological collectivism has been apparent for decades. To meet this crisis and, in a most general sense, the total crisis of metaphysical awareness in the life of modern man, it will be necessary to develop new and bold conceptions of religious education. But in order to be productive, the new requires the knowledge of the past. To provide such knowledge has been the purpose of this book.

Notes

CHAPTER 1

1. Of the rich literature on the Old Testament and the Commandments, see: Robert H. Pfeiffer, *Introduction to the Old Testament* (New York: Harper & Brothers, 1941); Arthur P. Davies, *The Ten Commandments* (New York: New American Library of World Literature, 1956); Harry E. Fosdick, *A Guide to Understanding the Bible* (New York: Harper & Brothers, 1956); Lewis J. Sherrill, *The Rise of Christian Education* (New York: Macmillan Co., 1944).

2. *The Wisdom of Confucius,* ed. Lin Yutang (New York: The Modern Library, 1938), pp. 104–105.

3. The Sacred Books of China: *The Texts of Tâoism,* trans. James Legge, in The Sacred Books of the East (Oxford: 1891), XXXIX, 47: Part I: "The Tâo Te King."

4. *Josephus,* trans. H. St. J. Thackeray (London-New York: Putnam's Sons, The Loeb Classical Library, 1936), I, 187, 361, 363. Reprinted by permission of the publishers.

5. (Baltimore: Johns Hopkins Press, 1940), p. 37. Reprinted by permission of the publisher.

6. *New Edition of the Babylonian Talmud,* trans. Michael L. Rodkinson (New York: 1900), "Section Jurisprudence," I (IX), 133.

7. *Geschichte des Erziehungswesens und der Cultur der Juden in Frankreich und Deutschland von der Begründung der jüdischen Wissenschaft in diesen Ländern bis sur Vertreibung der Juden aus Frankreich (X–XIV Jahrhundert* [Wien: 1880]). The English quotations are taken from a not-yet-published translation by Hedwig Schleiffer, Cambridge, Mass.

8. *The Rise of Christian Education* (New York: Macmillan, 1944), p. 69.

9. Israel Abrahams, *Jewish Life in the Middle Ages,* new edition by Cecil Roth (London: E. Goldston, 1932).

   Louis Finkelstein (ed.), *The Jews; Their History, Culture, and Religion* (New York: Harper & Brothers, 1949).

   Louis Ginzberg, *Students, Scholars, and Saints* (New York: Meridian Books, 1958).

   The Living Talmud. The Wisdom of the Fathers and Its Classical Commentaries, trans. J. Goldin (Chicago: Chicago University Press, 1957).

   Jacob Rader Marcus, *The Jew in the Medieval World; A Source Book, 315–1791* (Cincinnati: Union of American Hebrew Congregations, 1938).

   Leo Walder Schwarz (ed.), *Great Ages and Ideas of the Jewish People* (New York: Random House, 1956).

   Harry Austryn Wolfson, *The Philosophy of Spinoza* (New York: Meridian Books, 1960).

10. *The Daily Prayer Book*, revised edition, with Hebrew text and English translation, commentary and notes, ed. Dr. Joseph H. Hertz (New York: Bloch Publishing Co., 1948).

11. See Herman Wouk, *This Is My God* (Garden City, N.Y.: Doubleday, 1959).

CHAPTER 2

1. Clement, "The First Epistle to the Corinthians," *The Apostolic Fathers,* trans. K. Lake (Cambridge, Mass.: Harvard University Press, Loeb Classical Library, 1945), I, 115, 117 (Chs. lx, lxi). Reprinted by permission of the publisher.

2. Tertullian, *Writings,* in *Ante-Nicene Christian Library: . . . ,* eds. A. Roberts and J. Donaldson (Edinburgh: 1869), XI, 304–05.

3. *Ibid.,* p. 290.

4. St. Chrysostom, *On the Priesthood,* trans. T. A. Moxon (London: Soc. f. Prom. Christ. Knowledge, 1932), p. 71. Saint Chrysostom learned about the power of women himself when he was deposed from the See of Constantinople by the influence of the Empress Eudoxia. *Cherchez la femme* is an old experience.

5. Augustine, *Confessions and Enchiridion,* trans. Albert C. Outler (Philadelphia: Westminster Press, The Library of Christian Classics, 1955), VII, p. 192. Reprinted by permission of the publisher.

6. K. Lake (trans.), *The Apostolic Fathers* (Cambridge: Harvard University Press, 1945), I, 309, 311 (ch. i). Reprinted by permission of the publisher. See also James A. Kleist, *The Didache* (Westminster, Md.: Newman Press, 1948). For the rich literature on early Christianity see: Ernst von Dobschütz, *Christian Life in the Primitive Church* (New York: Putnam's Sons, 1905); Adolph von Harnack, *The Expansion of Christianity in the First Two Centuries,* trans. James Moffat (New York: 1904), and his *The Constitution & Law of the Church in the First Two Centuries,* trans. F. L. Pogson (New York: Putnam's Sons, 1910); Ernst Troeltsch, *The Social Teaching of the Christian Churches,* trans. Olive Wyon (London: Allen & Unwin, 1956); Rudolf Bultman, *Primitive Christianity in its Contemporary Setting,* trans. R. H. Fuller (New York: Meridian Books, 1959); Jaques Zeiller, *Christian Beginnings,* trans. P. J. Hepburne-Scott (New York: Hawthorne Books, 1960).

7. K. Lake (trans.), *The Apostolic Fathers* (Cambridge: Harvard University Press, 1945), II, 359, 361, 363 (Chs. v–vi). Reprinted by permission of the publisher.

8. Tertullian, *ibid.,* XI, 118–19.

CHAPTER 3

1. Harry A. Wolfson, *Philo; Foundations of Religious Philosophy in Judaism, Christianity, and Islam* (Cambridge: Harvard University Press, 1948). For

more detailed information about the Ante-Nicene fathers, see *The Ante-Nicene Fathers, Translations of the Writings of the Fathers Down to A.D. 325* (Grand Rapids, Mich.: Eerdmans Publ. Co., 1951). Volume IX contains a bibliographical synopsis and a general index. For this entire chapter see also: Harry A. Wolfson, *Religious Philosophy. A Group of Essays* (Harvard University Press, 1961); furthermore Werner Jaeger, *Early Christianity and Greek Paideia* (Harvard University Press, 1961).

2. St. Basil's *Address to Young Men on the Right Use of Greek Literature;* Gregory of Nyssa's *Great Catechetical Sermon;* Gregory of Nazianzus' *Eulogy for Basil the Great.* Moreover, Max L. M. Laistner, *Christianity and Pagan Culture in the Later Roman Empire Together with An English Translation of John Chrysostom's Address on Vainglory and the Right Way for Parents to Bring Up their Children* (Ithaca: Cornell University Press, 1951).

3. Tatianus, "Address to the Greeks," in *The Ante-Nicene Fathers . . . ,* eds. A. Roberts and J. Donaldson (Buffalo: 1885), II, chs. ii and xxvi.

4. "Most of all it is credible because it is an offence /to reason/ . . . and it is certain because it is impossible" (*On the Flesh of Christ,* ch. 5); see also his *Apologeticus,* ch. 7, for the often quoted phrase *"anima naturaliter Christiana."*

5. *"De Idolatria,"* Caput x, in Migne, *Patrologiae Latinae,* I, col. 761.

6. Justin's "Hortatory Address to the Greek" (ch. xx) in *The Ante-Nicene Fathers,* eds. A. Roberts and J. Donaldson (Grand Rapids, Mich.: W. W. Eerdmans, 1956), I, 281. Reprinted by permission of the publishers.

7. Clement of Alexandria, *Writings* I, in *Ante-Nicene Christian Library,* eds. A. Roberts and J. Donaldson (Edinburgh: 1867), IV, 111–346: "The Instructor (*Paedagogus*)."

8. For a discussion of the relation between faith and reason, see Harry A. Wolfson, *The Philosophy of the Church Fathers,* Volume I, *passim.*

9. Clement of Alexandria, "The Miscellanies; or Stromata" (Bk. vii, ch. 10), in his *Writings* II, *Ante-Nicene Christian Library,* XII (1869).

10. *Ibid.,* (Bk. iii, ch. 5).

11. *Ibid.,* (Bk. vi, ch. 17).

12. Origen, *Contra Celsum,* trans. Henry Chadwick (Cambridge: Cambridge University Press, 1953), p. 12.

13. For a discussion of literalism and freedom of interpretation of the sacred sources, see Harry A. Wolfson, *The Philosophy of the Church Fathers,* pp. 46, 58 ff., 74 ff.; and furthermore, Werner Jaeger, *Early Christianity and Greek Paideia,* pp. 47 ff. and 52 ff.

14. Origen, *The Writings* I, in *Ante-Nicene Christian Library . . . ,* eds. A. Roberts and J. Donaldson (Edinburgh: 1869), X, 300–301.

15. Gregory Thaumaturgus, *Address to Origen,* by W. Metcalfe (London-New York: Macmillan Co., 1920) (Translations of Christian Literature, Series 1: Greek Texts), pp. 51–52 ff., 57–58, 59–60. Reprinted by permission of the publisher.

16. *Ibid.,* pp. 89–90, 92–93. Reprinted by permission of the publisher.

17. See articles on "Baptism" in Hastings, *Encyclopedia of Religion and Ethics*

and in the *Encyclopaedia Britannica;* furthermore, Oscar Cullmann, *Baptism in the New Testament,* trans. J. K. Reid (London: SCM Press Ltd., 1950); see also article on "Catechumen" in Hastings, *Encyclopedia.*

CHAPTER 4

1. Gregorius, The Great (Pope), *Registrum Epistolarum,* in *Monumenta Germaniae Historica; Epistolae* (Berlin: 1899), II, 303.

2. St. Jerome, "To Laeta; Letter cvii," in *The Principal Works of St. Jerome,* trans. W. H. Fremantle, in *A Select Library of Nicene and Post-Nicene Fathers* (New York: 1893), 2nd series, VI, 189–95; reprinted in Robert Ulich, *Three Thousand Years of Educational Wisdom* (Harvard University Press, 1954), pp. 164–69.

3. Saint Benedict, *The Rule,* trans. Cardinal Gasquet (London: Chatto & Windus, 1925), pp. 1–2, 6–22, 84, 102–103. Reprinted by permission of the publishers.

4. "Accomplished though unlearned, and wise though unlettered," Gregorius I, *Opera* (Basel: 1564), *"Dialogi liber secondus,"* I, col. 1351.

5. Cassiodorus, *Institutiones . . . ,* ed. R. A. B. Mynors (Oxford: Clarendon Press, 1937).

6. *Capitularia Regum Francorum* in *Monumenta Germaniae Historica; Legum Sectio* II (Hannover: 1883), I, 103, No. 30: *"Ut omnis populus Christianus fidem Catholicam et dominicam orationem memoriter teneat"* ("That the whole Christian people may know by heart the creed of the Church and the Lord's prayer").

7. Theodulf, *Capitula ad Presbyteros Parochiae Suae,* in Migne, *Patrologiae Cursus Completus* (Paris: 1851), CV, col. 196: No. 20.

8. The following translation by the author follows the Latin edition of her *Manual* by Edouard Bondurand (Paris: 1887).

9. Friedrich Vogt and Max Koch, *Geschichte der Deutschen Literature* (Leipzig: Bibliographisches Institut, 1930), I, 59; Roswitha, *The Plays,* trans. Christopher St. John (London: Chatto & Windus, 1923); Latin edition: Migne, *Patrologia Latina* (Paris: 1870), CXXXVII, cols. 939–1196; see also Alice Kemp-Welch, *Of Six Mediaeval Women* (London: Macmillan & Co., 1913).

10. Hrabanus Maurus, *Education of the Clergy* (New York: American Book Co., 1905). See Robert Ulich, *Three Thousand Years . . . ,* pp. 174–80.

11. Assen (Bishop of Sherborne), *Life of King Alfred,* trans. L. C. Jane (London: Chatto & Windus, 1908).

12. *King Alfred's West Saxon Version of Gregory's Pastoral Care,* ed. Henry Sweet (London: 1871), pp. 2–8.

CHAPTER 5

1. *The Little Flowers of Saint Francis,* trans. T. W. Arnold (London: Aldine House, 1908), chapter xiii.

2. *Florilegium Patristicum Tam Veteris Quam Medii Aevi Auctores Complectens* (Bonn: P. Hanstein, 1921), IX, XIII, 1–36; "De Magistro" (in English trans.), in Mary Helen Mayer, *The Philosophy of Teaching of St. Thomas Aquinas* (St. Paul, Minn.: Bruce Publ. Co., 1929), pp. 39–86; see also Robert Ulich, *History of Educational Thought* (New York: American Book Co., several eds.), p. 94.

3. Hugo de Sancto Victore, *Didascalicon De Studio Legendi,* ed. Charles H. Buttimer (recent edition; Washington, D. C.: The Catholic University of America, 1939) ("Studies in Medieval and Renaissance Latin," X).

4. *Didascalicon,* Book III, ch. xix, p. 60 (translated by the author).

5. In the previous chapter Hugh says: "For work that is not preceded by study, is of little foresight, and theory is of little use which is not followed by good work."

6. *Ibid.,* Book I, ch. viii.

7. The expression *"mechanica, id est adulterina,"* is caused by Hugh's derivation of *mechanica* from the Greek *moichos* (adulterer). See J. Chr. G. Schumann, *Kleinere Schriften über Padagogische und Kulturgeschichtliche Fragen* (Hannover: 1878). This etymological absurdity (of which many can be found in medieval writers, especially in those who boast of a knowledge of Greek, generally not known before the fourteenth century) was ridiculed in the famous sixteenth-century satire against monkish ignorance, the so-called *Letters of the Dark Men (Epistolae Obscurorum Virorum),* epistle xxv.

8. Vincentius Bellovacensis, *Opus Praeclarum quod Speculum Morale . . .* (Cologne: 1494). For an analysis of Vincent's educational theories, see John Ellis Bourne, *The Educational Thought of Vincent of Beauvais* (Thesis, Harvard Graduate School of Education, 1960).

9. Ludwig Lieser, *Vinzenz von Beauvais als Kompilator und Philosoph* (Leipzig: Felix Meiner, 1928), p. 54.

10. Ed. Arpad Steiner (Cambridge, Mass.: Medieval Academy of America, 1938).

11. *De Eruditione,* pp. 5–6. (Translated by the author.) Compare Milton's *Tractate on Education* (Cambridge: 1883), pp. 3–4: "The end then of learning is to repair the ruins of our first Parents by regaining to know God aright, and out of that knowledge to love Him, to imitate Him, to be like Him, as we may the nearest by possessing our souls of true vertue, which being united to the heavenly grace of faith makes up the highest perfection."

12. *De Eruditione,* p. 13.

13. *Ibid.,* p. 52.

14. *Ibid.,* p. 25.

15. Gabriel Meier, *Ausgewählte Schriften von Columban, Alkuin . . . und Peraldus* (Freiburg i.B.: 1890), Bibliothek der Katholischen Paedagogik, III, pp. 213–14. (Translated by the author.)

16. Joannes Gerson, *Opera omnia,* 5 vols., ed. L. Ellies du Pin (Antwerp: 1706).

17. *Opera omnia,* III, col. 287. For a large extract of Gerson's "On Leading Children to Christ," see *Three Thousand Years of Educational Wisdom,* ed. Robert Ulich (Cambridge: Harvard University Press, 1950), pp. 181–90.

18. *Ibid.,* III, cols. 291–92.

19. *Ibid.*, IV, cols. 717–20.

20. To beat a cleric is an offence of which an ordinary confessor cannot absolve without special authority.

21. "Fathers, provoke not your children to anger, lest they be discouraged" (*Colossians* iii, 21).

22. *Contra perfidiam Machometi et contra multa dicta Sarracenorum* (Cologne: 1532 and 1533); see also *Disputatio inter Christianum et Sarracenum de Lege Christi et contra perfidiam impiissimi Machometi* (Cologne: 1532 and 1533).

23. A careful essay on Dionysius has been written by Heinrich A. Keiser. It contains a German translation of some of his educational writings: *Dionys des Kartäusers Leben und Pädagogische Schriften,* in *Bibliothek der Katholischen Pädagogik* (Freiburg: 1904), V, 173–336.

24. *"De Doctrina Scholarium"* in his *Opera Omnia* (Tornacia-Tournay: De Pratis, 1909), XXXVII, 337–71.

25. *Ibid.*, XXXVII, 185–207.

26. See especially Juan Luis Vives, *De Causis Corruptarum Artium, libri septem* (Antwerp: 1531).

27. Josef Frey, *Ueber das Mittelalterliche Gedicht "Theoduli Ecloga . . . "* (Münster: 1904).

28. Johannes Geffcken, *Der Bilderkatechismus des fünfzehnten Jahrhunderts* (Leipzig: 1855); Arthur M. Hind, *An Introduction to a History of Woodcuts with a Detailed Survey of Work Done in the Fifteenth Century* (London: Constable & Co., 1935).

29. Rudolphus Agricola, *De Inventione Dialectica* (Cologne: 1538).

30. See Johann Huizinga, *The Waning of the Middle Ages: A Study of the Form of Life, Thought and Art in France and the Netherlands in the Fourteenth and Fifteenth Centuries* (London: E. Arnold, 1937).

31. Translated from: *Meister Eckeharts Schriften und Predigten,* ed. Hermann Büttner (Jena: Eugen Diederichs, 1923), II, 163; there exists an English edition of his selected works: *Master Eckhard, A Modern Translation,* by Raymond B. Blakney (New York: Harper & Brothers, 1941).

32. *Schriften und Predigten,* I, 71.

33. "Defense" in R. B. Blackney's edition, p. 358.

CHAPTER 6

1. In spite of a large and critical literature, Jakob Burckhardt's *Civilization of the Renaissance in Italy,* first published in 1860, still remains one of the best introductions into the spirit of the period. For extracts from educational literature of this period see Robert Ulich, *History of Educational Thought* and *Three Thousand Years of Educational Wisdom.*

2. Leon Battista Alberti, *I Primi Tre Libri della Famiglia,* ed. F. C. Pellegrini (Firenze: Sansoni, 1911), pp. v, vi, 21, 24.

3. Jacopo Sadoleto, *On Education; a Translation of De Pueris recte Instituendis,* by I. I. Campagnac and E. L. Forbes (Oxford University Press, 1916); see

also Richard M. Douglas, *Jacopo Sadoleto, 1477–1574. Humanist and Reformer* (Cambridge: Harvard University Press, 1959).

4. *On Education*, p. 86.

5. *Ibid.*, p. 12.

6. *Ibid.*, p. 63.

7. *Ibid.*, p. 64.

8. *Ibid.*, pp. 90–91.

9. *Ibid.*, pp. 103 f.

10. *Ibid.*, p. 126.

11. "Epistola No. 13, *Venetiis, Cal. Novembris,* 1532" (Brixen: 1745), I, 397–402; among the many correspondents of Sadoleto was Calvin. See his letter on the unity of the Church, September, 1539, in his *Opera quae supersunt omnia* (Braunschweig: 1866), V, cols. 385–416 (*Corpus Reformatorum,* XXXIII).

12. "De Tradendis Disciplinis, seu de Institutione Christiana, libri V," in his *Opera omnia,* ed. Gregorius Majans (Valencia: 1785), VI, 243–437.

13. *Opera Omnia, cura* T. Clerici (Leyden: 1703), III, 694: "*Epistola* dcxiii, 1522."

14. For a more explicit description of Erasmus' pedagogy and extracts from his *Education of a Christian Prince* and *Praise of Folly,* see Robert Ulich, *History of Educational Thought* and *Three Thousand Years of Educational Wisdom.* Of the works of Erasmus which deal more with a general spiritual reform of Christianity than with education proper, see especially his *Enchiridion.* Modern edition: *A Book Called in Latin Enchiridion Militis Christiani and in English The Manual of the Christian Knight* (London: Methuen & Co., 1905).

15. "*Declamatio de Pueris Ad Virtutem ac Literas Liberaliter Instituendis,*" in Erasmus, *Opera omnia,* I (1703), col. 497.

16. *Adagia,* Pauli Manutii studio . . . (Florence: Giunta, 1575).

17. Taken from James Anthony Froude, *Life and Letters of Erasmus* (London: 1894), p. 312 (abridged).

18. *The Whole Familiar Colloquies,* trans. Nathan Baily (Glasgow: 1877), p. vii; See also Percy S. Allen, *The Age of Erasmus* (Oxford: Clarendon Press, 1914); Johan Huizinga, *Erasmus* (New York: Charles Scribner's Sons, 1924); John J. Mangan, *Life, Character and Influence of Desiderius Erasmus of Rotterdam* (2 vols.; New York: Macmillan Co., 1927); Desiderius Erasmus, *Opus epistolarum,* ed. Percy S. Allen (12 vols.; Oxford: Clarendon Press, 1906–1958).

19. Elizabeth L. Forbes (trans.), in *The Renaissance Philosophy,* ed. Ernst Cassirer a.o. (Chicago: University of Chicago Press, 1948), pp. 213–54.

20. (London-New York: Longman's, Green, 1923), pp. 208 f.

CHAPTER 7

1. "Letter to the Mayors and Aldermen of all the Cities of Germany in Behalf of Christian Schools," in Franklin V. N. Painter, *Luther on Education*

(Philadelphia: 1889), p. 186; see also Robert Ulich, *Three Thousand Years* . . . , pp. 218–38.

2. Friedrich Paulsen, *Geschichte des Gelehrten Unterrichts auf den Deutschen Schulen und Universitäten* (Berlin-Leipzig: Vereinigung wissenschaftlicher Verleger, 1921), I, Book 1, ch. iv.

3. See especially Luther's letter to the Elector John of Saxony, dated Wittenberg, November 22, 1526, "Letter No. 743," in Luther's *Correspondence and other Contemporary Letters,* trans. and ed. Preserved Smith . . . (Philadelphia: The Lutheran Publication Society, 1918), II, 383.

4. The standard edition of Luther's writings is his *Werke. Kritische Gesamtausgabe,* approximately 58 vols. (Weimar: Böhlau, 1883); a small, but good edition is his *Werke,* 3 vols., hg. Arnold E. Berger (Leipzig-Wien: Bibliographisches Institut, 1917); there is a large English edition of approximately 55 volumes in process: *Works,* ed. Jaroslav Pelikan (St. Louis: Concordia Publishing House, 1958).

5. "Letter No. 580" of March 29, 1523, in Luther's *Correspondence,* ed. Preserved Smith, II, 176.

6. Franklin V. N. Painter (Philadelphia: 1889), pp. 210–71; also in Robert Ulich, *Three Thousand Years* . . . , pp. 238–49.

7. *Smaller Catechism,* meant for children and laymen, and *Larger Catechism,* for clergymen and teachers.

8. (2d rev. ed.; Philadelphia: The United Lutheran Publ. House, 1935; 1960.) Sections are reprinted by permission of the publisher.

9. *Ibid.,* Preface.

10. *Ibid.,* pp. 17–22.

11. "*Commentarius in Epistolam Pauli ad Corinthios I,*" in *Opera quae supersunt omnia* (Braunschweig), XLIX, col. 497 (*Corpus Reformatorum,* LXXVII).

12. Dated 1619. *Ibid.,* XIV (1875), col. 314 (C. R., XLII) (Author's translation).

13. *Institutes of the Christian Religion,* trans. John Allen, 2 vols. (6th American ed.; Philadelphia: Presbyterian Board of Publication, 1928), I, 22f.

14. "*Projet d'Ordonnances ecclesiastiques. Septembre et Octobre 1541,*" *Opera,* X/1 cols. 15–30. (C. R., XXXVIII/1) (translated by the author).

15. Max Weber, *The Protestant Ethic and the Spirit of Capitalism,* trans. Talcott Parsons, with a foreword by R. H. Tawney (London: G. Allen & Unwin, 1930). Ernst Troeltsch, *Protestantism and Progress. A Historical Study of the Relation of Protestantism to the Modern World,* trans. W. Montgomery (New York: P. Putnam, 1912).

16. *St. Ignatius and the Ratio Studiorum,* ed. Edward A. Fitzpatrick, trans. Mary H. Mayer (New York: McGraw-Hill, 1933). For description of the Jesuit system of education, see Robert Ulich, *History of Educational Thought*; for extracts from *Ratio,* see Ulich's *Three Thousand Years* . . . , pp. 272–86.

17. *The Spiritual Exercises of Saint Ignatius of Loyola,* ed. W. Longridge. With a commentary and translation of the *Directorium in Exercitia* (rev. ed.; London-Milwaukee: The Morehouse Publishing Co., 1930), pp. 24 ff. Reprinted by permission of the publisher.

18. *Introduction to the Devout Life,* trans. John K. Ryan (New York: Harper & Brothers, 1949).

19. St. Francis de Sales, *The Spiritual Conferences,* trans. Canon Mackey, O.S.B. (Westminster, Md.: The Newman Bookshop, 1943), pp. 74–79, 84–87. Reprinted by permission of the publisher.

20. Pedro Juan Perpiñan, "*Epistola* xvi," in *Opera* (Rome: 1749), III, 88–110.

21. I am indebted to Georg Fell, S.J., for his careful description of Possevino's life and translation of his work: *Pädagogische Schriften von Antonio Possevino,* in *Bibliotheck der Katholischen Paedagogik* (Freiburg i.B.: 1901), XI, 275–560. (American libraries contain few of Possevino's writings.)

22. *Bibliotheca Selecta, qua agitur de Ratione Studiorum in Historia, Disciplinis et Salute omnium procuranda* (Rome: 1593).

23. *Epistola de Necessitate Utilitate que ac Ratione Docendi Catholici Catechismi* (Rome: 1593).

24. *Opera Omnia,* ed. Giulio Maffei (Venice: 1721–1728).

25. See Paul Hazard, *The European Mind; The Critical Years 1680–1715* (New Haven: Yale University Press, 1953).

26. All the leading encyclopedias of the various European nations have articles either under heading "Mission," or in connection with the history of the Churches.

CHAPTER 8

1. We refer here especially to Sanford Fleming, *Children and Puritanism. The Place of Children in the Life and Thought of the New England Churches; 1620–1847* (New Haven: Yale University Press, 1933).

2. Thomas Shepard, *Works* (3 vols.; Boston: 1853), I, 45.

3. *Massachusetts Missionary Magazine,* II (1804–1805), 227.

4. Massachusetts Historical Society, *Collections,* ed. W. G. Ford (Boston), 7th series, VII–VIII (1896); see also Cotton Mather, *Magnalia Christi Americana; or The Ecclesiastical History of New England* (London: 1702).

5. Cotton Mather, *Diary, I (1681–1708),* in Massachusetts Historical Society, *Collections* (Boston), 7th series, VII (1911), 471. Reprinted by permission of the Society.

6. Fleming, p. 133.

7. Cotton Mather, *op. cit.,* pp. 239–40. Reprinted by permission of the Society.

8. Samuel Sewall, "Diary, 1674–1729," in Massachusetts Historical Society, *Collections* (Boston), 5th series, V (1878), 15–16.

9. *An Epistle to the Christian Indians, giving them a short account of what the English desire them to know and to do in order to their happiness* (Boston: 1700), p. 3.

10. Juan Estarellas Ripoll, *Cultural Foundations of Mexico. A Study of the Educational Aims, Institutions and Practices of the Spanish Colonization*

in the Sixteenth Century Central New Spain. (Thesis, Harvard Graduate School of Education, 1956.)

11. Bk. IV, ch. xv, par. 20 and ch. xvi, par. 26, in *Opera Omnia quae Supersunt* (Braunschweig), IV (1866), cols. 955–56, 963–64, (C. R., XXXII).

12. *Complete Works* (London: 1843), IV, 358.

13. Orville Dewey, *Letters of an English Traveller to His Friend in England on the "Revival of Religion" in America* (Boston: 1828), p. 120.

14. *New England's First Fruits* (London: 1643); see also Massachusetts Historical Society, *Collections* (Boston), I (1792), 242–50.

15. For documentary evidence of early New England, see the *Collections* of the Massachusetts Historical Society. For extracts, see Edward P. Cubberley, *Readings in Public Education in the United States* (Boston: Houghton Mifflin Co., 1943); furthermore Lydia A. H. Smith, *Major American Children's Readers.* (Thesis, Harvard Graduate School of Education, 1960.)

16. Massachusetts Historical Society, *Collections* (Boston), I (1792), 243, 245; Cubberley, *Readings,* p. 34.

CHAPTER 9

1. John Amos Comenius, *The Way of Light,* trans. E. T. Campagnac (Liverpool: The University Press; London: Hodder & Stoughton, 1938), pp. 10–11, 22–23. Reprinted by permission of the publishers.

2. Selig Brodetsky, *Sir Isaac Newton; A Brief Account of his Life and Work* (Boston: John W. Luce & Co., 1928), p. 153.

3. *De la Démonomanie des sorciers* (Paris: 1580).

4. For an extensive analysis of Comenius' didactical method see the chapter on Comenius in Robert Ulich's *History of Educational Thought;* furthermore an English translation with careful introduction by N. W. Keatinge, entitled: *The Great Didactic of John Amos Comenius* (London: 1896). *The Great Didactic* was first written in Czech and later published in Latin as a part of Comenius' *Opera Didactica Omnia.*

5. George Fox, *An Autobiography,* ed. Rufus M. Jones (Philadelphia: Ferris & Leach, 1905).

6. *Ibid.,* pp. 84, 89.

7. *Ibid.,* pp. 29, 545.

8. *Ibid.,* p. 349.

9. *Ibid.,* p. 94.

10. *Ibid.,* p. 48.

11. *Ibid.,* pp. 38–39.

12. *A Catechism and Confession of Faith Approved of and Agreed Unto by the General Assembly.*

13. (Pendle Hill: Wallingford, 1940.)

14. Both in Wiliam Penn, *The Select Works* (5 vols.; London: 1782), V, 120–21, 164–67, 441–42.

15. Kuno Francke, "Cotton Mather and August Hermann Francke," in *Harvard Studies and Notes*, V (1896), pp. 60–61.

16. *Pädagogische Schriften*, hg. G. Kramer, 2 *Ausgabe* (Langensalza: 1885).

17. *"Idea Theologiae oder Abbildung eines der Theologie Beflissenen, wie derselbe sich zum Gebrauch und Dienst des Herrn und zu allen guten Werk gehörigermassen bereitet." Ibid.*, pp. 369–435; see also August Hermann Francke, *Schriften über Erziehung und Unterricht*, ed. Karl Richter (Leipzig: 1871–1872), pp. 579–655. *Timotheus, Zum Fürbilde Allen Theologiae Studiosis* was first published in 1693 and the *Idea Studiosi Theologiae*, in 1712.

18. *Kurtzer und Einfältiger Unterricht, Wie Die Kinder zur wahren Gottseligkeit und Christlichen Klugheit anzuführen sind, ehemals Zu Behuf Christlicher Informatorum entworffen, und nun auff Begehren zum Druck gegeben* (Halle, 1702) (ed. Kramer, pp. 15–89; ed. Richter, pp. 47–147).

19. Similar ideas were expressed already in the Middle Ages. Vincent of Beauvais says in his *De Institutione Puerorum Regalium:* "Correction should proceed from pity and the zeal of love" (*"Correctio debet procedere ex misericordia sive caritatis zelo"*).

20. Especially see Thomas Aquinas, *De Magistro*.

21. John Wesley, *The Journal*, ed. Nehemiah Curnock (8 vols.; London: 1910–1916), II, 16: "July 24, 1738."

22. John W. Bready, England, *Before and After Wesley; the Evangelical Revival and Social Reform* (London: Hodder & Stoughton, 1938), *passim*.

23. *Journal*, I, 141: "January 25, 1736"; I, 123: "November 23, 1735"; I, 151: "February 8, 1736."

24. *Ibid.*, I, 475: "May 1738"; III, 409: on July 19, 1745, Wesley writes about Luther: "I finished the translation of Martin Luther's *Life*. Doubtless he was a man highly favoured of God, and a blessed instrument in His Hand. But, Oh what a pity that he had no faithful friend—none that would, at all hazards, rebuke him plainly and sharply for his rough untractable spirit and bitter zeal for opinions, so greatly obstructive to the work of God."

25. John Bunyan, *The Pilgrim's Progress* (London: 1903), p. xvii.

26. Wesley, *Journal*, III, 178: "May 29, 1745."

27. *Ibid.*, V, 458: "May 5, 1765."

28. *Ibid.*, V, 523.

29. *Ibid.*, II, 13.

30. *Ibid.*, IV, 188: "October 11, 1756."

31. John Wesley, *The Works* (14 vols.; London: 1872), XIII, 412–16: "Thoughts upon Baron Montesquieu's 'Spirit of Laws.'"

32. *Journal*, V, 252–53: "February 3, 1770."

33. *Works* (ed. 1872), V, 296; Bready, *England*, p. 197.

34. Quotations are from "The Principles of a Methodist; Occasioned by a Pamphlet Entitled 'A Brief History of the Principles of Methodism.'" *Works* (ed. 1872), VIII, 362f.; *Ibid.*, XIII, 150.

35. John Wesley, *Works* (10 vols.; New York: 1827), X, 464: "Letter to a

Lady." See also Wesley's "Answer to Mr. Rowland Hill's Tract, Entitled 'Imposture Detected,'" in *Works* (ed. 1872), X, 449.

36. *Works* (ed. 1872), I, 251f.; II, 101, 235, 385; III, 414–17, 505; VIII, 333.

37. *Ibid.*, VIII, 482.

38. *Ibid.*, VIII, 484 f. The Methodists, Moravians, and other sects, part of them also coming from France, were "The Enthusiasts" whom the Earl of Shaftesbury in his *Letter on Enthusiasm* (1707) wanted to be made harmless by ridicule. Wesley himself had to answer the charge of "enthusiasm" (which in his time had the negative connotation of "rapture") in several letters. *Works* (ed. 1872), IX, 1–14, 15–60: "A Letter to the Author of 'The Enthusiasm of Methodists and Papists Compared' and 'A Second Letter to the Author of Enthusiasm.'"

39. *Works* (ed. 1872), XI, 206–207.

40. *Ibid.*, XIII, 473–77.

CHAPTER 10

1. See Galileo's profound and touching letter to the Grandduchess of Toscany, imploring her to intervene for him in his conflict with the Church and to protect freedom of scholarship. (Extracts from the letter are in Robert Ulich, *Three Thousand Years of Educational Wisdom*, pp. 323–36.)

2. Large extracts from the works of Bacon, Locke, Berkeley, Hume, Gay, Bentham, James Mill, and John Stuart Mill may be conveniently found in the anthology, *The English Philosophers from Bacon to Mill*, ed. Edward A. Burtt (New York: The Modern Library, 1939). Extracts from Bacon and Locke related to education are in Robert Ulich, *Three Thousand Years* . . . , pp. 306–11, 355–82.

3. Francis Bacon, *Works*, ed. J. Spedding a. o. (15 vols.; Boston: 1853), VIII.

4. The following quotation is taken from Thomas Hobbes, *Leviathan*, pt. III, ch. 43; see also pt. II, ch. 31.

5. Benedict de Spinoza, *The Chief Works*, trans. R. H. M. Elwes (2 vols.; London, 1883–1884), I, 259: "No, the object of government is not to change men from rational beings into beasts or puppets, but to enable them to develop their minds and bodies in security, and to employ their reason unshackled. . . . In fact, the true aim of government is liberty."

6. *Ibid.*, I, 1–11.

CHAPTER 11

1. John Wesley, *Journal*, IV, 51: "January 20, 1753": IV, 190: "November 9, 1756."

2. *Ibid.*, V, 194: see also VI, 46: "November 4, 1774": according to which a now forgotten preacher, Mr. Downes, "was by nature full as great a genius as Sir Isaac Newton."

3. Wesley, *Works* (ed. New York: 1827), VIII, 165–74: "Serious Thoughts Occasioned by the late Earthquake at Lisbon."

4. An interesting example of this kind of literature is Robert Fleming (supposed author), *A Discourse on Earthquakes; as they are Supernatural and Premonitory Signs to a Nation: With a Respect to what has Occured in this Year 1692* (London: 1693).

5. John Locke, *The Works* (10 vols.; London: 1823), VI, 9–13.

6. Charles Louis de Montesquieu, *Persian Letters,* trans. John Davidson (2 vols.; London: 1892), I, 99–102.

7. Gotthold E. Lessing, *Briefe,* hg. Julius Petersen (Leipzig: Insel Verlag, 1911), p. 296: "Letter to Elise Reimarus."

8. Ellen Frothingham (trans.), (New York, 1876).

9. For the development of the "gentleman idea," see Robert Ulich, *The Education of Nations* (Harvard University Press, 1961), pp. 97ff.

CHAPTER 12

1. *Emilius, or a Treatise of Education,* trans. from the French (3 vols.; Edinburgh: 1773), II, bk. iv. 101–107; an easily available translation, largely based on the above, can be found in Everyman's Library, No. 518, *Émile,* trans. Barbara Foxley, pp. 219 f.

2. For a more detailed description of Pestalozzi's life and work, see Robert Ulich, *History of Educational Thought* and for larger extracts from his writings, Robert Ulich, *Three Thousand Years . . . ,* pp. 480–507. In contrast to the Japanese, the English-speaking nations, though educationally deeply influenced by Pestalozzi, possess only a few translations of his work. Even these are abridged and unsatisfactory. See also Käte Silber, *Pestalozzi, The Man and His Work* (London: Routledge and Paul, 1950).

3. *"Schwanengesang"* (Swan Song), in Heinrich Pestalozzi, *Sämmtliche Werke,* hg. L. W. Seyffarth (Liegnitz: 1902), XII, 423 ff. It may be said in advance that Pestalozzi's extremely involved and picturesque style would be unbearable if translated verbally into English. The following translations by the author are rather free renderings.

4. *"Uber die Idee der Elementarbildung,"* *ibid.,* X, 213 f. Pestalozzi's term "Elementarbildung" should by no means be confused with "elementary education." It denotes the elements or fundamental principles on which education should be based. In view of the whole context of Pestalozzi's thought the term "organic education" might be the best rendering, provided the word organic, just as Pestalozzi's concept of nature, is not understood in a materialistic or "naturalistic" sense. Also the term "elemental education" could be an adequate rendering.

5. *"Lienhard und Gertrud; Ausgabe von 1781–1787,"* *ibid.,* IV. There exists an abridged translation by Eva Channing (Boston: 1901).

6. *Ibid.,* IX, 3 ff.

7. *"Ueber die Idee der Elementarbildung,"* *ibid.,* X, 313 ff.

8. *"Schwanengesang," ibid.*, XII, 356 and 402 ff. See also John C. Osgood, *Johann Heinrich Pestalozzi, My Fate and Experiences as Director of My Educational Institutes in Burgsdorf and Ifferten.* An annotated translation with Introduction. (Thesis, Harvard Graduate School of Education, 1959.)

9. *Sämmtliche Werke,* IV, 597ff.

10. *Ibid.,* VIII, 465.

11. The following extracts are taken from Friedrich Schleiermacher, *On Religion, Speeches to its Cultured Despisers,* trans. John Oman (New York: Harper & Brothers, 1958), pp. 1–2, 49–50, 20, 41, 45, 56, 87–88. Reprinted by permission of the publishers.

12. *Erziehungslehre* . . . , hg. von C. Platz (Berlin: 1849).

13. *Ibid.,* p. 183. For Schleiermacher's ideas about higher education, see his memorandum regarding the foundation of the University of Berlin: *"Gelegentliche Gedanken über die Universitäten im deutschen Sinn"* (Berlin: 1808); reprinted in Eduard Spranger (ed.), *Fichte, Schleiermacher, Steffens über das Wesen der Universität* (Leipzig: Dürr, 1910). This memorandum, written in the spirit of idealist humanism, ascribes to the scholar the role of a "priest of truth." There is no mention of a theological faculty in his memorandum.

14. *Ibid.,* p. 184.

15. Immanuel Kant, *Education,* trans. Annette Churton (Ann Arbor: University of Michigan Press, 1960).

16. Friedrich Schleiermacher, *Sämmtliche Werke* (Berlin: 1835), 3. Abtlg., V.

CHAPTER 13

1. Barbara M. Cross, *Horace Bushnell; Minister to a Changing America* (Chicago: University of Chicago Press, 1958), p. 125.

2. "Our Gospel a Gift to the Imagination," in his *Building Eras in Religion.* (*Literary Varieties,* 3 [New York: 1881]), pp. 249–85.

3. *Ibid.,* pp. 258–60.

4. (New York, 1861.)

5. *Christian Nurture,* pp. 10 ff.

CHAPTER 14

1. ". . . an indispensible condition /for establishing a European moral and religious order/ is to efface from the European dictionary that fatal word, Protestantism." See Comte Joseph de Maistre, *Du Pope* (Lyon, etc., 1867–1868), p. 469.

2. *Ibid.,* p. 154.

3. (Paris: 1822.)

4. *The Five Great Encyclicals—Labor, Education, Marriage, Reconstructing the Social Order, Atheistic Communism*—ed. Rev. Gerald C. Tracey, S.J. (New York: The Paulist Press, 1939), pp. 48–49, 53–57.

5. Philip Sharper, "The Teaching of Religion," *The Commonweal* (Educational Issue) (April 3, 1959), p. 16. Reprinted by permission of the editors. This article relates especially to the book *Shaping the Christian Message*, ed. Father Gerard S. Sloyan (New York: Macmillan, 1959). Among the twelve contributors are Gustave Weigl, S.J., Johannes Hofinger, S.J., and Joseph A. Jungmann, S.J.

6. (New York: Sheed & Ward, 1953), pp. 3 ff.; see also Christopher Dawson, *Education and Christian Culture* (New York: Sheed & Ward, 1961).

7. See, for example, *The Catholic Mind* (July-August, 1960).

8. See the articles by Sister Josephina, C.S.F., "A Study of Some Common Religious Terms for Six Year Old Children," *Religious Education*, LVI (January, 1961), 24–25; "Retention of Religious Knowledge," *Ibid.*, LIV (July, 1959), 372.

9. *Modern Catechetics*, NCEA Convention, 1961 (New York: Herder & Herder, 1961).

10. (Freiburg i.B.: Herder, 1957.)

11. (New York: Herder & Herder, 1957.)

12. *Ibid.*, p. 166.

13. Joseph B. Collins, *Teaching Religion. An Introduction to Catechetics. A Textbook for the Training of Teachers of Religion* (Milwaukee: Bruce, 1953).

14. George A. Coe, *A Social Theory of Religious Education* (New York: Scribners, 1917) and his *What Is Christian Education?* (New York: Scribners, 1929). The following quotations from Coe's *A Social Theory of Religious Education* are to be found on pp. 28, 249, 313, 315. Even the more conservative of the outstanding writers of Religious education no longer take Christian faith within the younger generation for granted. They struggle with the modern issues of "living" versus "conventional" Christianity and of religion versus "secularism" in its various intellectual and political forms. In this respect see: Randolph C. Miller. *The Clue to Christian Education* (New York: Scribners, 1950) and his *Biblical Theology and Christian Education* (New York: Scribners, 1956). Harry S. Munro, *Protestant Nurture* (Englewood Cliffs: Prentice-Hall, 1956). Lewis J. Sherrill, *The Rise of Christian Education* (New York: Macmillan & Co., 1944) (historically oriented). The same author has contributed a brief outline on the "History of Religious Education in America" to *Orientation in Religious Education*, ed. Philip H. Lotz (New York: Abingdon Press, 1950); James D. Smart, *The Teaching Ministry of the Church* (Philadelphia: Westminster Press, 1954); D. Campbell Wyckoff, *The Gospel and Christian Education* (Philadelphia: Westminster Press, 1959). On the liberal or "progressive" side we find in addition to George A. Coe: Ernest Chave, *A Functional Approach to Religious Education* (Chicago: University of Chicago Press, 1947); Harrison S. Elliott, *Can Religious Education Be Christian?* (New York: Macmillan, 1940). Significant signs of a new approach to religious education are also the following publications: Ernest R. Koenker, *The Liturgical Renaissance in the Roman Catholic Church* (Chicago: University of Chicago Press, 1954); Van Ogden Vogt, *Art and Religion* (Boston: Beacon Press, 1948); *Highlights of Recommendation for Research*, ed. Herman

E. Wornom (New York: The Religious Education Assoc., 1959); Wesner Fallaw, *Church Education for Tomorrow* (Philadelphia: The Westminster Press, 1960). In order to improve the quality of religious teaching, Mr. Fallaw recommends that the Protestant minister include religious instruction into his ministerial duties and that the divinity schools in conjunction with schools of education prepare prospective ministers systematically for this obligation. A source of information on the various aspects of religious education is a collection of essays—different in quality: *Religious Education; A Comprehensive Survey*, ed. Marvin J. Taylor (New York: Abingdon Press, 1960). As one of the signs of growing interest of scientists in religion should be mentioned "The Institute of Religion in an Age of Science," 280 Newton Street, Brookline, Massachusetts. See also the journal *Religious Inquiry; Exploratory Studies on Empirical Approaches to Religion*, ed. James Houston Shrader and Roger W. Mann (Waterville, Vermont). The best source of information on the current issues of religious education is the journal *Religious Education; A Platform for the Free Discussion of Issues in the Field of Religion and their Bearing on Education*, ed. Randolph C. Miller (New York: The Religious Education Association). A comprehensive survey on the religious situation in America has now been provided by the four volumes *Religion in American Life*, ed. James W. Smith and A. Leland Jamison (Princeton: Princeton University Press, 1960), Vol. I, "The Shaping of American Religion," Vol. II, "Religious Perspectives in American Culture," Vol. III, "Religious Thought and Economic Society," Vol. IV, "A Critical Bibliography of Religion in America."

Of great help to those who prefer a cosmic-humanist approach to religious education will be the publications of the Beacon Press, Boston, especially the various books by Sophia L. Fahs and Bertha Stevens. The most recent book by Sophia Fahs is *Worshipping Together with Questioning Mind* (1965).

A valuable guide to religious education is *Theological Bibliographies. Essential Books for a Minister's Library* (The Andover Newton Quarterly, September, 1963).

15. "We've got to learn to talk their language," see *Antics . . . Or Semantics. The Answer to the Problem of our Young People* (Philadelphia: Board of Christian Education of the United Presbyterian Church in the U.S.A., 1959).

16. For a vivid analysis of the predicaments of our spiritual situation, see Gerhard Szczesny, *The Future of Unbelief*, trans. Edward B. Garside (New York: George Braziller, 1961).

POSTSCRIPTUM

1. E. T. Campagnac (trans.) (Liverpool: The University Press; London: Hodder & Stoughton, 1938), p. 18.

2. Martin Buber, *Between Man and Man*, trans. Ronald Gregor Smith (New York: The Macmillan Company; Second Printing, 1966), p. 18.

Index